THE GREAT CUMBERLAND FLOODS

THE GREAT CUMBERLAND FLOODS

DISASTER IN THE QUEEN CITY

ALBERT L. FELDSTEIN

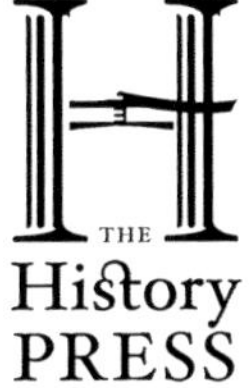

Published by The History Press
Charleston, SC 29403
www.historypress.net

All photographs are courtesy of the collection of Albert and Angela Feldstein unless otherwise noted.

First published 2009

Manufactured in the United States

ISBN 978.1.59629.688.6

Library of Congress Cataloging-in-Publication Data

Feldstein, Albert L., 1949-
The great Cumberland floods : disaster in the queen city / Albert L.. Feldstein.
p. cm.
Includes bibliographical references.
ISBN 978-1-59629-688-6
1. Cumberland (Md.)--History. 2. Floods--Maryland--Cumberland--History. I. Title.
F189.C9F44 2009
975.2'94--dc22
2009015772

CONTENTS

ACKNOWLEDGEMENTS

There are many individuals who helped me with this publication and who need to be acknowledged. Thanks go to the former director of the Allegany County Historical Society, the late Martha Hahn; the former director of Cumberland's Community Development Department, Michael Pearce; and to Jeff Griffith and Denis Gillen, formerly of the U.S. Geological Survey—all of whom in 1986 originally made available to me the collections from their respective organizations. I also acknowledge their successors, Sharon Nealis from the historical society and Kathy McKenney, historic preservation planner for the City of Cumberland, who again made these collections available to me. I would also like to mention Nadeane A. Gordon, who contributed several historic depictions. The late Danny B. Thomas and the late Kathleen "Kenny" Lear also assisted me greatly in the 1986 effort on which this book builds. I miss them both.

The wonderful flood control construction projects were made available to me in both 1986 and recently by the director of the City of Cumberland's Engineering Department, John DiFonzo. Along with John, other folks in that department over the years, including Dave Curry, the late Jackie Powell, John DeVault, William Moyer and Kim Twigg, are also recognized. Appreciation is also given to the *Cumberland Times-News*, via its managing editor, Jan Alderton, for its cooperation, as well as Rita Knox of the Chesapeake and Ohio Canal National Historical Park, the Dewitt Camera Center and James Rada, author of *The Rain Man*.

Others who either provided photographs or assisted in a variety of ways include Wayne Babb, Jeff Repp, Allen Blank, David Cotton, Bill Atkinson and Vicki Day.

Though credited within the work itself, the 1936 flood photographers of the period whose work is included here should also be singled out. Among those whom I was able to identify were Eleanor Gerkins of 501 Beall Street in Cumberland, the Eyerman Photographic Studios located at 5 South Mechanic Street, Elmer E. Thrasher at 221 Race Street and the Goldfine Photography Studio at 117 Baltimore Street.

Finally, I need to thank my two daughters, Natasha and Josinda, and my stepson, Michael Mulligan, who at various times assisted me in myriad ways on one or more of my efforts over the years: proofreading, looking for tombstones, accompanying me on research expeditions or selecting photographic images for publication. Thank you. And most of all, to my long-suffering wife of over twenty-eight years, Angela. This is it for me. Really.

INTRODUCTION

In 1986, I self-published *Feldstein's Fiftieth Anniversary Commemorative Edition of the St. Patrick's Day Flood, March 17, 1936*. The book was a one-time limited edition printing and quickly sold out. Over the years, local bookstores and many individuals have asked me to revisit this topic. The publication you hold in your hands not only meets this request but also greatly exceeds the scope of the original work.

Obviously, the 1936 flood is covered mightily within chapter three. And to paraphrase my 1986 introduction, this photographic and definitive journal captures much of the devastation, nostalgia and history that characterized the natural phenomenon known as the St. Patrick's Day Flood. The deluges of 1924 are also "honored" with the dedication of a chapter solely to the twin flooding events of that year. Naturally, chapter one begins at the beginning with an overview of some of the historic floods of Cumberland, such as the great flood of 1889. For the sake of simplicity, I also incorporated images from other Cumberland-related floods from the early 1900s up to 1937 and 1942.

In working on this introduction, I was struck by a sentence from the 1986 effort that states, "As one reads local history, it becomes quite obvious that beginning with records from the early 1800s this area was, *and continues to be to this day*, deluged with floods on an all too frequent reoccurring basis." The publisher of this book, The History Press, obviously specializes in historical publications. Although disasters occurring within the last twenty years or so are a little too recent to be a major focus of this work, the publisher graciously agreed to let me include an additional chapter briefly highlighting some of the more contemporary flooding events. I am grateful for that. Furthermore, I appreciate the opportunity to occasionally step outside Cumberland's corporate limits and include immediately adjacent or nearby communities within the text and occasional imagery. Floodwaters do not adhere to political boundaries, and neither do I when recounting their impact.

In conclusion, I would point out three items that really "excite" me (I need to get a life, I know). In addition to the obvious "flood scenes," make sure you notice and pay attention to the streetscapes, businesses, homes, public buildings, churches and more in the background of the desolation and havoc. As much as anything else, this is a photographic exhibition of downtown Cumberland and its adjacent residential neighborhoods as they have evolved at certain intervals over the last one hundred years. I am also excited to note that I have expanded on the flood control construction photographs in the final chapter. This covers a period between 1949 and 1959 and provides a whole new perspective to an area we visit, work in and drive by every day prior to the levee and flood wall erection. Finally, I would note that I attempted to incorporate within the introductory text of each chapter the best darn existing historical narrative covering the region as it pertains to floods that you will find in one work. That said, there are obviously overlooked facts and details, outright omissions and even, possibly, mistakes. For these I apologize.

On a personal note, the Metro Clothes Store is depicted in several of these early flood scenes. Metro Clothes was established in 1932 and was originally located in the basement of the old Olympia Hotel on the northwest corner of Baltimore and North Mechanic Streets. Metro suffered through both of the floods of 1936 and 1937. In late 1937, the owner relocated across the street to the corner of Baltimore and South Mechanic and extensively remodeled an existing building. This was just in time for the flood of 1942. The store closed in 1984. The owner was Joseph Feldstein, my father.

The final two sentences from the 1986 introduction read as follows: "To those who remember the 1936 flood, I hope this brings back some memories. To those who are too young, I hope this journal provides a glimpse of the way things were." It has been twenty-three years since that was written and seventy-three years since that great flood. Only the very young of that era remain. This book is dedicated to them.

Albert L. Feldstein
March 17, 2009

Chapter 1

THE HISTORIC CUMBERLAND DELUGES OF 1889 AND BEYOND

The city of Cumberland is located in Allegany County in far Western Maryland. Established by an act of the Maryland state legislature on January 20, 1787, it has often historically been referred to as the "Queen City": the Queen City of the Potomac in the nineteenth century by the Baltimore & Ohio Railroad due to its position as the second largest city on the Potomac River behind Washington, D.C.; and the Queen City of the Alleghenies, honoring its position as the one-time second largest city in the Allegheny Mountains behind Pittsburgh, Pennsylvania. These references, to this day, clearly underscore the historical and continuing geographical relationship that we of this region have with nature. For it seems that every time the mountain snows melted and the rains came, the rivers and streams would overflow their banks, resulting in the region, with Cumberland at its center, being deluged with raging floodwaters.

In a report issued on November 22, 1940, by the Army Corps of Engineers for a North Branch Potomac River Flood Protection Project for Cumberland, Maryland, it was written that the earliest recorded flood known to have occurred at Cumberland was the "Great Freshet" of 1810. Accounts at that time noted that Wills Creek rose to unprecedented heights. Along with several bridges being washed out in Cumberland, this flood caused damage along the entire North Branch of the Potomac River, as well as portions of the Georges Creek region. A freshet, which is defined as the overflowing of a stream by heavy rainfall or melting snow, was also stated in the report to have occurred in Cumberland in 1840, again with disastrous consequences. In addition to those in the Corps report, there were other early major floods noted in Cumberland, including those occurring in the years 1816, 1828 and 1836, when flooding from Wills Creek led to some thought as to relocating the city to the higher ground west of the creek. The building of the Chesapeake and Ohio Canal from Georgetown in Washington, D.C., to Cumberland between the years 1828 and 1850 was plagued by a series of floods during the 1830s and 1840s resulting in several financial and construction setbacks.

Quite obviously, along with flooding, these early events sometimes also brought disease in their wake. It was in the aftermath of a major flood on August 16, 1853, that the city of Cumberland, which had an estimated population of 6,067, was covered with mud and other types of filth. The following excerpt from Lowdermilk's *History of Cumberland* provides some details:

> *A heavy rain of several days' duration caused the river and creek to overflow their banks, and a great part of the town was inundated. Bedford, Centre, Liberty, Mechanic, Frederick, and Baltimore Streets were covered with water, and a great mass of filth and ooze was deposited in the streets, cellars, etc, on which the hot sun poured down for several days, generating disease. On the 17th a case of cholera occurred, and this was followed by others, the scourge soon becoming epidemic, and producing a panic. Thousands of people fled to the country, and to distant cities. For two weeks the town was almost depopulated, business having been abandoned. Those who remained, and escaped the disease, devoted themselves heroically to the care of the sufferers. At the expiration of two weeks frost came, fortunately somewhat earlier than usual, and the epidemic terminated. During that time there were fifty-five deaths from cholera.*

One local person specifically remembered from the ravage resulting from the 1853 flood was Dr. John Andrew Reinhard, a leading Cumberland physician at the time of the epidemic. Reinhard worked extremely hard during the cholera outbreak to help save the sick and dying citizens of Cumberland. Several years later, his own health began to deteriorate. He became gravely ill and soon passed away.

In 1889, a major storm hit the region, resulting in what popularly became known as the "Johnstown Flood" in Pennsylvania. Historical records show that the storm lasted two days, from May 31 to June 1, 1889, with most of the rainfall coming within a period of thirty hours. The rainfall, runoff and resulting deluge on June 1, 1889, caused great decimation and financial and property havoc throughout the Potomac River Valley. This mammoth flood heavily damaged the Chesapeake and Ohio Canal, scattered boats, cost hundreds of jobs and caused enough ruination to close the canal for a period of time, with almost two years required to complete the repairs. Although major in its impact, Weather Bureau gauges at the Johnson Street Bridge in Cumberland and the C&O Canal Dam indicate 1889 flood marks about four feet below the future 1936 level. Other notable floods from the late nineteenth and early twentieth centuries occurred in 1894, 1902, 1903 and 1907. The flood of February 28, 1902, occurred generally throughout the Potomac River Basin from the last day of February through the first two days in March. Though not considered to be "extensive," as characterized in the earlier referenced Corps report, downtown Cumberland was underwater, as seen by the images in this publication.

Cumberland experienced two floods in 1937. The first of these was on April 26, 1937, and was the result of significant rainfall. Although the crests were well below the recorded 1889, 1924 and 1936 Cumberland flood gauge levels, the water did exceed the 1924 flood along various other portions of the Potomac River, where roads were damaged and several bridges were washed out. Portions of downtown Cumberland were also flooded to some extent. A second and lesser flooding event occurred on October 28 of that year.

Five years later, on October 15, 1942, Cumberland would again be hit by swelling floodwaters overflowing the North Branch of the Potomac River near the city. Though the crest was several feet below the great floods of June 1889 and March 1936, it was still significant enough to flood Cumberland's downtown to a depth of four to five feet. As in 1936, business was suspended, and the Maryland State Guard was called in to assist with maintaining order. The Red Cross provided assistance in the form of shelter and food to over three hundred people. Over six hundred telephones were out of service due to cable and line damage. The cellars of many homes and businesses adjacent to Wills Creek, which was out of its banks for ten hours, were flooded, as was the basement of city hall. The Cumberland Chamber of Commerce estimated well over $50,000 in property damage.

Although the focus of this book is on Cumberland, it is appropriate to provide some historical perspective pertaining to the Georges Creek region of Allegany County. As with Cumberland, the earliest recorded floods within the area go back to 1810. This was at a time when there was extensive flooding in the area now known as Lonaconing. Other early deluges followed within the Georges Creek region, specifically in the years 1823, 1861, 1884, 1912 and 1918.

The flood of 1884 was particularly devastating in Lonaconing, an incorporated town within the Georges Creek Valley of western Allegany County. Three days and three nights of flooding resulted in the destruction and loss of many homes and businesses. Alexander Park was inundated, the citizens of the "Island" evacuated and numerous bridges washed out. Houses were lifted from their foundations, and some were even swept away down Georges Creek. It was this disastrous flood of 1884 that led, in part, to the town incorporating in 1890 so as to provide paved streets and other public improvements. Floodwaters struck the Georges Creek region and Lonaconing again in 1918. Trucks and horse-powered wagon teams worked many hours transporting people away, through or around the flooded locations, particularly in the Jackson and Railroad Streets areas, where ice and flood debris from the swelling Georges Creek blocked the roads.

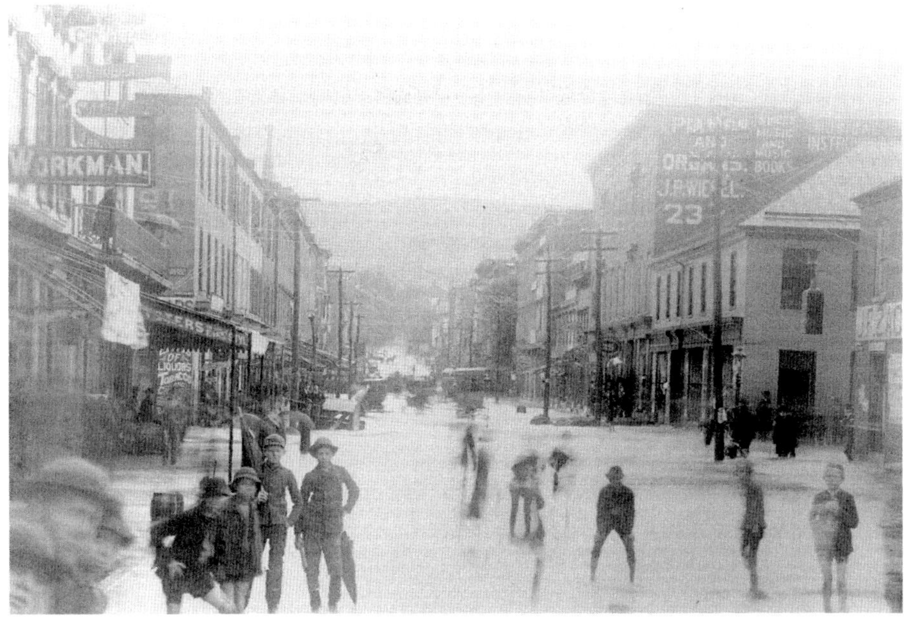

Children pose for the camera in this 1889 flood photograph looking east on Baltimore Street just west of its intersection with Mechanic. *Courtesy City of Cumberland.*

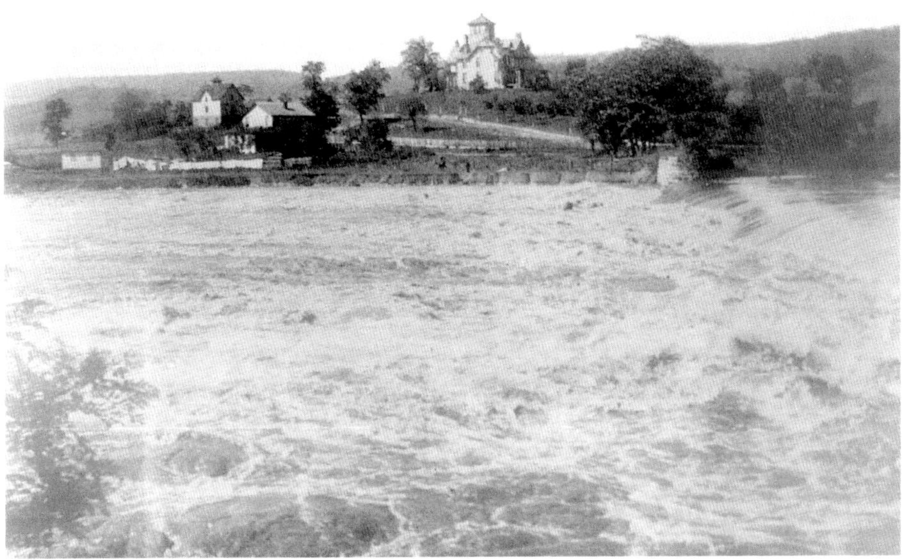

With Ridgeley, West Virginia, in the background, the Potomac River rages during the 1889 flood. Atop the hill stands the old Calmes Mansion, which was erected in the 1790s and was the residence of Dr. George Carpenter at the time of this photograph. In the early 1900s, it became known as the Potomac Club, a social venue for wealthy Cumberland industrialists and businessmen who lived across the river. *Courtesy U.S. Geological Survey.*

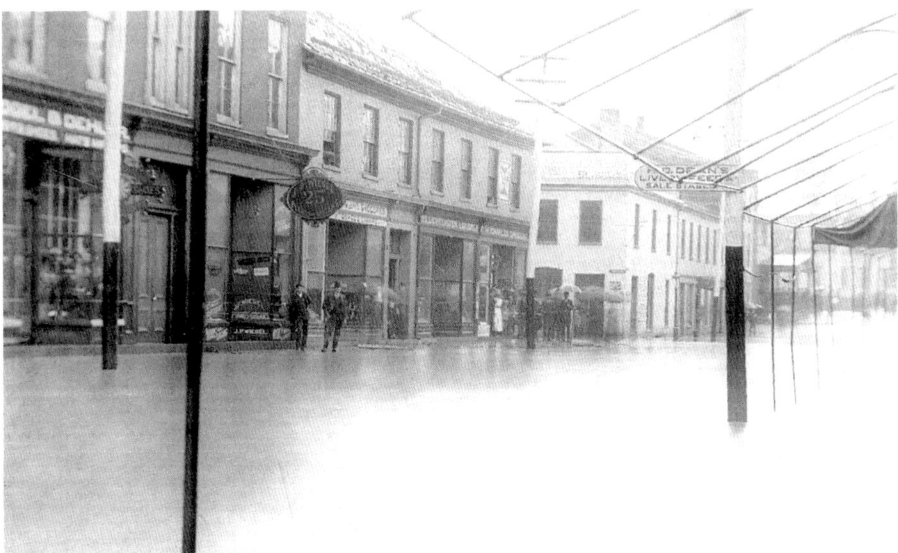

Certain elements within this photograph, such as the white telephone poles and the building at the corner of Baltimore and South Mechanic Streets, lead us to believe that this watery scene occurred somewhere between the floods of 1889 and 1902, most likely during the flood of 1894. Note the livery, feed and stable sign on the left.

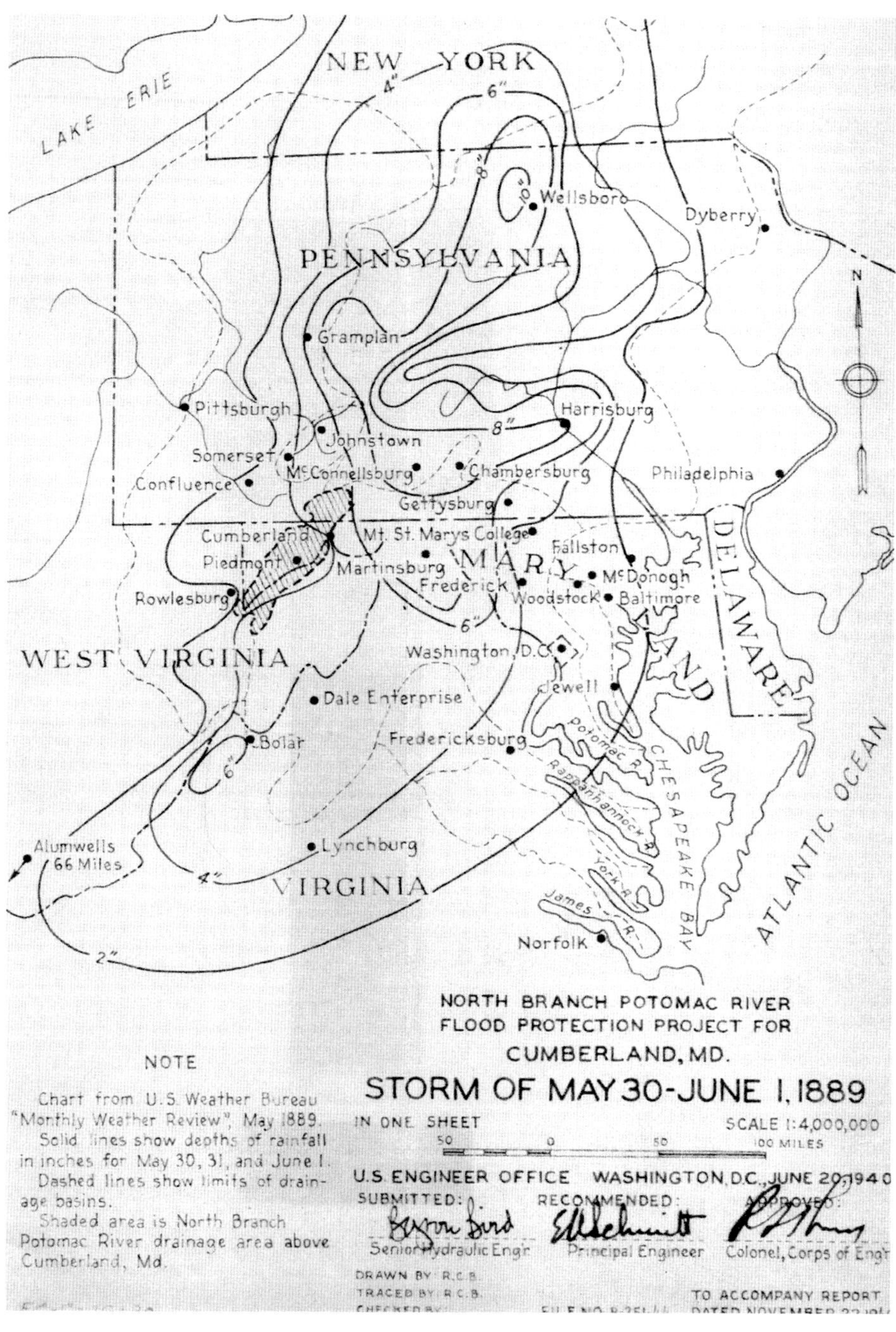

The solid lines on this 1940 Army Corps map show the depth of rainfall in inches for the time period May 30 through June 1, 1889. The shaded area depicts the North Branch Potomac River drainage area just above Cumberland. *Courtesy U.S. Army Corps of Engineers.*

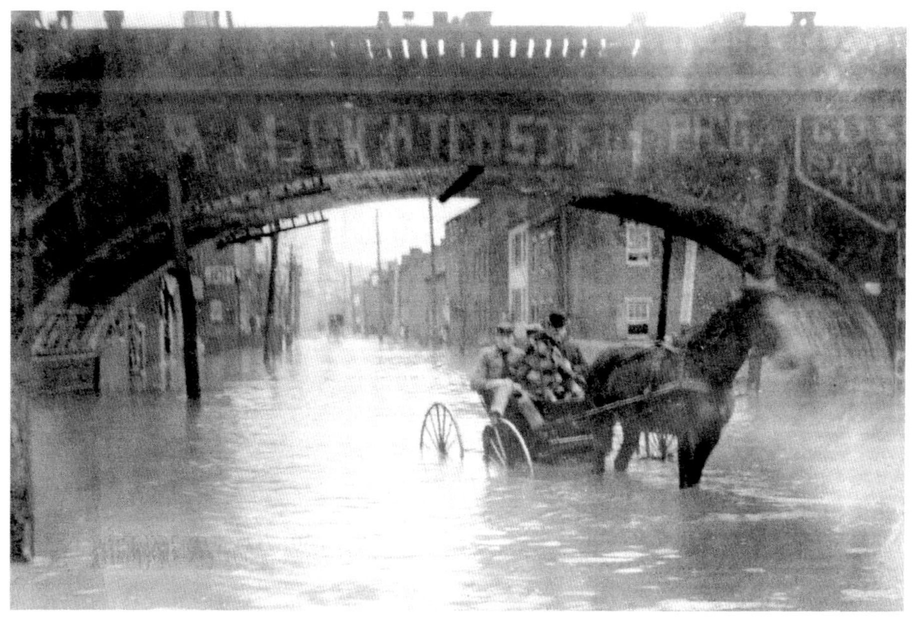

Students in uniform from the Allegany County Academy negotiate their way home in a horse-drawn buggy during the flood of 1894. The scene is looking south from North Centre Street below the Baltimore & Ohio (B&O) Railroad viaduct, which had been constructed through Cumberland in 1851. *Courtesy Nadeane A. Gordon.*

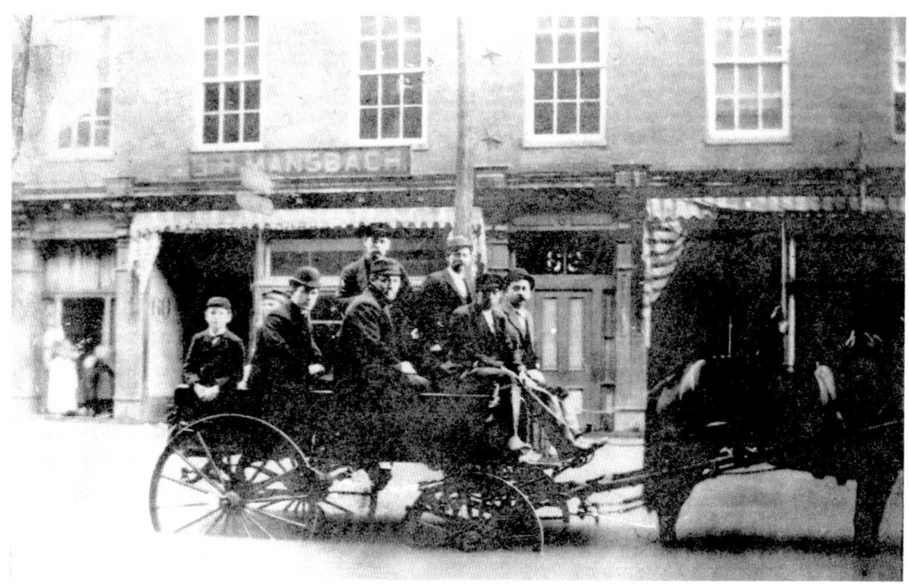

A single horse attempts to haul eight men through the floodwaters on Baltimore Street in 1902. *Courtesy City of Cumberland.*

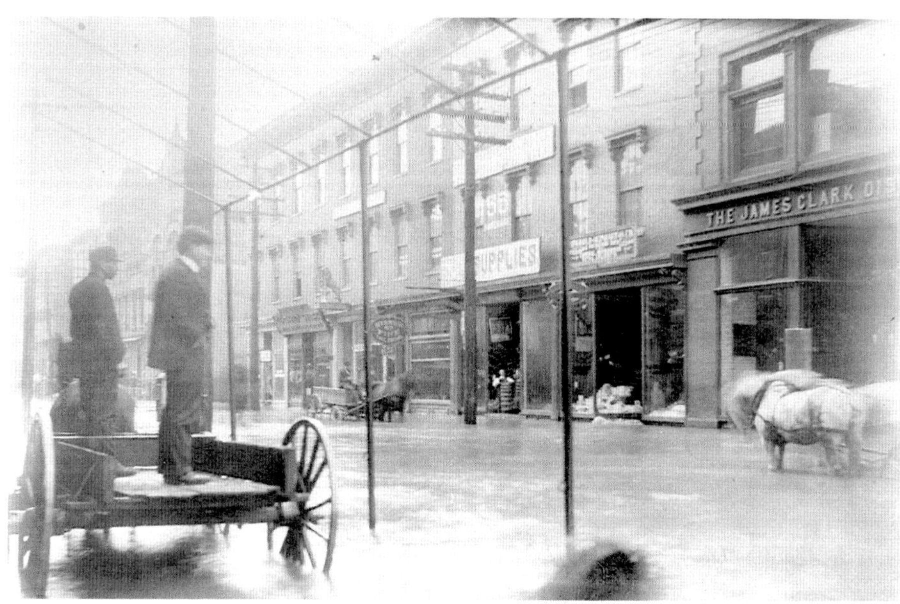

It is the flood of 1902. On the right is the James Clark Distilling Office Building, located at 55 Baltimore Street. This company produced Braddock's Pure Rye Maryland Whiskey at its distillery in LaVale. In the distance, just beyond the intersection of Baltimore and South Liberty Streets, is the old Second National Bank (now Susquehanna Bank), which was erected in 1890. *Courtesy City of Cumberland.*

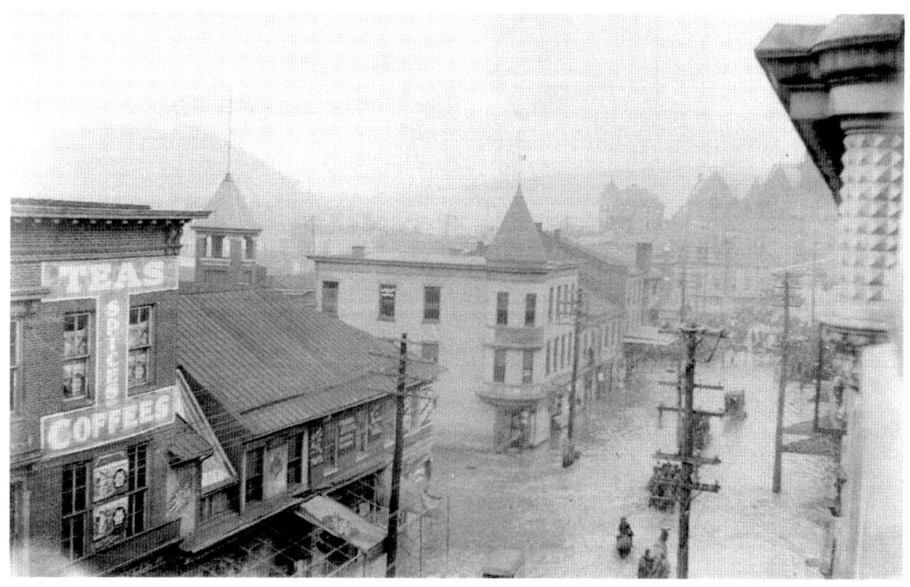

A February 28, 1902 dated bird's-eye view depicts the flooding near the southwest corner of Baltimore and Mechanic Streets. *Courtesy City of Cumberland.*

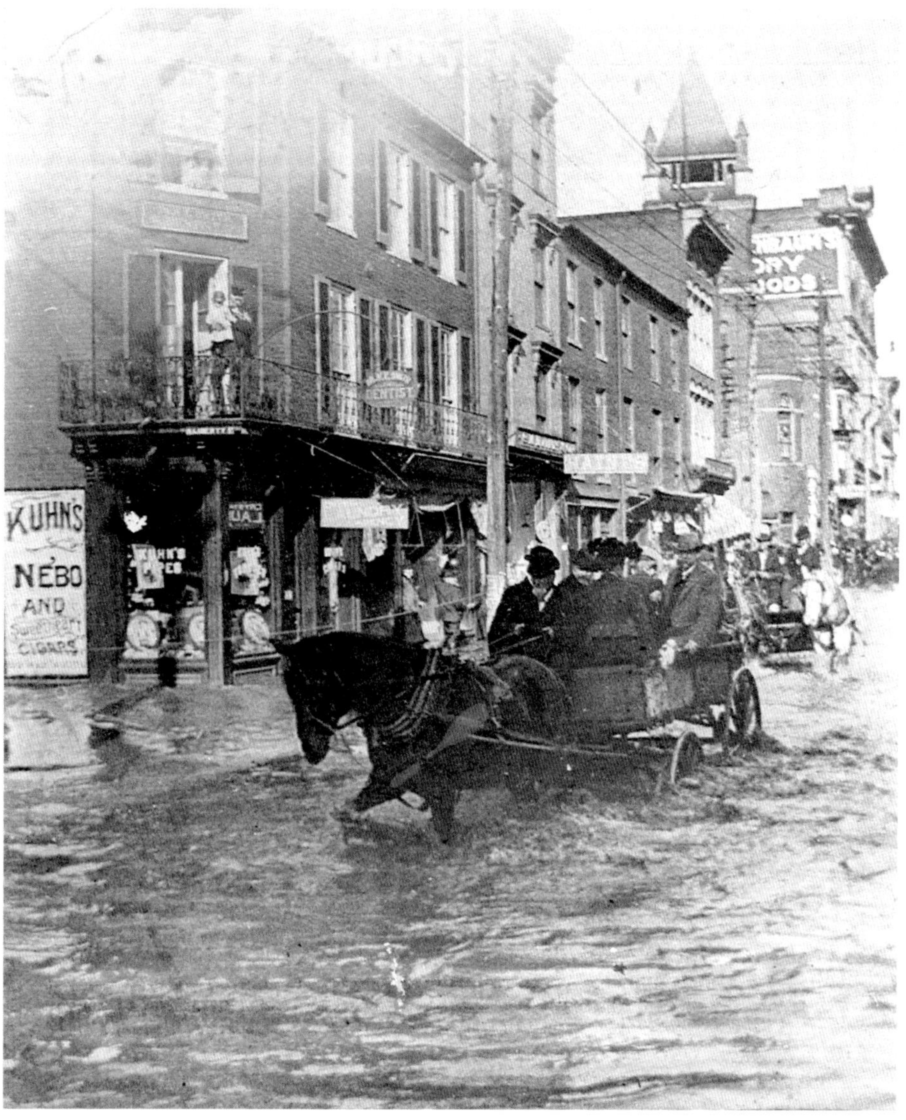

This February 28, 1902 depiction was taken on Baltimore Street at its intersection with North Liberty. Note the old Saint Paul's English Lutheran Church at the corner of Baltimore and Centre Streets, which had been dedicated in 1895 and was later razed in 1957. *Courtesy Allegany County Historical Society.*

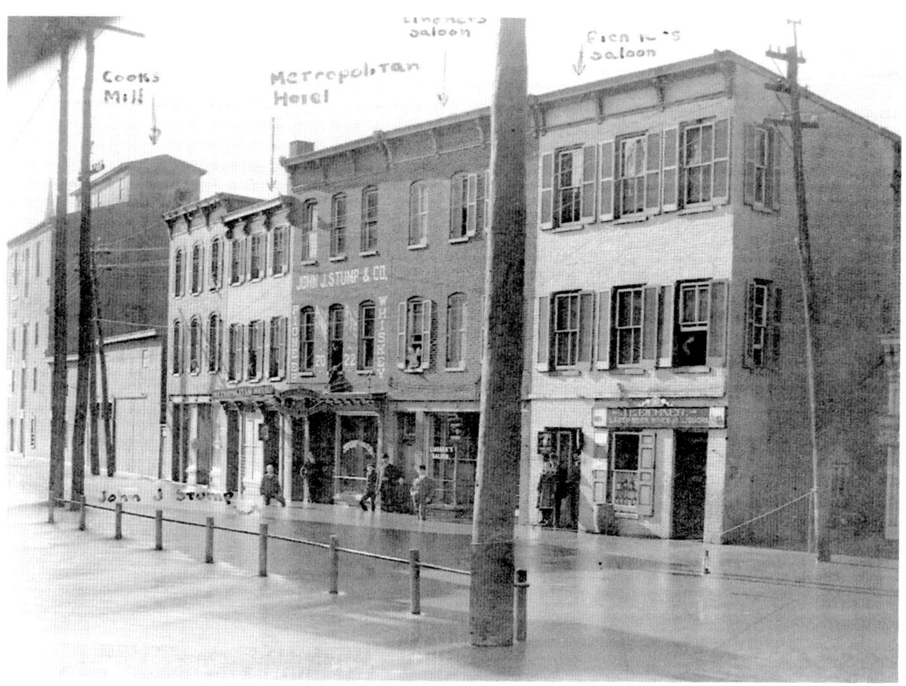

In 1903, floodwaters submerged lower Frederick and Bedford Streets. The buildings shown here are long gone, and the site is now occupied by the Cumberland Public Safety Building. *Courtesy Allegany County Historical Society.*

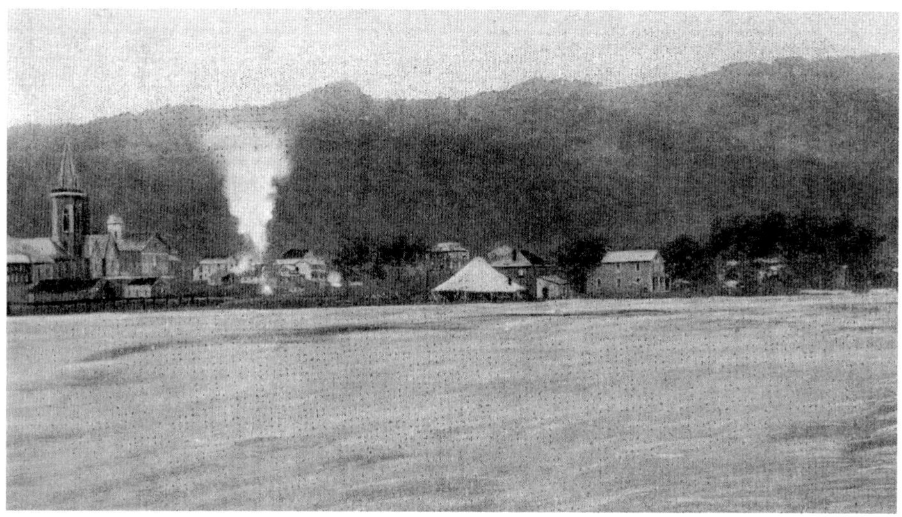

The flood of July 23, 1912, was one of several that have inundated Westernport over the years. Looking across the Potomac River, on the left is Westernport's St. Peter's Roman Catholic Church, which was built during 1870–72.

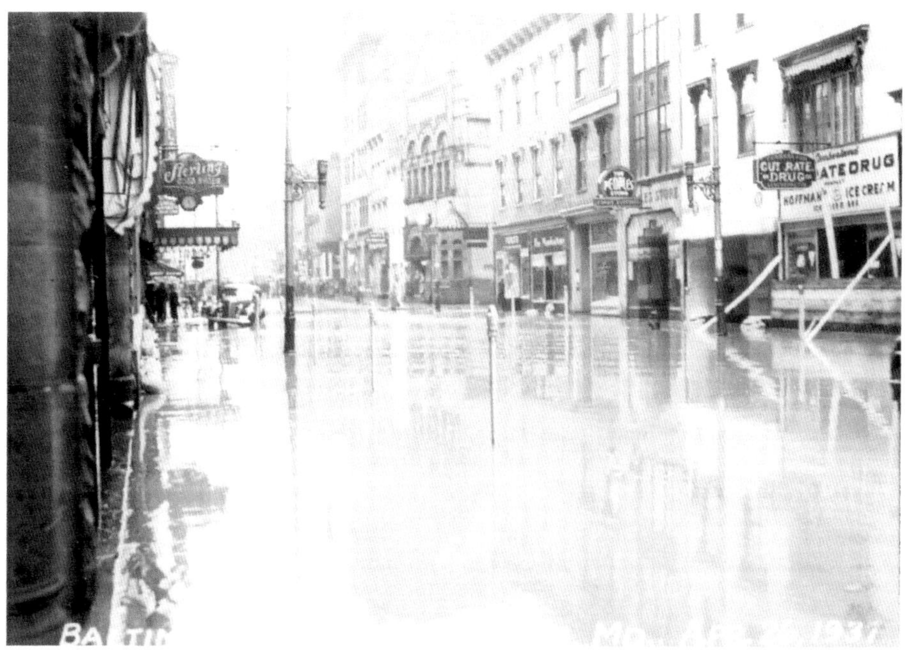

It is April 26, 1937, and we are looking east on Baltimore Street in the flood. The back of this postcard sent on May 5 from New York reads, "How are things going old man? Neither the Cumberland studios nor mine have heard from you for weeks. Hope everything is perfectly all O.K. (signed) Tomcat."

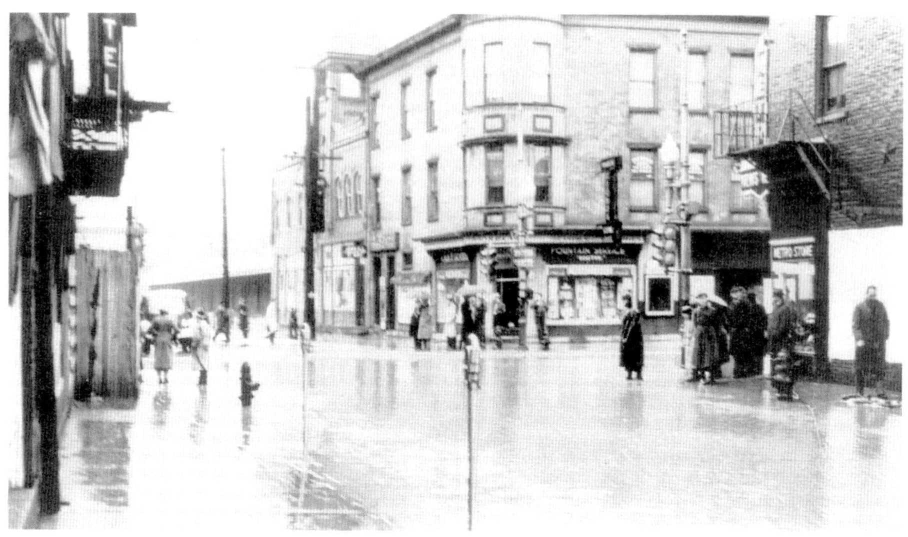

The date, again April 26, 1937, and floodwaters have receded to ankle depth at the intersection of Baltimore and Mechanic Streets. The Metro Clothes Store on the right was established in 1932 and was located in the basement of the old Olympia Hotel. It suffered through both the floods of 1936 and 1937. In late 1937, the owner, Joseph Feldstein, the author's father, relocated across the street to the corner of Baltimore and South Mechanic. Metro closed in 1984. *Courtesy City of Cumberland.*

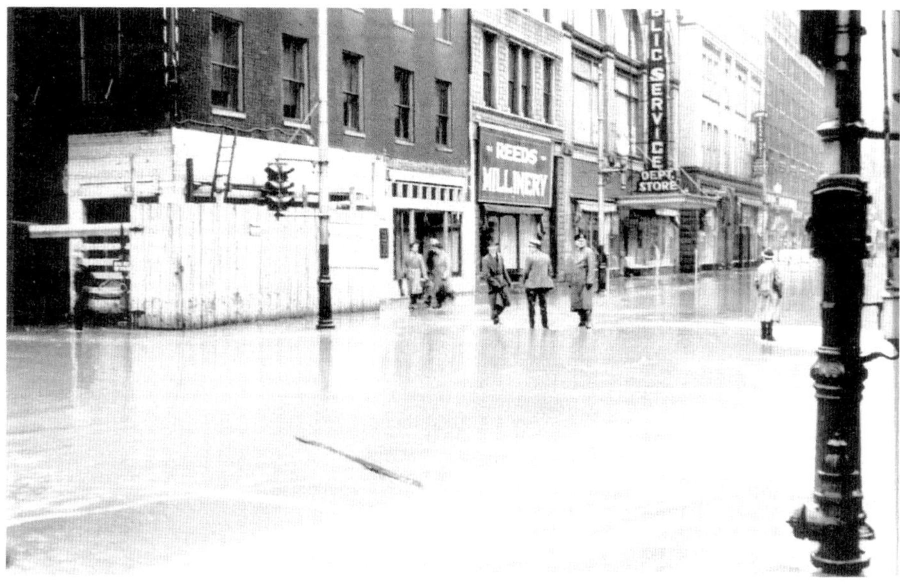

Now a parklet, the businesses located at the corner of Baltimore and North Mechanic Streets fortify themselves for the 1937 flood. Note the old Reeds Millinery and Public Service Department Store buildings, both sites now occupied by CBIZ. *Courtesy City of Cumberland.*

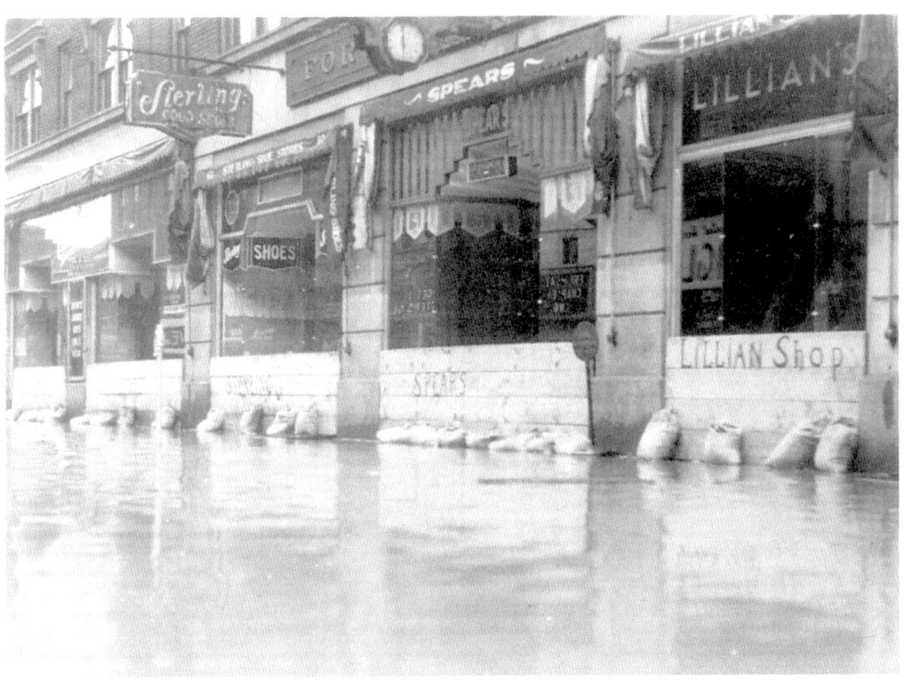

Boarded-up storefronts along Baltimore Street just below its intersection with Liberty Street are ready for the 1937 flood. These businesses—including Spears Jewelry, Sterling "Good" Shoes and the Lillian Shop—are located on the first floor of the Fort Cumberland Hotel. *Courtesy U.S. Geological Survey.*

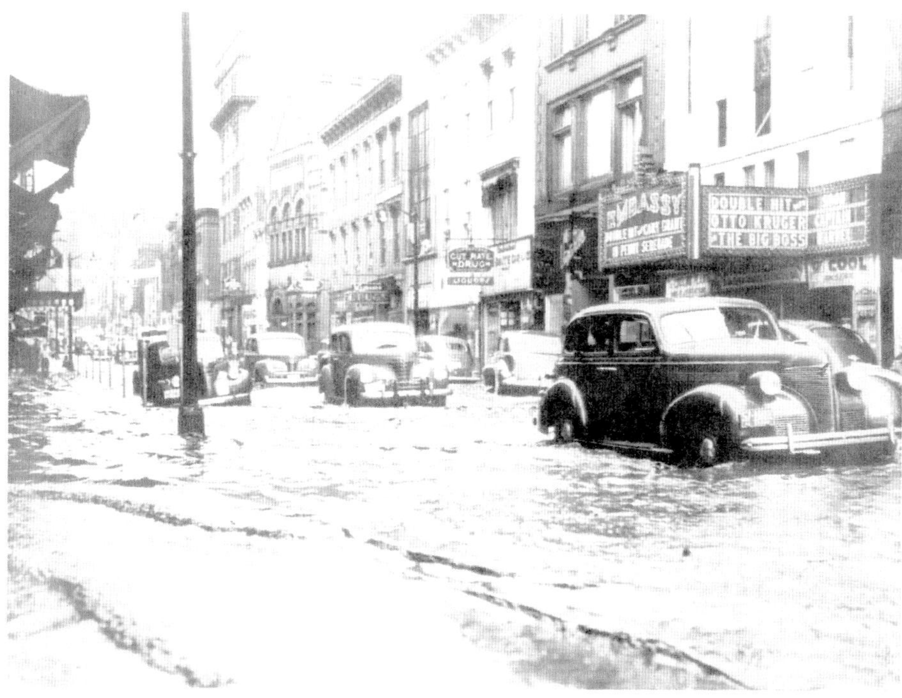

It is 1942 and *The Big Boss* is playing at the Embassy Movie Theatre, while outside traffic traverses Baltimore Street and floodwater. The Embassy had opened in 1931. Closed in 1957, it has been restored as the New Embassy Theatre and is now producing various live stage productions and presenting classic movies.

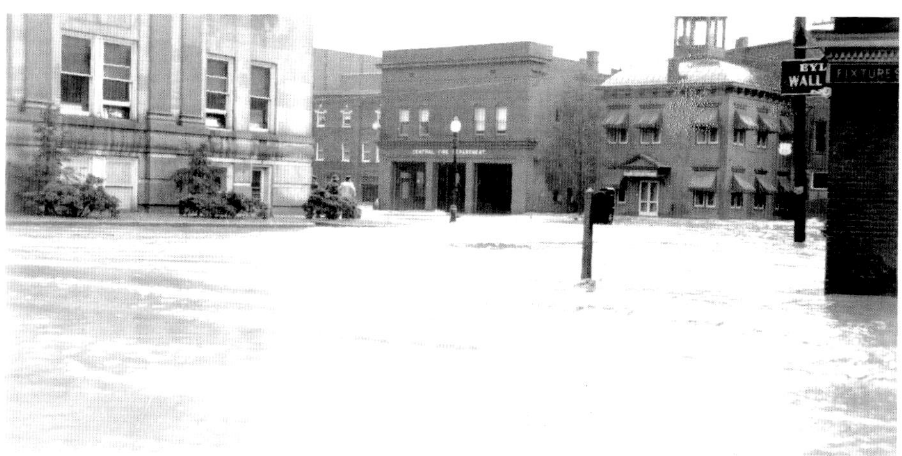

The flood of October 15, 1942, saw water rising all the way to City Hall Plaza. Note the old Central Fire Department building in the center, which was razed in 1978, and the old City Jail Bell Tower Building, which was built in 1885 and is now home to the Allegany County Chamber of Commerce.

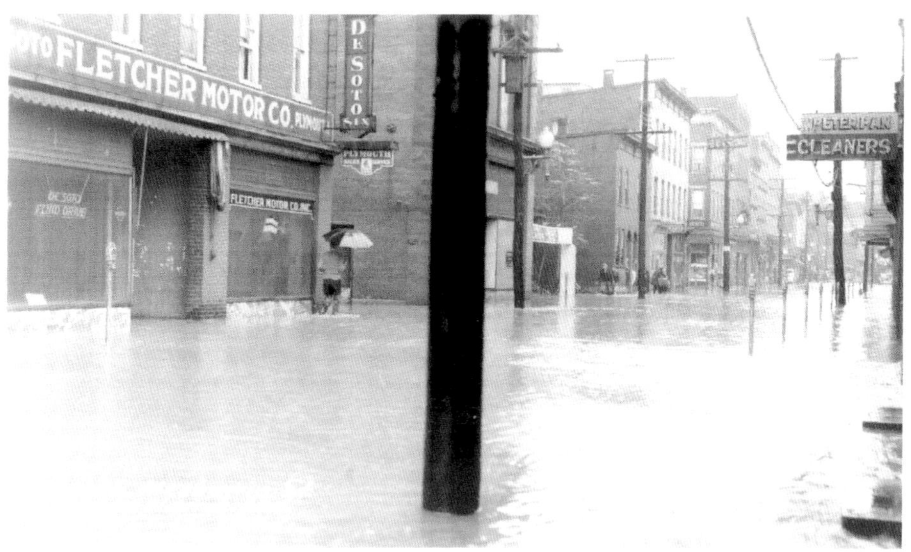

With the Fletcher Motor Company, sellers of DeSotos and Plymouths, on the left and the Peter Pan Cleaners on the right, water remains almost a foot deep in this 1942 portrayal of North Centre Street.

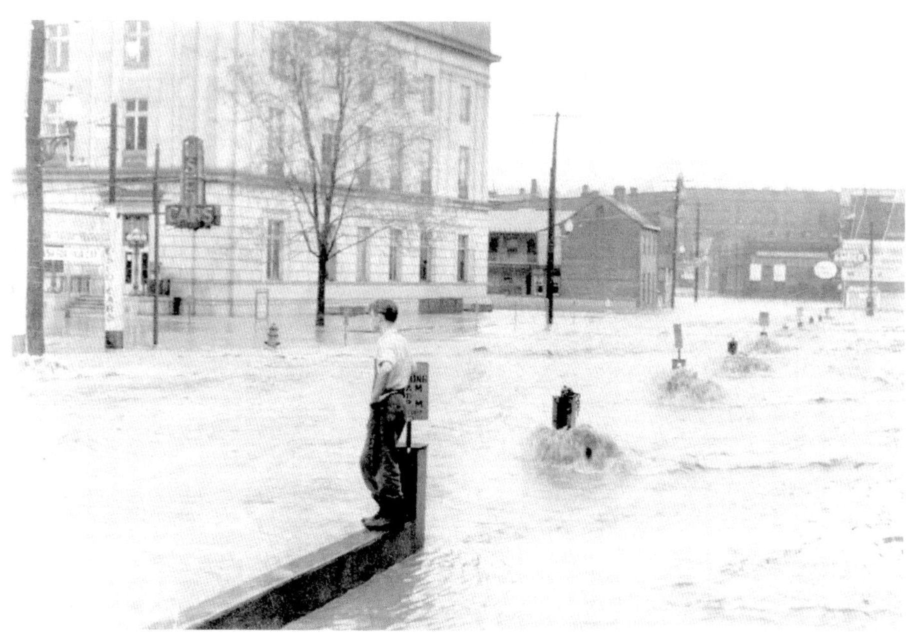

Floodwaters remain high in this 1942 scene from South Mechanic at Pershing Streets. The former U.S. Post Office and courthouse, constructed in 1932, appears on the left. *Courtesy City of Cumberland.*

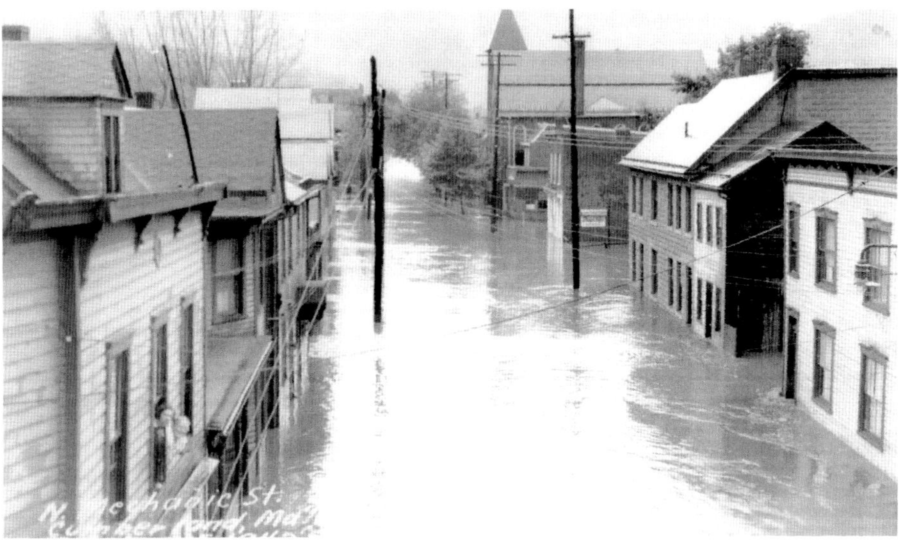

The date was October 15, 1942, and two women gaze out from their second-floor home on North Mechanic Street. The Zion Church appears in the distance. This photograph was most likely taken from atop the Baltimore & Ohio Railroad.

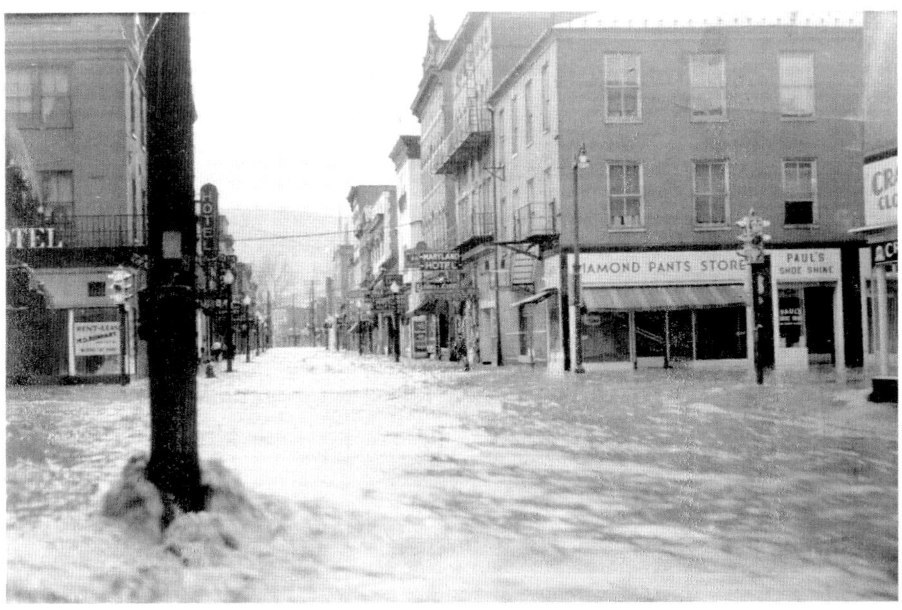

In 1942, the Diamond Pants Store and Paul's Shoe Shine stood at the corner of Baltimore and North Mechanic Streets while the waters raged. Over six hundred telephones were out of service due to cable and line damage. Stores were closed and business suspended. The Maryland State Guard was called in to restore order, and the Cumberland Chamber of Commerce estimated over $50,000 in property damage. *Courtesy City of Cumberland.*

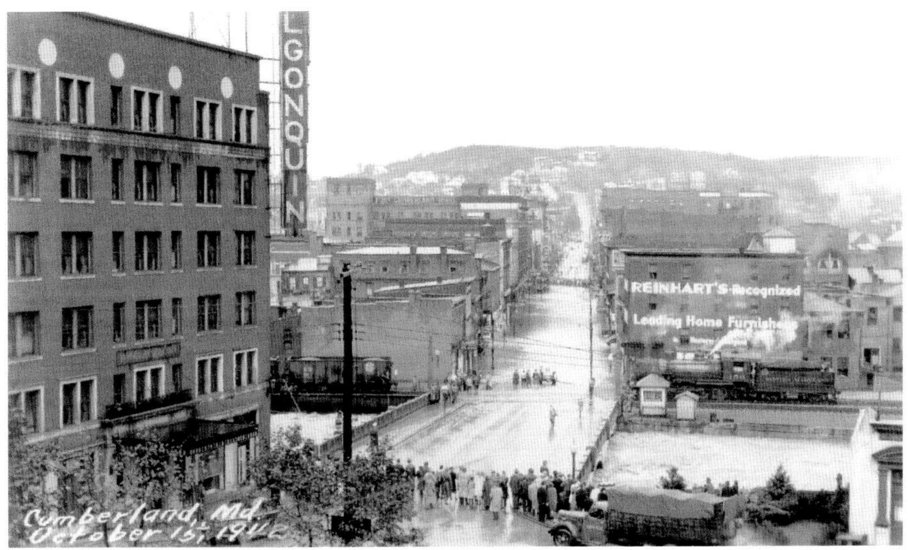

As seen from this October 15, 1942 depiction, a major concern was that the Baltimore Street Bridge would be swept away by the swift, rising water of Wills Creek. A crowd gathers to see the action. By 1949, work had begun on the Cumberland, Maryland–Ridgeley, West Virginia Flood Control Project. This was completed in 1959 at a cost of $18.5 million. On the left is the Algonquin Hotel, constructed in 1926 and now known as the Kensington-Algonquin.

Chapter 2

THE DEVASTATING FLOODS OF 1924

There were two floods occurring in early 1924, one resulting from a storm March 26–29, and the other from the storm of May 8–12. According to the Weather Bureau records at the time, the first five months of 1924 were the "wettest of record" since 1889. As noted in the following excerpt from a 1939 speech given in Cumberland by a representative from the Army Corps of Engineers, the March flood was particularly significant:

> *This storm of March 26–29, 1924 caused a particularly destructive flood in Cumberland. During March, heavy snowfall occurred throughout western Maryland. This snow piled up in drifts to twenty feet in height in some places and blocked the roads for most of the month. It is stated that the mountains were covered with at least three to four feet of snow. The total rainfall for the three days amounted to three to four inches. However, most of this occurred on March 29, 1924. On the previous day, the temperature had risen to 65 degrees. The relatively heavy rainfall, together with the melting snow from the mountains, brought down a tremendous amount of water which emptied into the Potomac River and caused the rapid rise and destructive damage at Cumberland.*

The following excerpt originally appeared in my 1986 work entitled *Feldstein's Fiftieth Anniversary Commemorative Edition of the St. Patrick's Day Flood*. I feel that the flood synopsis from that work, with one or two small additions incorporated, still provides the best overview in the space available.

> *Although the flood of March 29, 1924 was to be definitely exceeded by the 1936 flood in Cumberland, this flood is still characterized by*

its extraordinary severity along the North Branch of the Potomac River above the city. The towns of Westernport, which saw its Potomac River Bridge across to Piedmont, West Virginia washed away, and Luke, as well as the West Virginia Pulp and Paper Company [now the NewPage Corporation] *and the newly developing Amcelle* [American Cellulose and Chemical Manufacturing Company] *plant site all suffered physical damage, with the latter suffering further production delays and financial problems with an additional flooding of the Potomac River on May 12. As a matter of fact, it would not be until Christmas Day of that same year that Amcelle, or Celanese as it became commonly known, would after much effort produce its first cellulose acetate yarn. Just as historically significant, it was also the vast destructive nature of this flood upon the Chesapeake and Ohio Canal that caused the already financially troubled Canal's final termination of operations in 1924.* [Historically speaking, on July 4, 1828, President John Quincy Adams broke ground in Georgetown for the 184½-mile Chesapeake and Ohio Canal. It was completed and opened to Cumberland on October 10, 1850. In 1971, the Chesapeake and Ohio Canal was named a national historical park.] *It was the melting snow and heavy rains along the streams of the Allegheny Mountain region during March 28 and 29 that had caused the Potomac River to swell. By 8:30 a.m. on the 29th, Wills Creek was overflowing its banks resulting in tremendous havoc and property loss in the Cumberland vicinity. Telephone, telegraph, and electric wires were swept away and the city left in darkness. Cumberland's central business district was flooded to a height of four feet with most of the paving washed away and with a torrent of water rushing down Mechanic Street at a great velocity. With the Potomac River rising at a rate of one foot per hour until 3:00 p.m., and one and ½ feet per hour until 6:00 p.m., half of Cumberland's west side was flooded to a depth of five feet. Property loss, including Western Maryland and Baltimore and Ohio railroad damage and washed out bridges, was conservatively estimated at between four and five million dollars. Even the Strand Theatre, located at the corner of Pershing and South Liberty Streets, was required to close for one week while theatre seats were refurbished and new carpeting installed* [the Strand had opened in 1920 and closed in 1972]. *The flood of March 29, 1924 had been 2.5 feet higher than any previous flood in Cumberland's history. One Potomac River gauge had the river reaching a height of 19 feet, two and one-half inches. By 5:00 a.m. on March 30, the water had completely receded and clean-up operations began. The* *deluge which soon followed, on May 12, 1924, flooded many of the same sections of the city, but not to such a great depth. With water flows about four feet below the earlier March level, losses were approximated at only about $35,000 in Cumberland.*

The floods of 1924 initiated discussion for a flood control construction project. Plans were developed for the erection of a flood wall along Wills Creek, channel deepening and levee construction along the Potomac River. However, with the small exception of WPA (Works Progress Administration) crews removing debris from the islands of the Potomac during the early 1930s, no real work was undertaken. Nothing was done to protect the city from the devastation of the upcoming flood of March 17, 1936.

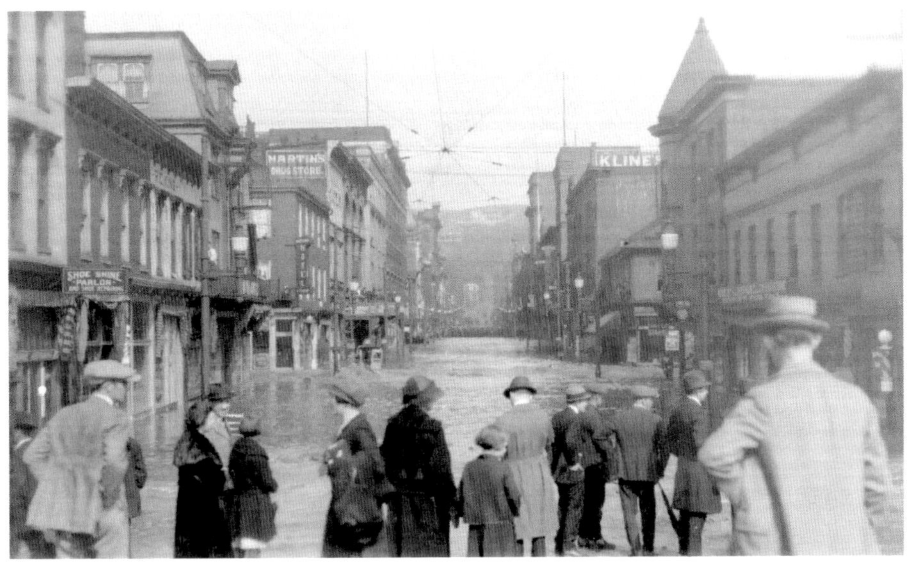

Crowds gather near the west end of Baltimore Street at the Western Maryland (WM) Railway tracks and consider how to negotiate a flooded downtown to the east. Note the Maryland Hotel sign on the left at the corner of Baltimore and North Mechanic Streets and the Shoe Shine Parlor and repair shop on the near left.

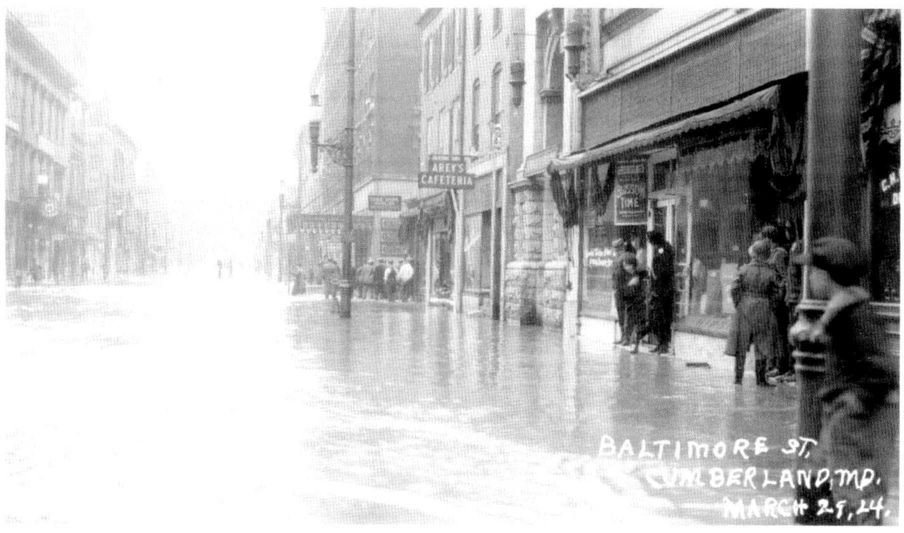

It is March 29, 1924, looking west on Baltimore from Centre Street. This flood had been 2.5 feet higher than any other in Cumberland's recorded history. A second flood, though not as severe, occurred on May 12 of the same year. It was the 1924 floods that caused the final closure of an already financially troubled Chesapeake and Ohio (C&O) Canal as a functioning waterway. Historically speaking, construction had begun on the C&O Canal in Georgetown on July 4, 1828. It was completed and opened to Cumberland in October 10, 1850.

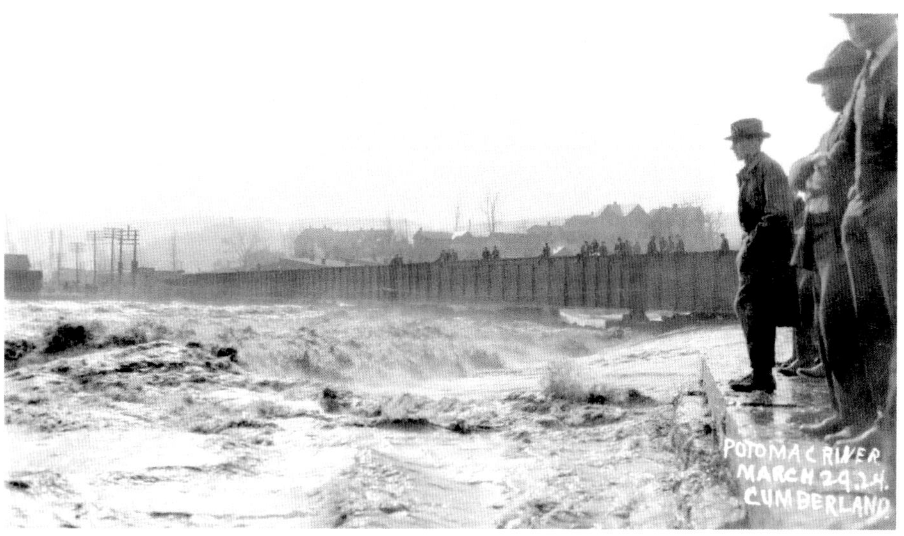

Spectators stand dangerously close at the confluence of Wills Creek and the Potomac River as they gaze in awe at the swelling waters. Significant damage would occur along the entire North Branch of the Potomac River, including at the towns of Westernport and Luke in Maryland, as well as Piedmont, West Virginia.

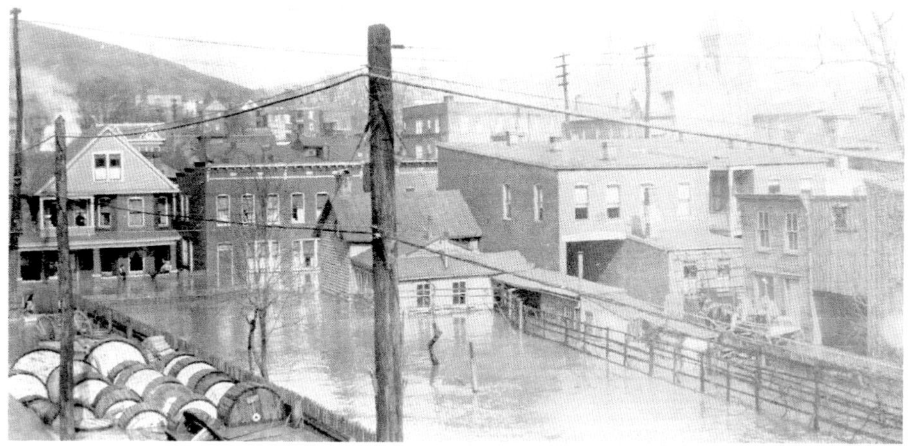

Taken from the B&O Railroad Viaduct, this image looks east toward Mechanic and Centre Streets. Note the Centre Street Methodist Church steeple and horse and wagon on the right.

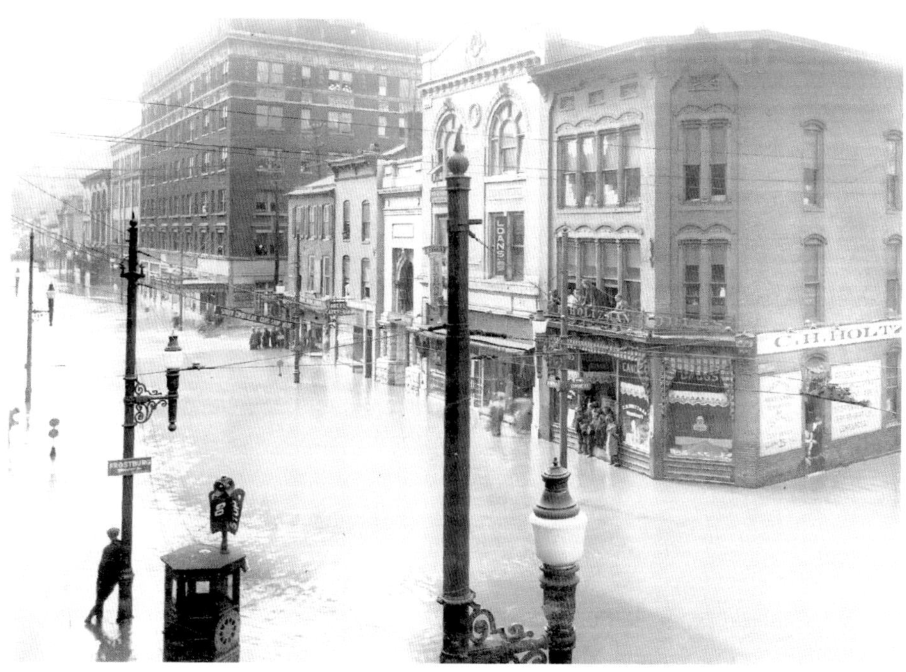

We are looking west on Baltimore Street at 1:30 p.m. on March 29, 1924. Wills Creek would rise an additional three and a half feet after this photograph was taken. Note the C.H. Holtzman Drug Store on the corner, now the site of Café Mark. A sign hung on the left notes a downtown stop for South Cumberland trolley cars. By evening the next day, the water had completely receded and cleanup operations had begun.

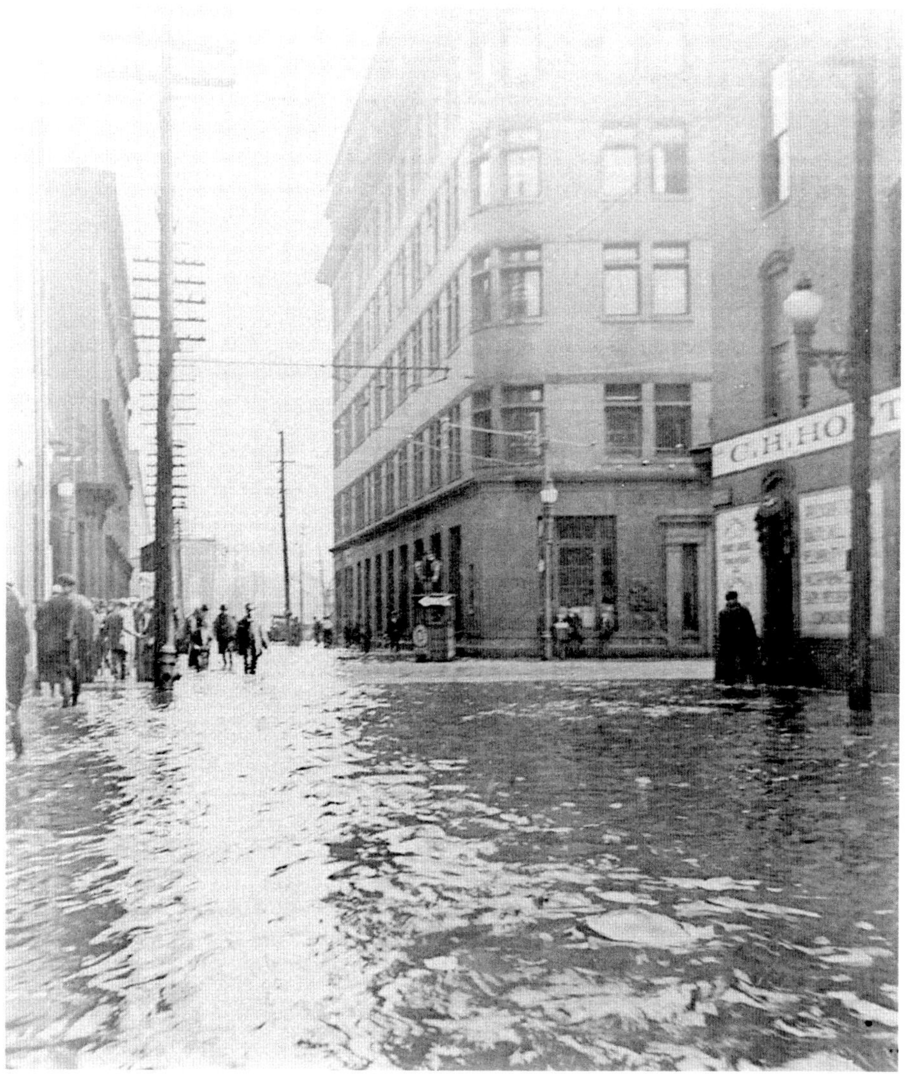

Constructed in about 1906–7 as the Third National Bank, the building depicted at the corner of Baltimore and South Centre Streets at the time of this photograph was known as the Liberty Trust. *Courtesy City of Cumberland.*

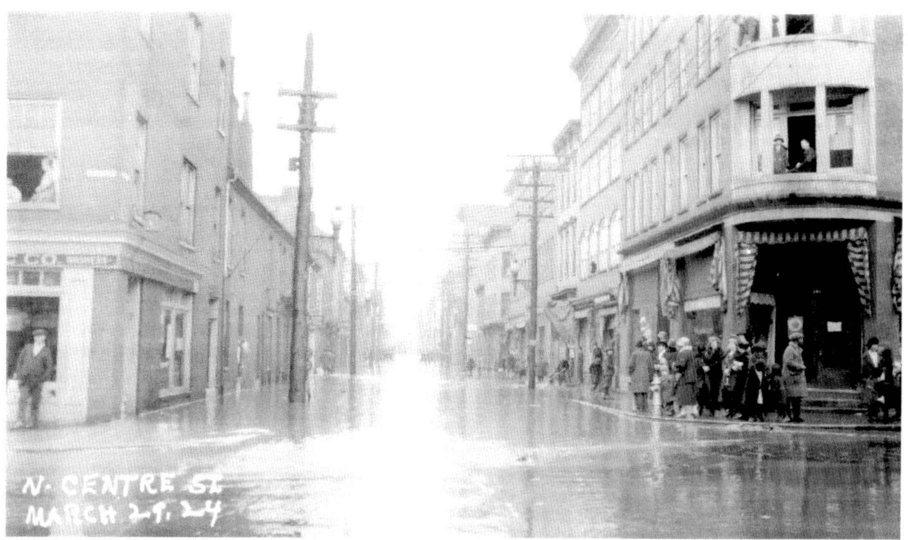

This view, looking north, depicts the corner of Bedford and North Centre Streets. The building on the left was the Sterling Electric Company, while in 1924, Ford's Pharmacy, now the Walsh-McCagh & Kellough Pharmacy, occupied the corner on the right.

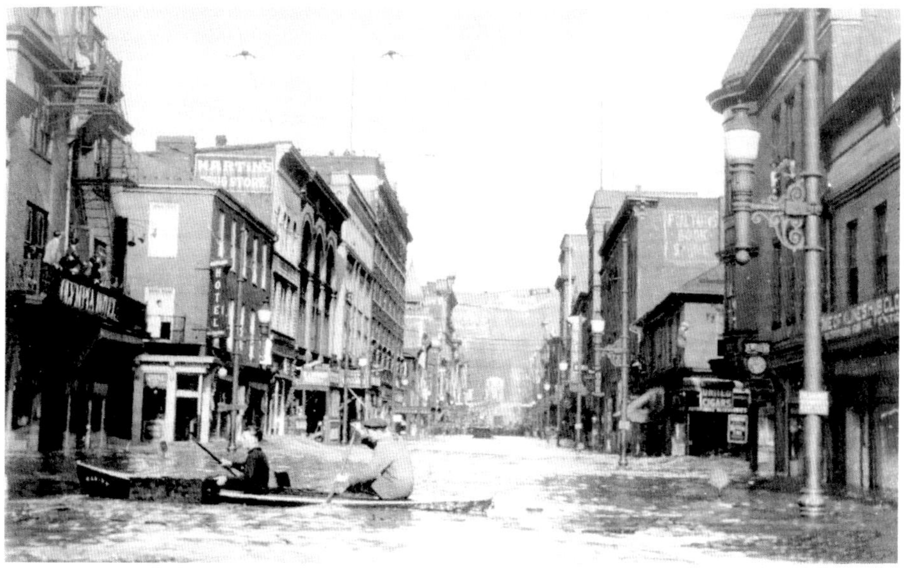

Heavy rainfall and melting snow had caused the Potomac River to rise, resulting in the flood of March 29, 1924. Within the city of Cumberland there was almost $5 million worth of destruction. Nearly half of Cumberland's West Side was flooded to a depth of five feet of water or more. Telephone, telegraph and electric wires were washed away, with much of the region left in virtual darkness. This canoeing scene is looking east on Baltimore Street from the Western Maryland Railway tracks.

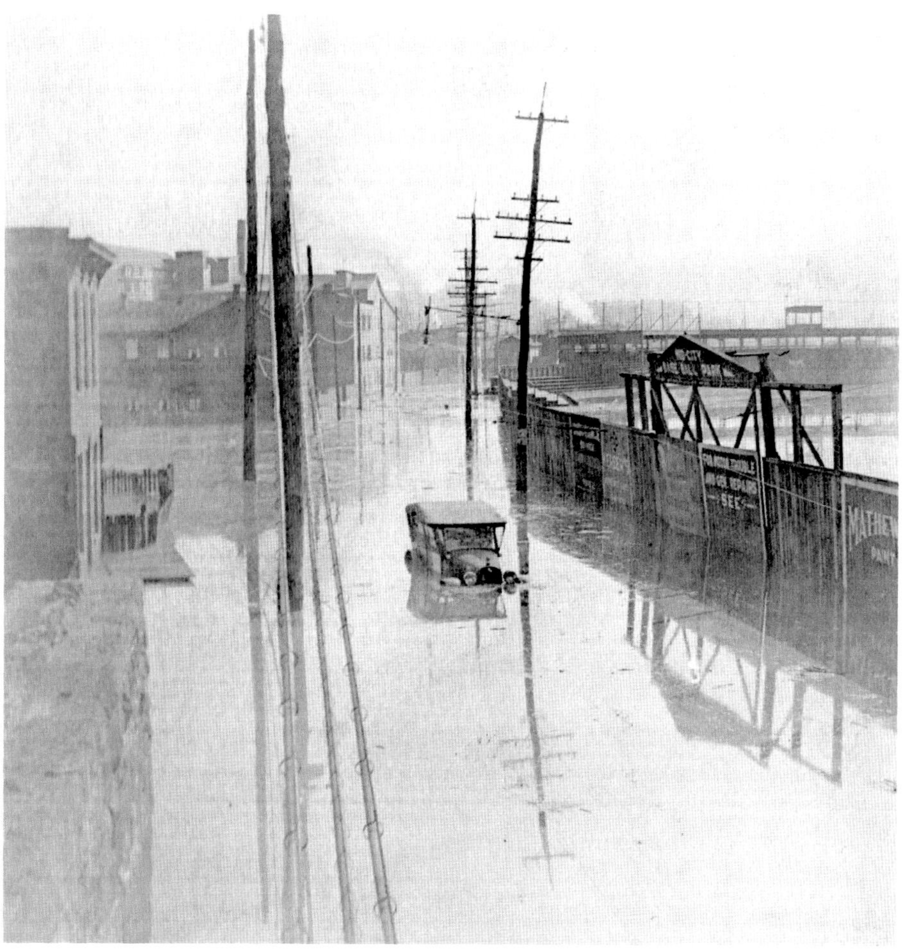

This is Wineow Street near the Baltimore and Ohio Railroad tracks. The old "Mid-City Base Ball Park" is depicted on the right. A Mathews Paint Company sign is on the wooden fence. The store was located at 110–112 North Mechanic Street, phone Cumberland-1237.

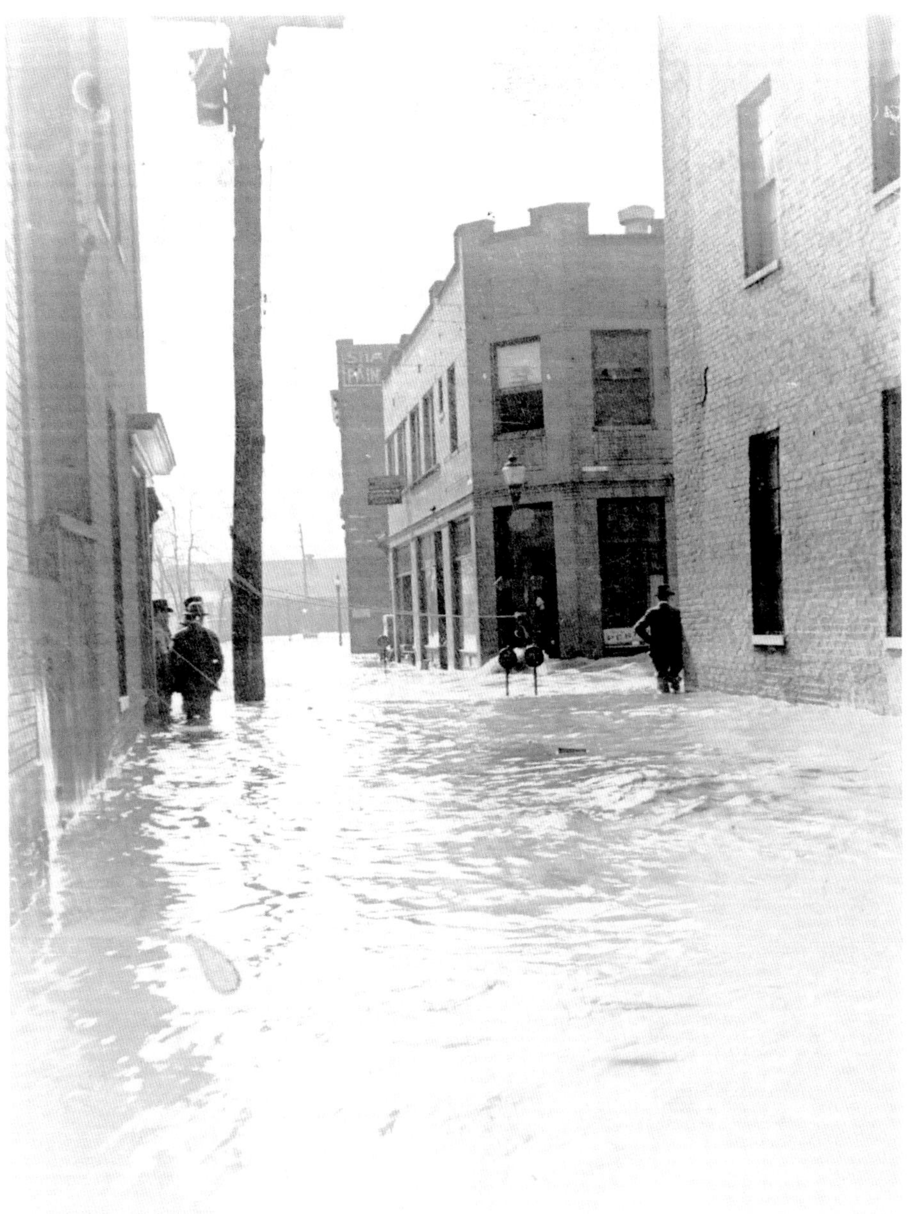

This view of Pershing Street is looking west from its intersection with North Centre. The building in the middle is now occupied by Keller-Stonebraker Insurance.

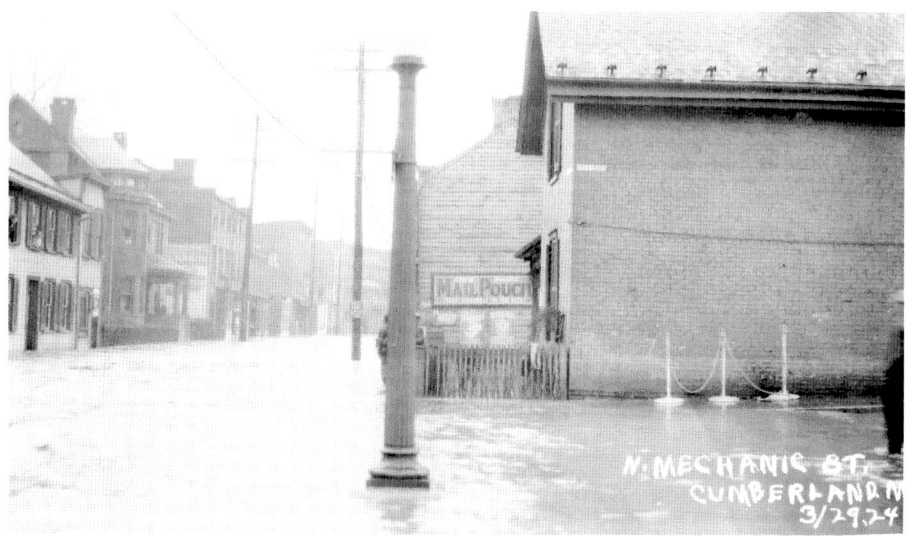

Water remains high, but calm, on North Mechanic Street.

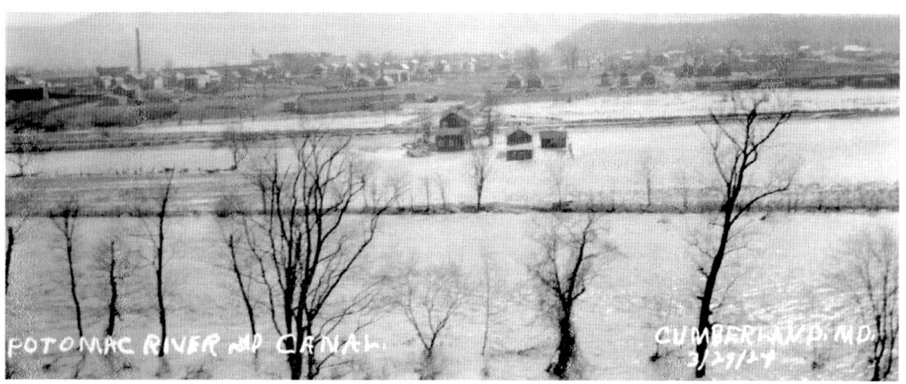

A flooded Potomac River, C&O Canal and South Cumberland are all portrayed in this photograph taken near the height of the flood on March 29, 1924.

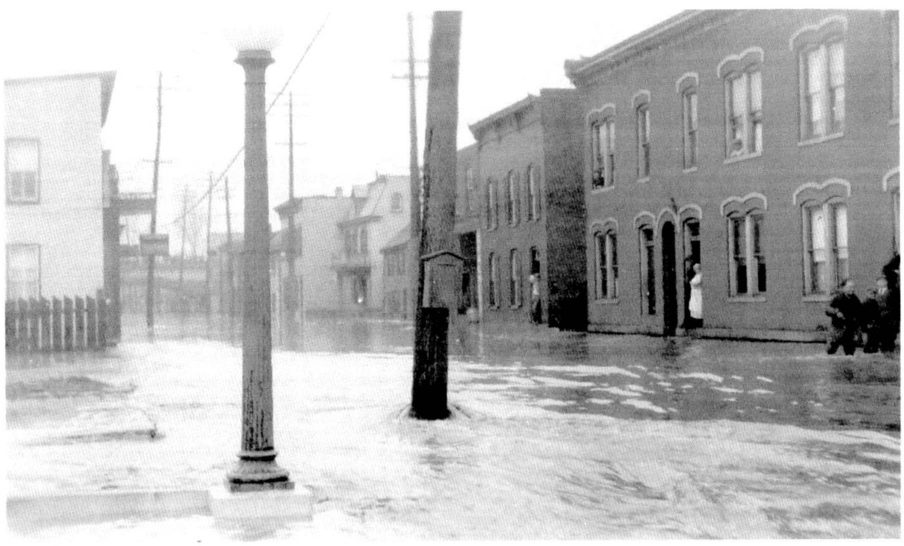

It is Saturday, March 29, 1924. The B&O Railroad viaduct is seen in the background of this North Mechanic photograph.

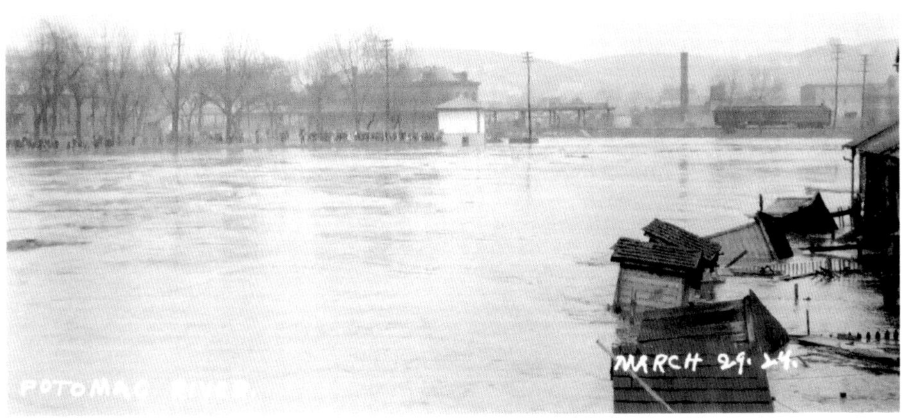

Shown on the left is the old Shriver Boat Basin, Riverside Park and, if you look closely, the George Washington Headquarters. Also visible in the distance is the Western Maryland Railway Station, while on the right are several submerged Ridgeley, West Virginia backyard structures.

Weather--Fair Tonight Tuesday, colder tonight with freezing temperature.

Cumberland Evening Times.

VOL. LVII.—NO. 77 | LAST CITY EDITION | CUMBERLAND, MD., MONDAY, MARCH 31, 1924 | Associated Press Direct Service | TWO CENTS

City Digs Self Out Of Worst Flood In History

DAMAGE FAR OVER MILLION

Many West Side Houses Are Completely Wrecked

Mountain Streams Formed From Melting Snow Pour Turbulent Rivers Into Heart of Cumberland Business District, Tearing Up Streets, Smashing Plate Glass Windows And Washing Away Tons Of Merchandise And Household Furnishings

The *Cumberland Evening Times* displayed this banner front-page headline from March 31, 1924. *Courtesy the* Cumberland Times-News.

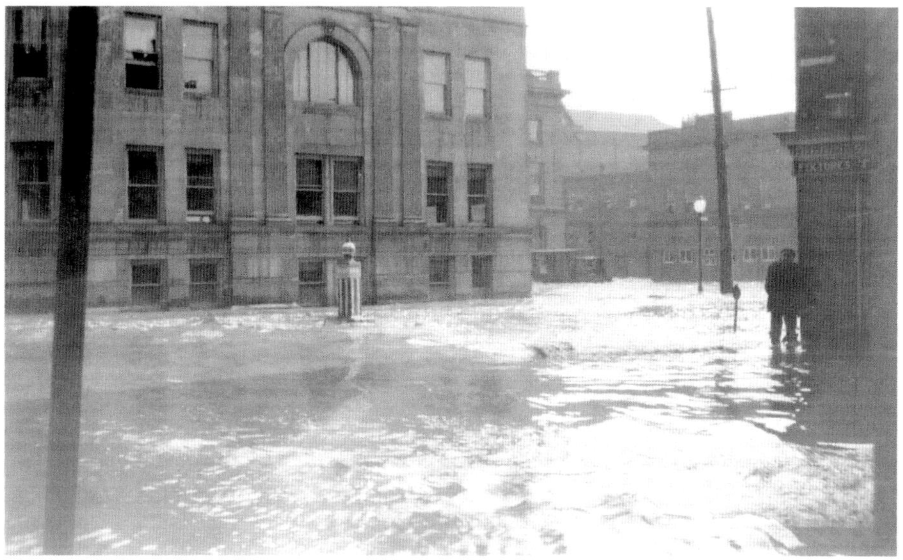

The Cumberland City Hall was constructed during 1911–12. It is seen here from the intersection of North Centre and Bedford Streets.

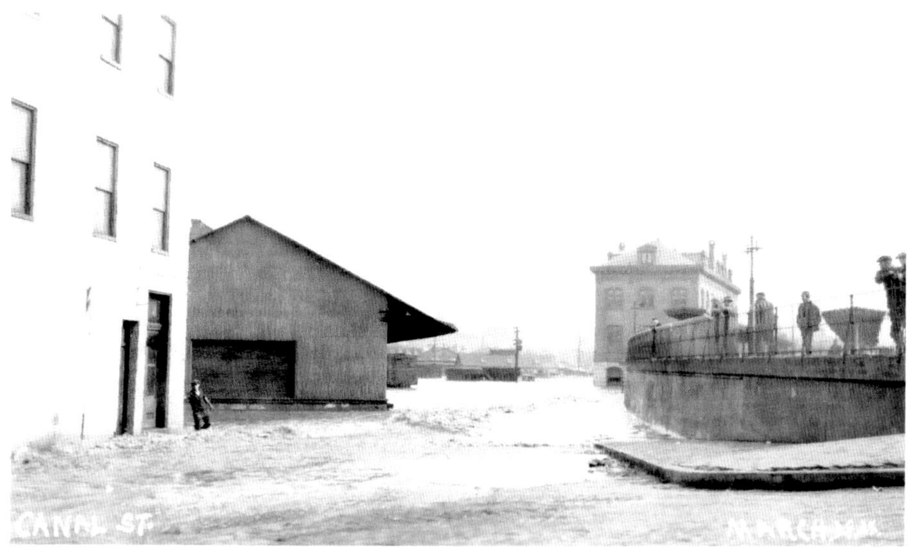

Floodwaters race along Canal Street just below its intersection with Baltimore Street. The Western Maryland Station stands in the distance.

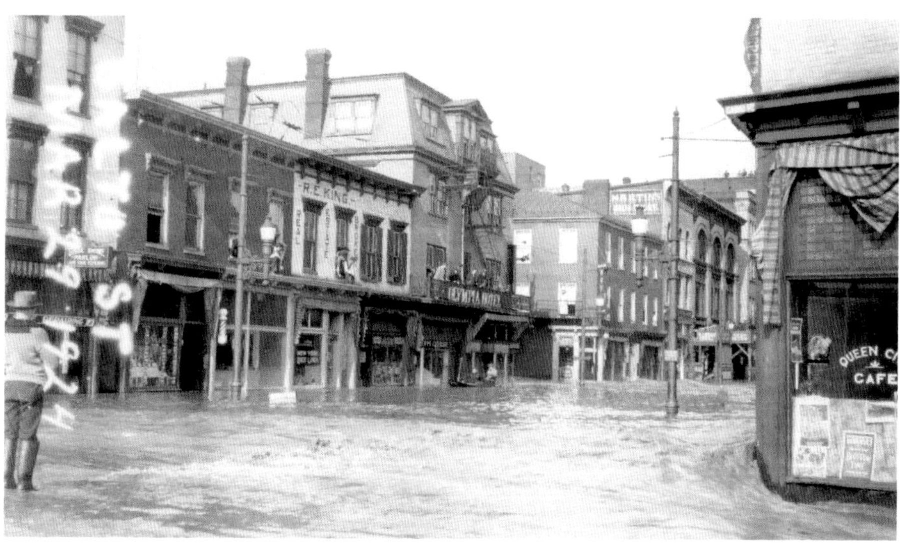

This view was taken from the corner of Baltimore and Canal Streets. Among businesses depicted, from the left, are the New York Quick Lunch and Olympia Hotel (razed in 1960) at the corner of Baltimore and North Mechanic Streets. The Queen City Café is on the right, where a parklet is now located.

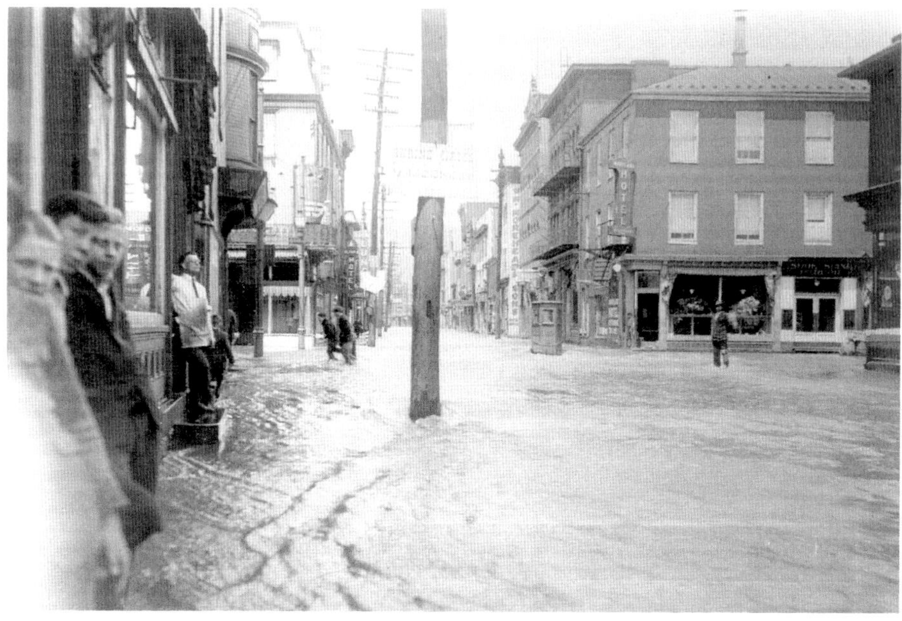

This portrayal of the flood of May 12, 1924, is looking north on Mechanic at its intersection with Baltimore Street. A poster advertising the Shrine Circus is vividly displayed on a telephone pole.

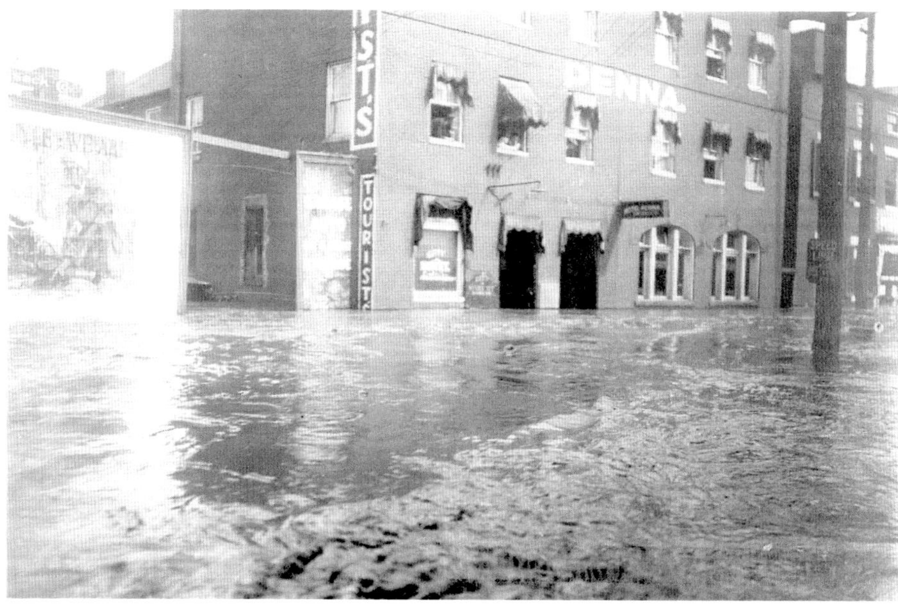

A torrent of water passes along the Pennsylvania Hotel at 133 North Mechanic Street. The hotel catered to transients and tourists.

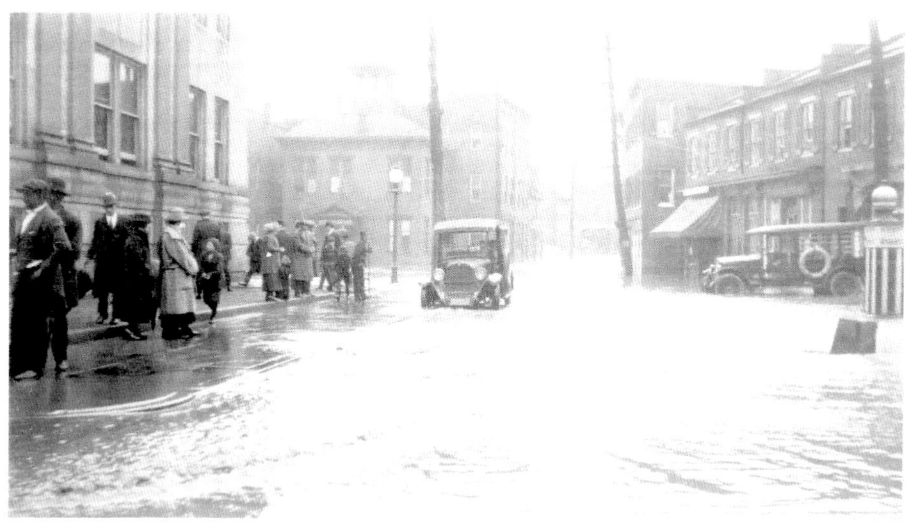

Several fine automobiles were abandoned in the flood, as seen in this scene of lower Bedford Street. At the time of this photograph, the "Bell Tower Building" was serving as Cumberland's police headquarters and city jail.

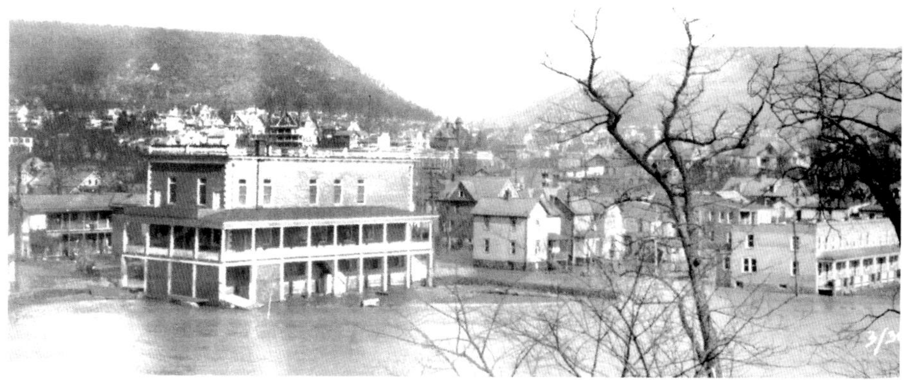

The Johnson Street area, long before the flood control construction project, was inundated during the March flood of 1924. This view was taken on March 30, 1924.

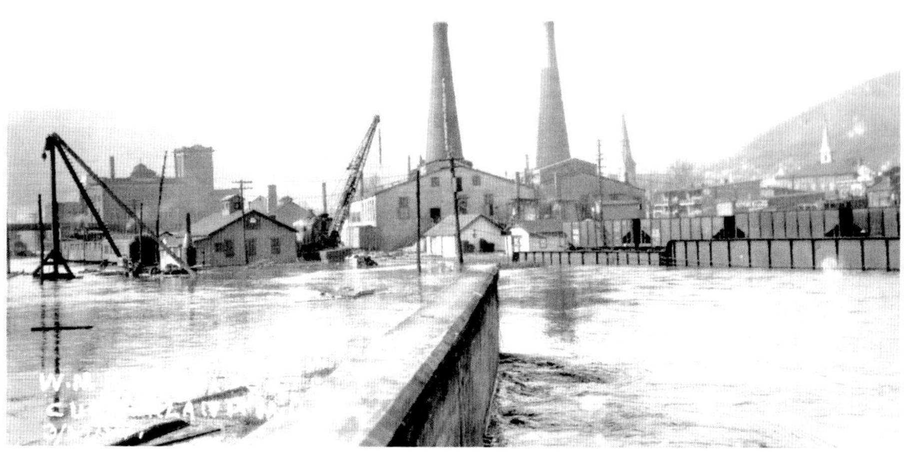

This scene from the flood of March 29, 1924, depicts the inundated Western Maryland Railroad Yard, which was located behind the present-day Kensington-Algonquin and along Wills Creek. Shown in the background, from the left, are the German Brewing Company, Potomac Glass Company, the steeples from Centre Street Methodist and St. Patrick's Churches and Carroll Hall.

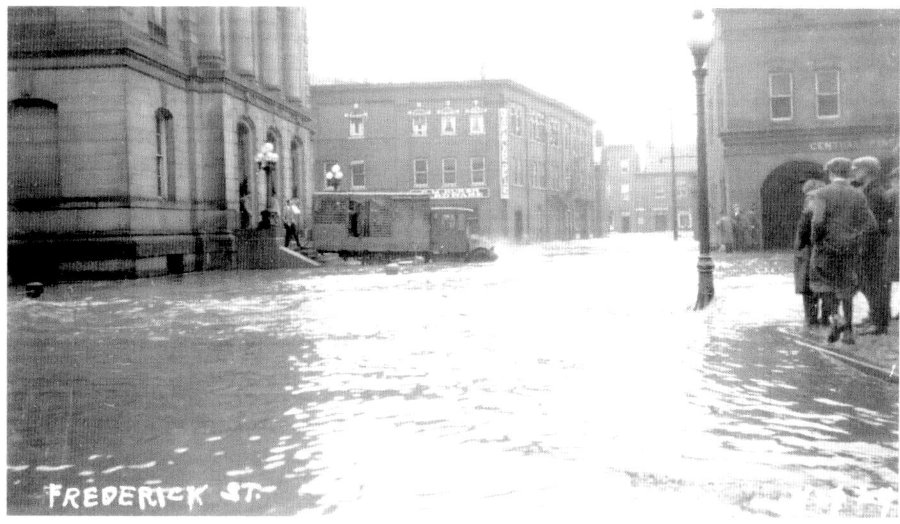

The date is March 29, 1924, and this is lower Frederick Street, looking toward North Mechanic. The building on the left was erected during 1902–4 and at the time of this photograph was serving as the Frederick Street Post Office and courthouse.

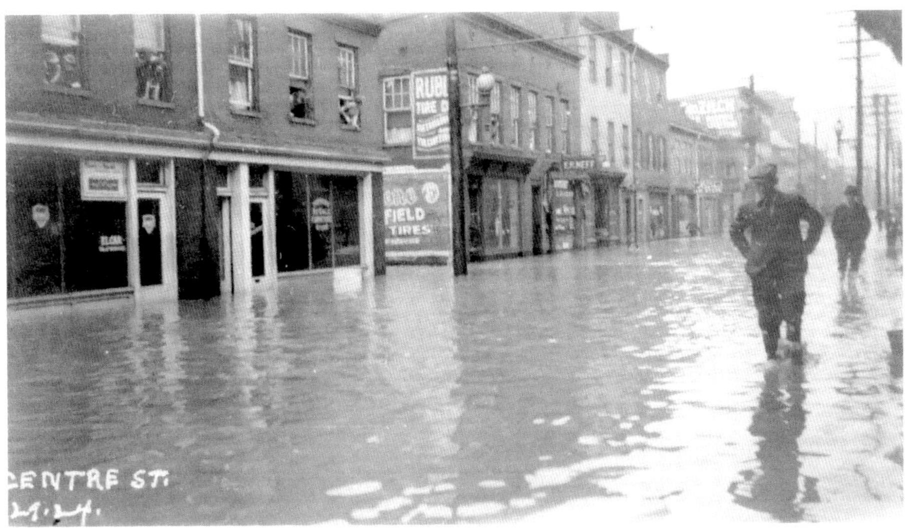

A pedestrian negotiates floodwaters on North Centre Street. The Elcar Auto Agency at 116 North Centre Street is on the left.

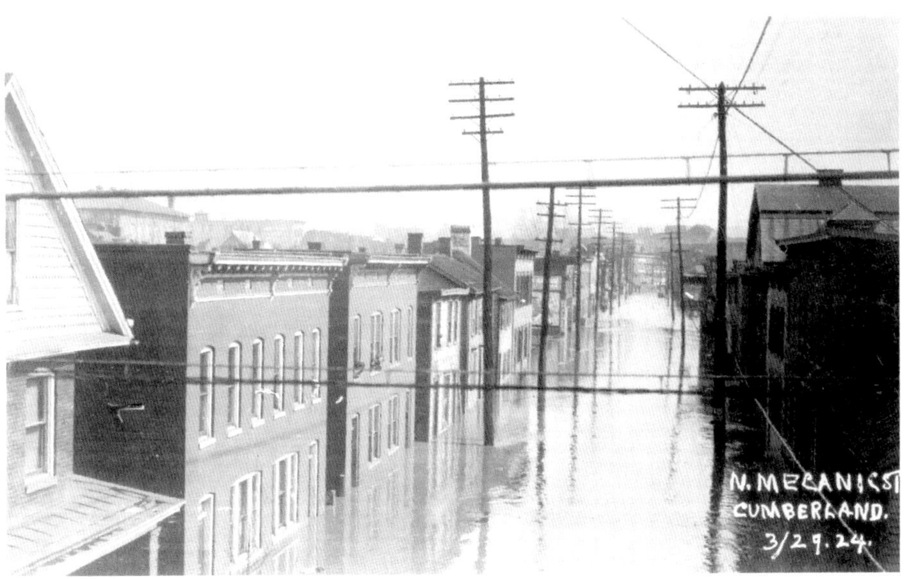

The torrent of water has ceased and appears to be receding on North Mechanic Street in this scene.

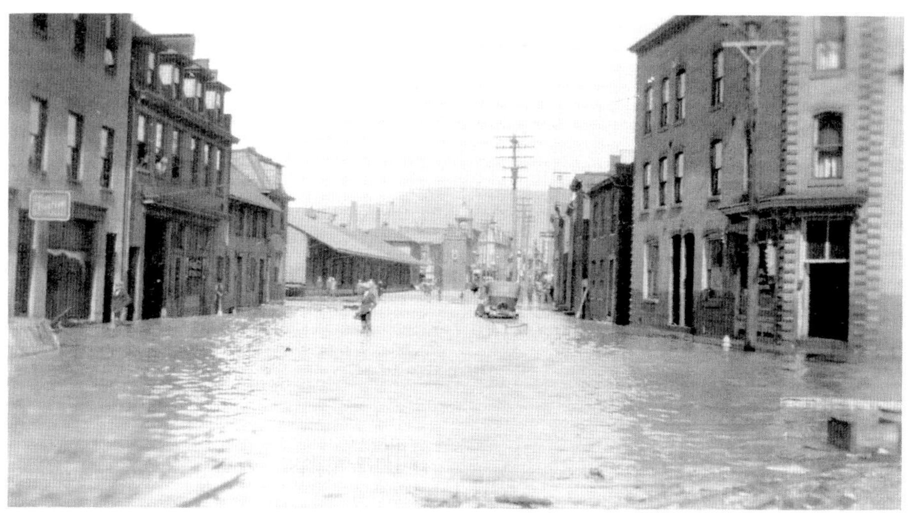

Lower South Mechanic Street, looking north at its intersection with Harrison Street, remains under water. *Courtesy Allegany County Historical Society.*

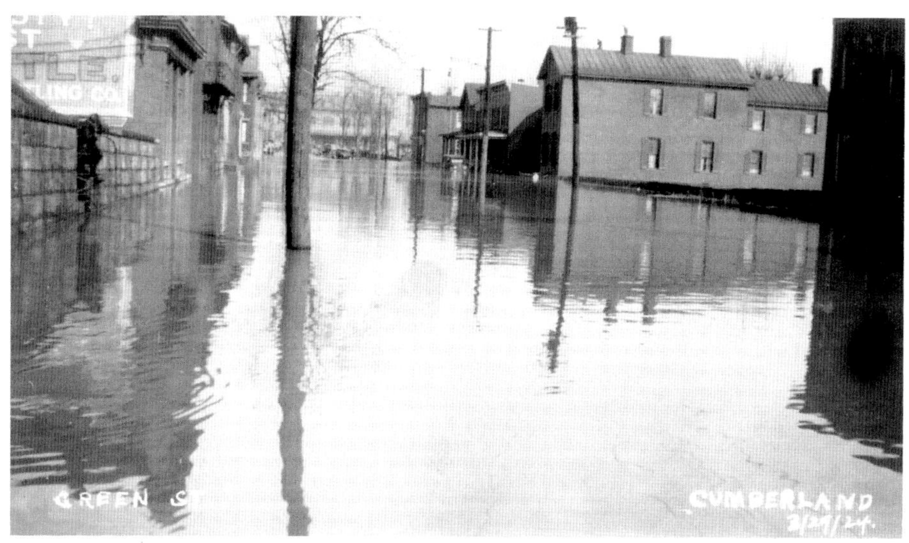

This is one of the few depictions of Greene Street under water during the flood of 1924. This view is looking east toward the Western Maryland Railway Station, which stands in the background.

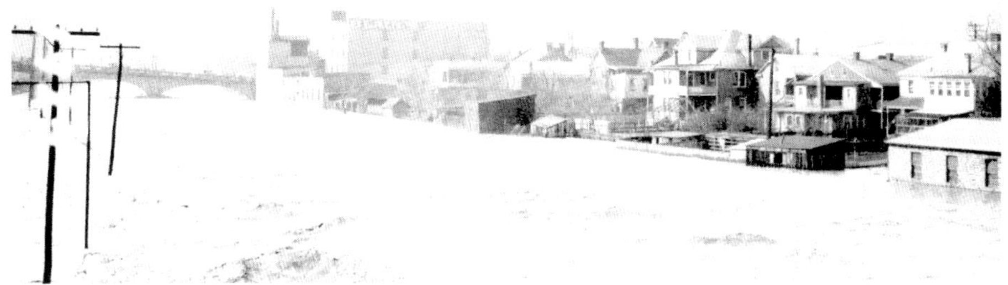

The waters rage as we look upstream along Wills Creek. The old Valley Street Bridge appears on the left. The back of this photograph notes that it was taken from atop the B&O Viaduct.

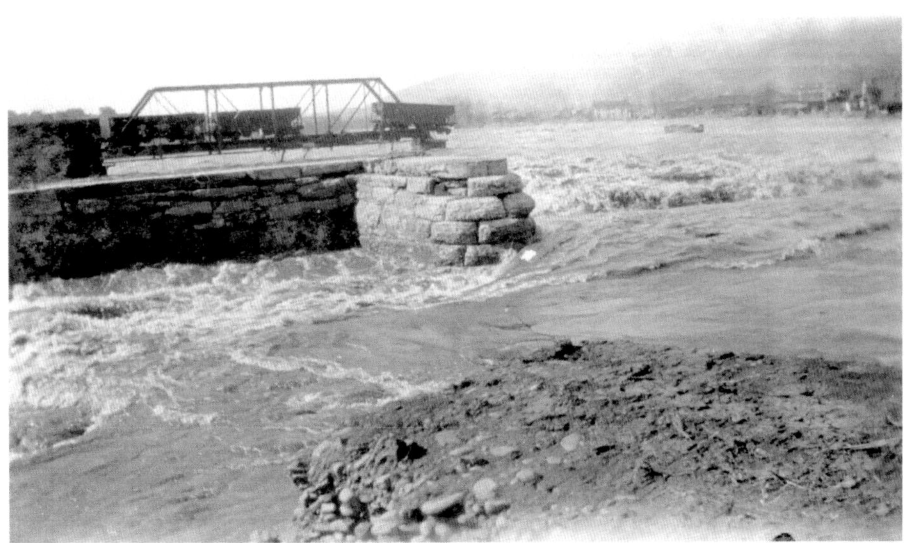

The back of this photograph by Joseph Edward Grabenstein states, "This is where the dam broke." It also portrays a wrecked Potomac River Western Maryland Railway Bridge to Ridgeley, West Virginia.

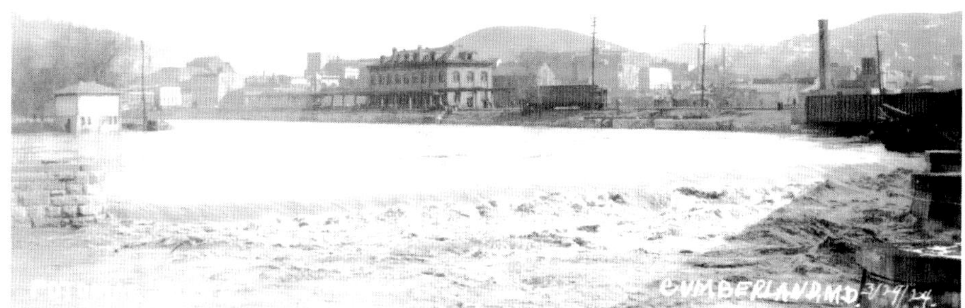

The old Potomac River dam stands in the forefront of this photograph, which depicts the confluence of Wills Creek and the Potomac River. The Western Maryland Railway Station stands in the distance.

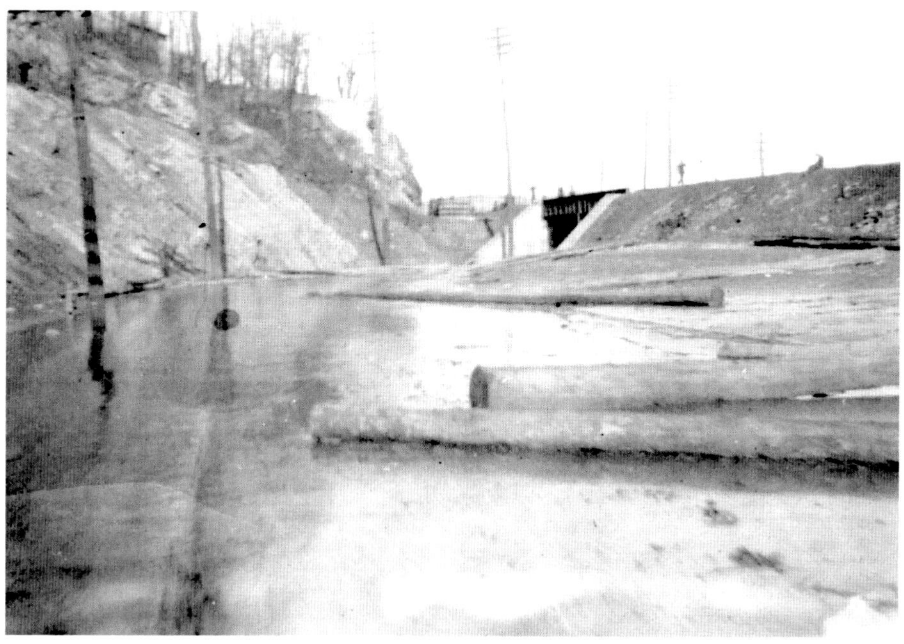

A rare scene, this photograph depicts the railroad underpass along Kelly Road. The hatch marks identify the water's heights during the flood.

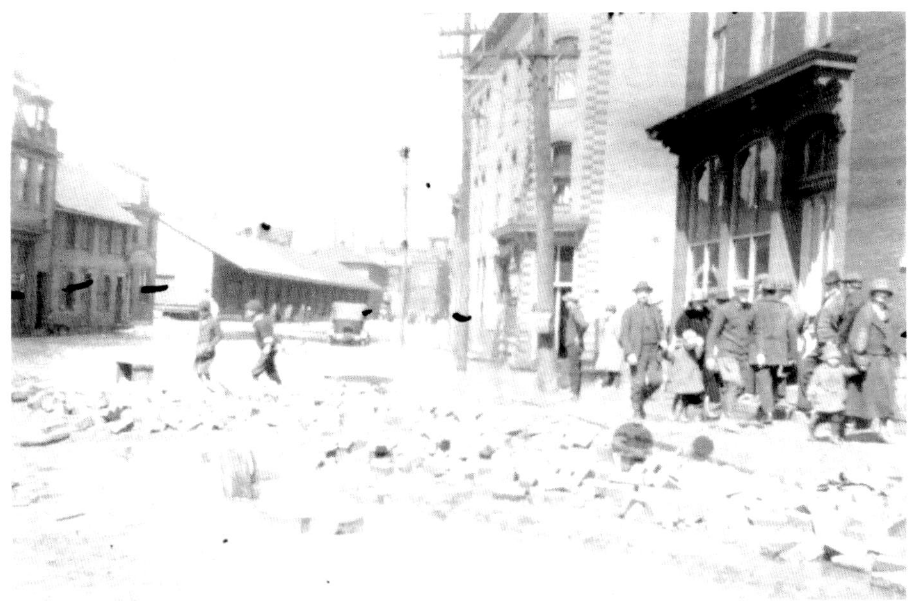

Hatch marks illustrate how high the water rose, this time along lower South Mechanic near its intersection with Harrison Street.

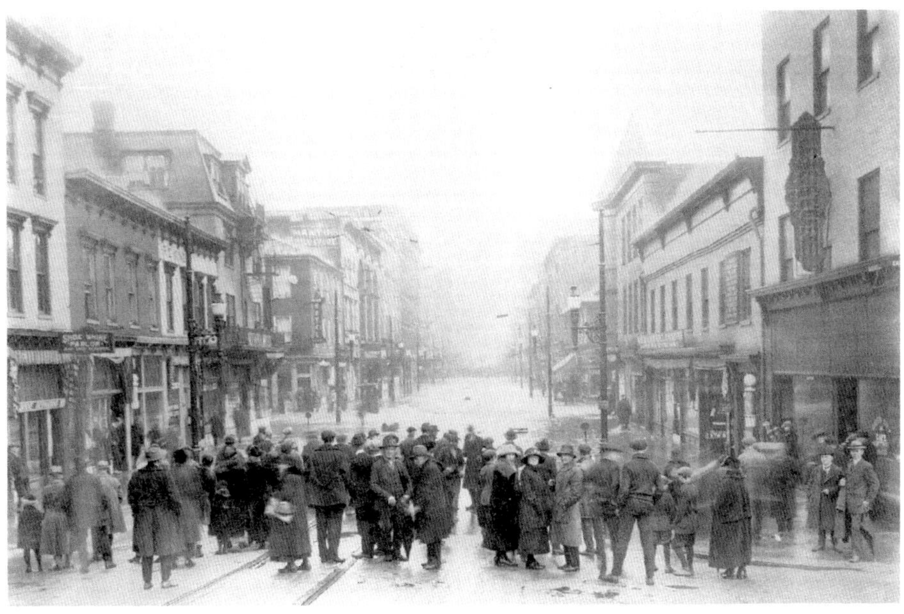

It is 11:30 a.m. on March 29, 1924. Crowds gather at the western end of Baltimore Street near the Western Maryland Railway tracks. Wills Creek would rise about four additional feet after this photograph was taken. Note the trolley car tracks in the lower left. *Courtesy Allegany County Historical Society.*

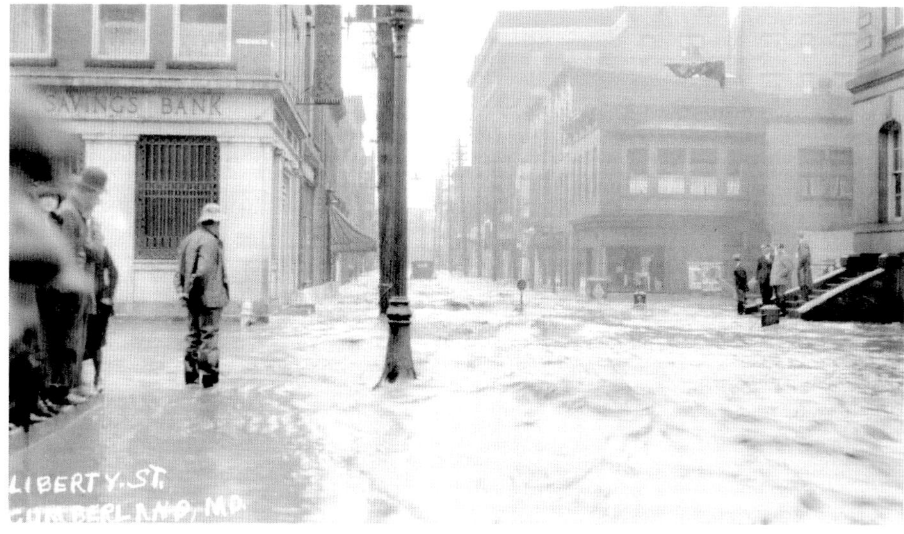

The former Cumberland Savings Bank, now home to Morgan Stanley Financial Services, stands on the left of this view of North Liberty at its intersection with Frederick Street. The deluge of water practically engulfs a car in the distance. *Courtesy Allegany County Historical Society.*

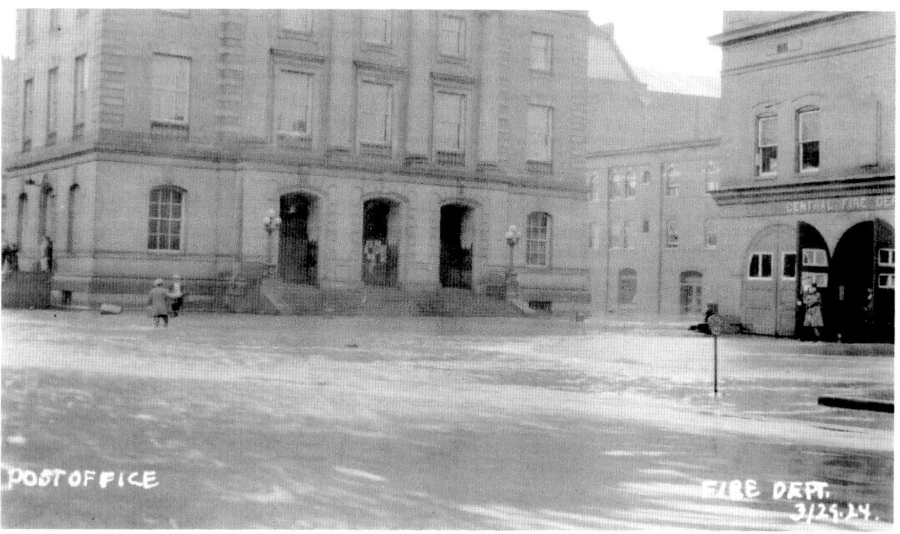

The old post office and Central Fire Department stand amidst a flooded lower Frederick Street.

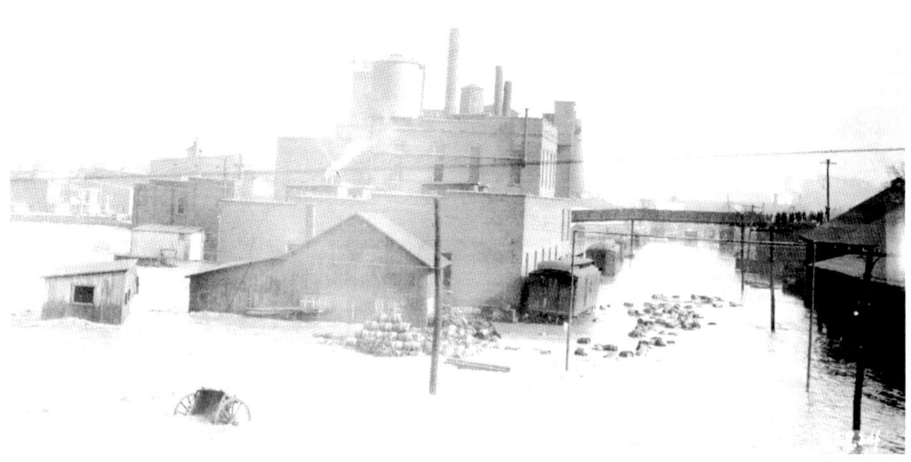

During Prohibition (1919–33), the German Brewing Company manufactured Queeno, a nonintoxicating cereal beverage. This is the Queeno Company plant, phone Cumberland-82, on Market Street adjacent to Wills Creek. Note the upturned wagon on the left and the floating "beer" barrels atop the flooded Western Maryland Railroad tracks on the right. Onlookers gather to the right at the foot of Cumberland Street.

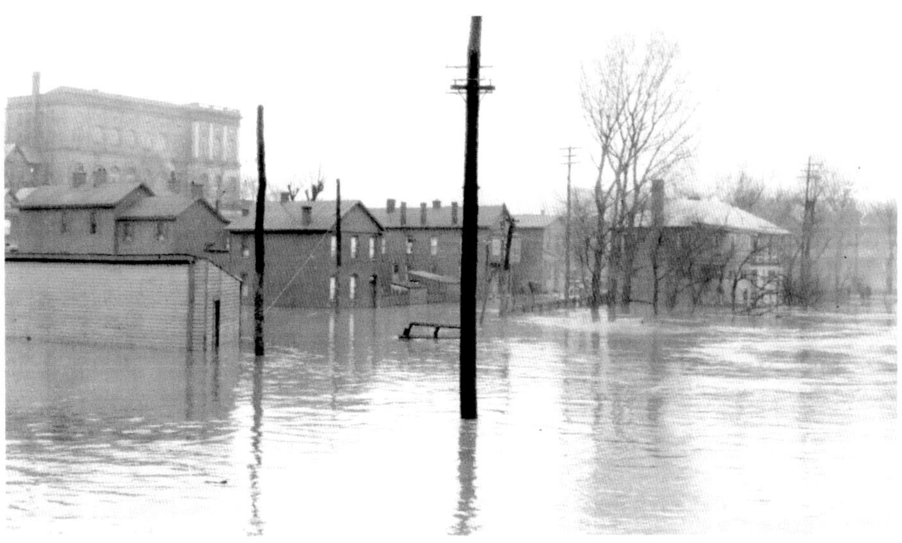

The Masonic Temple, constructed in 1911–12, stands safely on a hill on the left of this image, which portrays the receding Water Street floodwaters on Cumberland's west side.

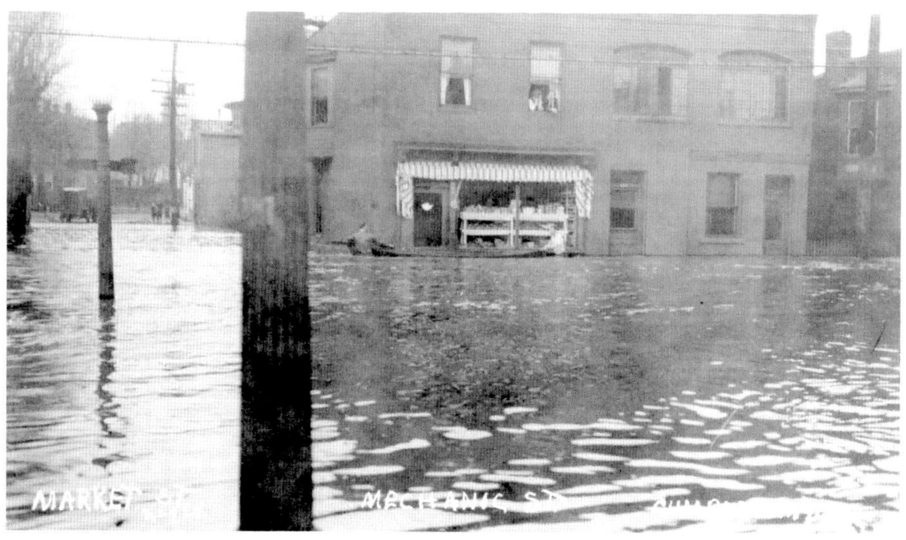

Two residents peer out a second-floor window at the corner of Market and Mechanic Streets. Note the men attempting to board a canoe in front of the store.

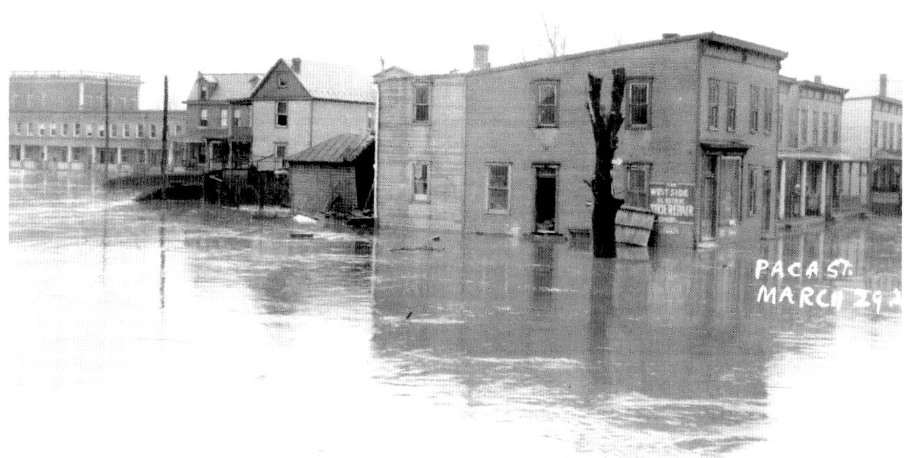

Paca Street looks calm but remains under water. The torrent is over and the waters recede.

AN EXPLANATION TO TIMES READERS

The Electric Power Company is unable to supply current for Running The Evening Times printing machines in day time. The type for news in the paper today had to be set last night

That is why news happenings of the past ten hours cannot be published before tomorrow. It will be necessary to print this paper on the press at the Daily News plant the use of which was very graciously offered the Evening Times by the publishers of the morning paper. The electric motor in Daily News pressroom fortunately was not damaged by the flood. The press motor at the Times plant may be out of commission for several days despite the efforts of loyal and expert electricians and helpers to restore it. We are all doing the best we can to give the public service and ask the patient indulgence of the people for a few days or until it is humanly possible to have normal conditions again.

The *Cumberland Evening Times* offered this explanation in its March 31, 1924 edition for any delays in publication. *Courtesy the* Cumberland Times-News.

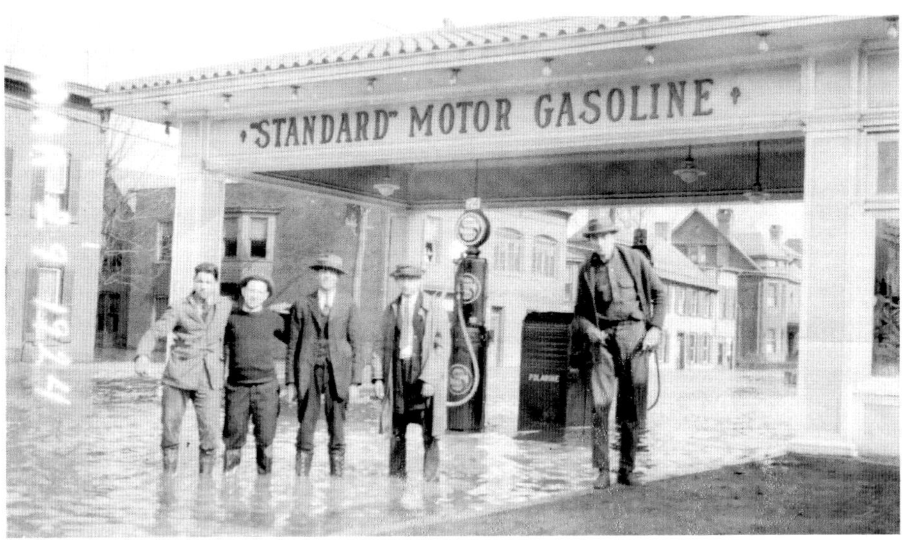

It is March 29, 1924, and this is the Standard Gasoline Station on North Mechanic at its intersection with Market Street. As noted on the back of the photograph, from left to right are Fred Dryer, Con Lashley, F. Johnson, Mike Paupe and Bill Connelly.

Chapter 3

THE GREAT ST. PATRICK'S DAY FLOOD OF MARCH 17, 1936

There had been general rainfall throughout the Potomac River Basin during the first two weeks of March 1936. Snow had also covered much of the watershed in early March. By mid-March, much of this rainfall and thawing snow had begun to find its way into the region's streams and creeks. Even with a saturated watershed and relatively high runoff, however, things were still relatively normal. On March 15, a major storm that had originated in Texas began to move in a northeasterly direction, resulting in heavy downpours throughout the Mid-Atlantic states and the Upper Ohio River Valley. Although the heaviest rainfall occurred on March 17, the rainfall continued until March 19 with a total rainfall depth during this period of five inches in the Wills Creek and North Branch of the Potomac River areas.

The following narrative originally appeared in a March 1936 issue of the *Cumberland Shoppers Guide*, a weekly publication published by Stanley Fields and William B. Kaldor. Richard T. Renshaw, who served as the guide's city editor, wrote this article. In my 1986 publication entitled *Feldstein's Fiftieth Anniversary Commemorative Edition of the St. Patrick's Day Flood*, I noted that this period piece, which immediately follows, describes the phenomenon surrounding this "catastrophe" better than anything I could write. I feel the same today.

Highlights of the 1936 Flood

Here is the story of the Great Flood of 1936—the flood that prostrated Cumberland, Queen City, and industrial leader of Western Maryland. Here is the story of the Catastrophe, a story that opens with rainy Monday,

March 16, and closes upon Cumberland, calm, and on the way to Recovery after the floodwaters had receded. Here is a story simply written, set forth chronologically in all its appalling detail, describing the situation as Cumberland met it and faced it…

Forecast

Because it had long been common belief that Cumberland was afflicted with a flood every twelve years, and because the snowfall was unusually heavy in the winter of 1935–36 while January and February had been a series of alternate hot and cold spells, a spring flood had been predicted as early as February, 1936.

Several false alarms had come as the result of thawing snow but it was a heavy and protracted rain which began to fall on Monday, March 16, continuing until late Tuesday night that caused Wills Creek to rise and inundate a large section of the City of Cumberland.

While the floods of 1924 were serious, particularly the May flood of that year; they were caused by the rising of the Potomac River, into which Wills Creek empties at a point just below Cumberland. In 1936, the Potomac was not dangerously high. The trouble was due to the creek being unable to empty into the river fast enough to disgorge the water which poured down from the mountains.

Early Tuesday morning, March 17, Cumberland authorities began to feel uneasy. By communicating with points throughout the "Creek Section" it became apparent that water was rising at a dangerous rate and a flood was on the way.

Throughout the day crowds gathered on the Baltimore Street bridge to watch the rising water, in spite of the heavy downpour.

Fire Chief Reid C. Hoenika began notifying property owners along Mechanic Street and in the low-lying parts of town to prepare for high water. At this time the water was still nearly eight feet lower than flood stage, but rising rapidly.

Precautions were taken but no one suspected the proportions the flood was to assume.

The day wore on; the rain continued; the creek rose; and a feeling of impending tragedy pervaded everyone. Baltimore Street soon resembled an ant hill; with people scurrying here and there, boarding up windows, placing sand-bags, and doing everything possible to prepare for the worst. If they had only known it, they were wasting energy for nothing in the world could have withstood the force of the torrent that was soon to follow.

By 3 p.m. every store along the lower end of Baltimore Street had suspended business. Employees rushed helter-skelter putting merchandise in high places. Unfortunately, the high places proved not high enough in many cases because people thought the water wouldn't go higher than in 1924.

Arrival

At 4 p.m. word began to circulate that Wills Creek had overflowed its banks at the Narrows and that upper Mechanic Street was flooded to a depth of 12 inches. This marked the actual beginning of the flood.

At Baltimore and Mechanic Streets the clear rain water that had been running in the gutters all day slowly changed to a muddy color. A trickle of brown that widened into a broad band on each side of the street began to come.

For nearly fifteen minutes the sewers absorbed this overflow but they were soon filled and the water turned the corner, running lazily along Baltimore Street, ankle deep. The bands on each side met. Mechanic Street was under water. Centre and Liberty Streets were in the same condition, but slightly less deep. Watchers at the Creek reported that it was still rising, and the rain continued.

It began to grow dark. Fear that the electric lights would soon go out grew. Candles became precious and even matches were in big demand.

The City Fathers realizing that Cumberland was in for a siege created flood headquarters at City Hall from which to direct emergency activities. The Red Cross, with its usual dispatch, set up emergency headquarters at the State Armory.

Water was two feet deep in the streets by this time, and was still rising. Every pair of hip boots in town was sold. Volunteer workers had to wade, soaked to the skin, in icy water.

As the water crept higher, many phones went dead, throwing switchboards into confusion. Trouble crews worked frantically disconnecting lights on dead phones so the operators could answer legitimate calls.

By five p.m. Mechanic, Centre and Liberty Streets were virtually tributaries of Wills Creek. Crossing them, even in a boat would have been a hazardous undertaking. City Hall was soon cut off by the rising water, and phones there went dead. Headquarters was washed out.

Sixteen were trapped in a building on South Mechanic Street. Several men were marooned in a cigar store on Centre Street, and later nearly drowned when the water broke the plate glass windows and swept them out into the stream. Nearly every store on Baltimore Street held refugees.

As the night wore on with the water growing higher, rescue crews were able to get food into the buildings by pulleys but evacuating the trapped victims was impossible.

Washouts

By six o'clock rumors of bridges being washed out were going the rounds. Nearly every dam within 100 miles was said to have broken. A siding with 13 freight cars on it did wash out. One railroad bridge gave way. No dams broke.

Trains, buses, and cars were stranded. Communications were cut off. The city was isolated for the duration of the high water, save for radio station WTBO, which obtained permission from the Communications Commission through Senator Millard E. Tydings, to remain on the air all night.

With headquarters cut off, the police found themselves temporarily without leadership but gallantly carried on. The Fire Department moved its equipment to higher ground. Floodwater, inundating all bridges, made it impossible to get to or from the West Side except by walking across the B & O viaduct.

Hotels outside of the flooded area were packed, as were all other available rooms and sleeping places. Hundreds of refugees spent the night in the Armory where they were cared for by the Red Cross, who estimated the number of families washed out at more than 1200, close to 6,000 people. These were in addition to those who were only temporarily cut off from their homes.

As word of the flood spread, offers of aid began to pour in from state, federal, and local officials of other communities.

8 p.m. found water spread, over the Western Maryland railroad bridge at Baltimore Street, and an ominous sag in the line of cars standing there told officers that the bridge had buckled. No one was allowed to approach within a few hundred feet of the structure which was expected to give way momentarily.

Mayor George W. Legge called on the National Guard to help preserve order and to prevent looting of damaged property. In a very short time they had mobilized and were swinging into action aiding the local police, and the special officers who had been sworn in. The town was under semi-Martial Law.

Meanwhile, the raging water was doing a first class wreckage job. Inadequately secured windows smashed under the impact of the water. Quickly the contents of these stores were swept out into the general confusion, to bump and slide along adding impetus to the water's charge. Soon articles of every description, including stoves, refrigerators, pianos, showcases, gasoline storage tanks and household furnishings could be seen bobbing along like straw on the crest of the waves.

Although it was Election Day, and the polls had long since closed, nobody knew and few cared who had been elected. It was purely and simply the day of the flood and nothing else was of even minute importance. Not even St. Patrick.

Barricades in front of stores gave way without much of a struggle against the force of the current. Water rose to a depth of ten feet and more in many places. Even Baltimore Street was covered by more than six feet at the height of the flood.

Rehabilitation

No sooner had the flood started to subside than Water Department employees began to rush the work of repairing water lines. The Street Superintendent quickly mobilized crews to clean away enough of the debris to allow trucks to get through the devastated sections. The City Engineer made a hurried survey to estimate the damage. The WPA [Works Progrss Administration] *Administrator received permission to use laborers on clean-up work. Whole companies of Civilian Conservation Corps (CCC) were rushed in to help. Scores of workers were hired by the city, and private contractors were pressed into service with both men and their equipment.*

The damaged area was set apart and roped off. No one was allowed to enter except on business. Unfortunately the first set of passes was issued indiscriminately and a second and a third set had to be issued before all the curiosity seekers had been weeded out.

The local company of National Guards were relieved by a company from Hagerstown. Mayor Legge issued a proclamation closing all places selling beer and liquor every evening at nine. All restaurants outside the flood area did a land-office business. No theatres escaped the flood, and as a result Cumberland was under a blanket of gloom with nothing to relieve the tragedy.

Reconstruction work progressed rapidly. Plate glass poured into town by the truckload and quickly replaced the 300 boarded up windows on the day after the flood.

Merchants piled debris on the curb and trucks hauled it away. Mails which were delayed for several days returned to normal. Salvaged merchandise was offered to the public at give away prices. Bargain hunters snapped it up. Citizens took their losses cheerfully.

The National Guard was recalled. State Police took over the job of patrolling the crippled area. A few days of frenzied activity saw an end to the worst. The State Police were recalled. The special officers were relieved of their duties. The flood area was opened. Business returned to normal. The Great Flood of 1936 faded into the past and became History. Cumberland marched ahead!!

There was a vast array of officials, volunteers and citizens who played a role in providing local relief during the 1936 flood. These included Maryland governor Harry W. Nice, who visited the flood sites and took steps to provide relief and funds. Our Congressional representatives, led by Congressman David J. Lewis, began to press for flood control protection funds from the federal government. State Senator Robert B. Kimble, of Allegany County, sought flood relief funds from the state. Allegany County commissioners A. Charles Stewart, James Holmes and Nelson W. Russler floated local bond bills for flood assistance. Cumberland mayor George W. Legge and Mayor-elect Thomas W. Koon, MD, worked together to raise funds and begin work with the Army Corps of Engineers to develop a long-term solution to flooding in Cumberland and the entire Potomac River Valley. The Allegany County's Flood Disaster Committee included Mrs. George Henderson of the Allegany County Red Cross, Dr. Joseph Franklin as the Allegany County Health Officer, Lieutenant Colonel George Henderson representing the Maryland National Guard, Harry Greenstein from the Maryland Emergency Relief Administration and J. Milton Patterson of the Allegany County Welfare Board.

It is important, at least from a textual perspective, to provide some understanding on the impact of the flood of March 17, 1936, on the Georges Creek region of Allegany County, including Midland, Barton and Westernport. All suffered heavily from the flood. In Lonaconing alone, Mayor William O. Jones estimated the destruction to be $50,000. Rail service of any kind (including trolley) ceased, and repairs to the Cumberland and Pennsylvania Railroad tracks were expected to take at least a week. The water not only damaged railroad lines, streets and sewers, but it also inundated many area mines. This calamity was the final straw for many of the local coal enterprises already in financial straits. Only the high ground municipalities, such as Frostburg, escaped the violent floodwaters.

From the *Cumberland Evening Times*, March 19, 1936:

Many houses along Railroad Street and in the "Island" section are flooded with all the Island residents having been moved out when the waters of

Georges Creek began to rise. The creek has swelled to several times its ordinary size and has torn away banks as much as twenty feet on both sides. Garages and out-houses are washed away, and several homes in Lonaconing and Pekin are moved from their foundations with the foundations of nearly all the buildings along the creek undermined, with retaining walls also battered to pieces. A huge fuel tank from the old glass works on Railroad Street broke loose about 11:00 AM Tuesday and banged into Stakem's bowling alley on Jackson Street, knocking the building from its foundation where it is left dangerously dangling over the creek.

From the *Cumberland Evening Times*, March 20, 1936:

More than 100 families of the Tri-Towns were left homeless from the flood waters that visited this vicinity. Piedmont suffered the least due to the flood wall that was built several years ago. The cellars of the houses belonging to the West Virginia Pulp and Paper Company on Maryland Avenue, Westernport were flooded, with numerous garages along the upper end of Main Street along the C&P Railroad tracks washed away. There was over three feet of water at the lower end of Main Street running through the business district from Georges Creek, with store owners placing stock and fixtures on the second floor. Although considerable, losses at the West Virginia Pulp and Paper Company plant were less than the great flood of 1924, with only one foot of water reported on the streets of Luke. The concrete bridge on the Bloomington Road which connects Bloomington with Luke is now gone, the road between Westernport and McCoole has been closed for over 24 hours due to slides, and the Westernport water line on the Savage River road had also been washed out.

From the *Cumberland Evening Times*, March 21, 1936:

Mayor E.J. Roberts of Westernport requests the patience and indulgence of the people due to inconveniences caused by the flood. All broken pipes, water mains, sewers, etc. will be repaired as soon as possible. Mayor Roberts requests all consumers to boil city water at least fifteen minutes before using it for drinking purposes. School will be resumed at Bruce High School Monday morning. Reports that the county road bridge at Bloomington had washed away were erroneous, with only about twenty feet of the approach being gone, which workmen are now filling with the expectations of the bridge opening for traffic this evening.

From the *Cumberland Daily News*, March 24, 1936:

> *Lonaconing Commissioner James Holmes has asked a state-wide committee appointed by Governor Harry Nice to study flood damage in Maryland, to approve a road repair program that would relieve the county of the cost of repairing and improving a number of county roads that have been damaged by the flood waters. Holmes stated that roads in the Georges Creek section were particularly bad, with one stretch of about two miles in which five bridges had been destroyed. Nathan Smith, Chief Engineer of the State Roads Commission, said that based upon a partial survey of the damage he had made of the roads in just Georges Creek since the flood, he would estimate the cost of repairs at $37,000. Allegany County Commissioner Nelson Russler and Lonaconing Commissioner Holmes both said this amount "would not even touch the work needed to be done."*

From the *Cumberland Daily News*, March 24, 1936:

> *Supper is held despite flood—With the church basement and kitchen flooded, the Ladies Guild of the Barton Presbyterian church served their supper last Tuesday night in the Odd Fellows Hall. The food and tables were later hastily removed. As the water rapidly rose in the creek, all of the available men, many donating the use of their trucks, were called away and frantically tried to divert the water from Main Street.*

Flooding would hit again in the "Crik" and the region with the downpour of April 1937, as well as in October 1942, 1957, 1985 and beyond.

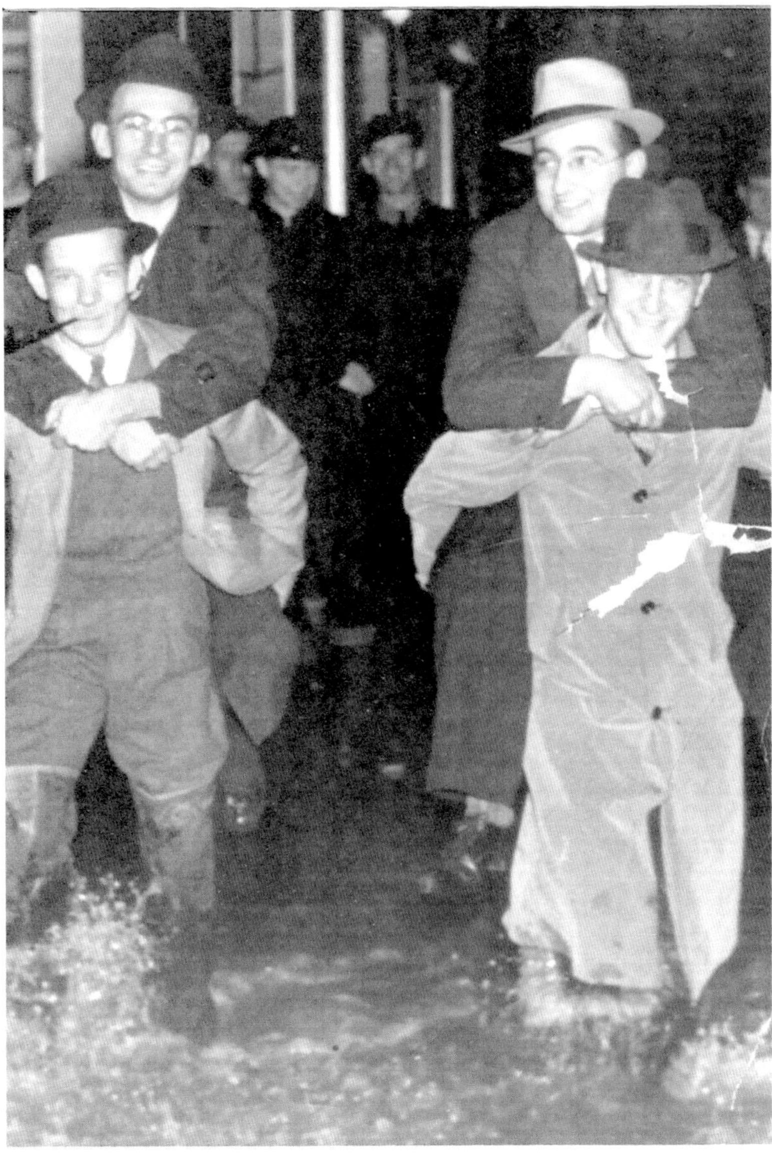

Making the best of a bad situation, four friends traverse a flooded Baltimore Street during the 1936 flood. *Left to right*: The "pack horses" are Richard Wilkinson and Cecil J. Northcraft, while the riders are Charles "Dutch" Haller and Joseph Feldstein, the author's father.

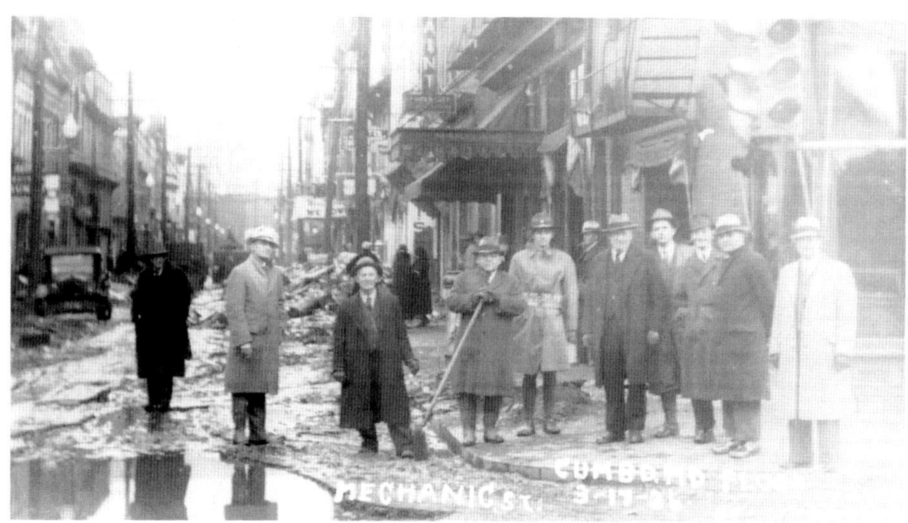

The sender of this postcard writes, "We live just up the street a space on Mechanic. I never seen so much water and refuse come down the street like an ocean. I prayed all night long so our house would still be here in the morning." Although the Georges Creek region in western Allegany County was also flooded, Cumberland suffered the most damage in the 1936 flood. This view looks north from the corner of Baltimore and North Mechanic Streets.

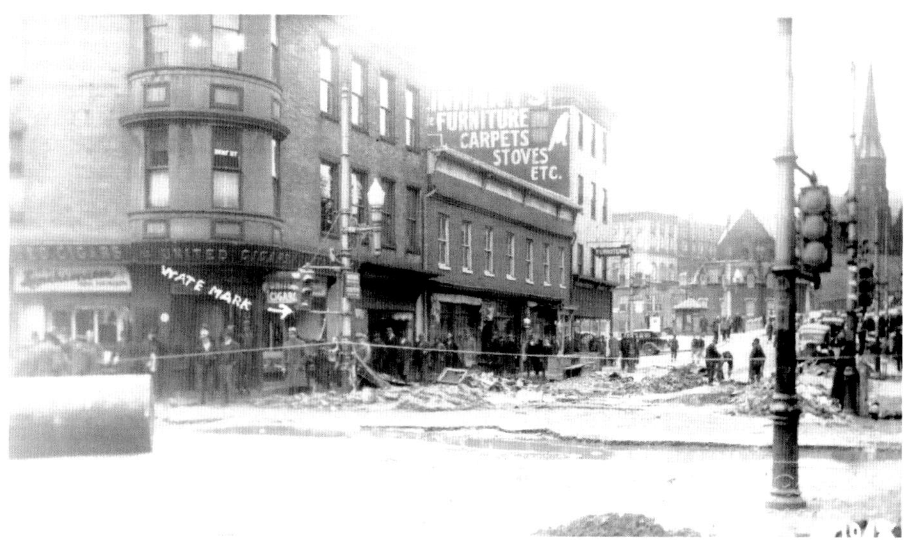

Many who lived or worked on Cumberland's West Side were trapped by the rising waters and used the B&O Railroad Viaduct to cross the city. Note the white arrow "watermark" at the corner of Baltimore and South Mechanic Streets in front of Troxell's Cigar Store, a site later occupied by Metro Clothes.

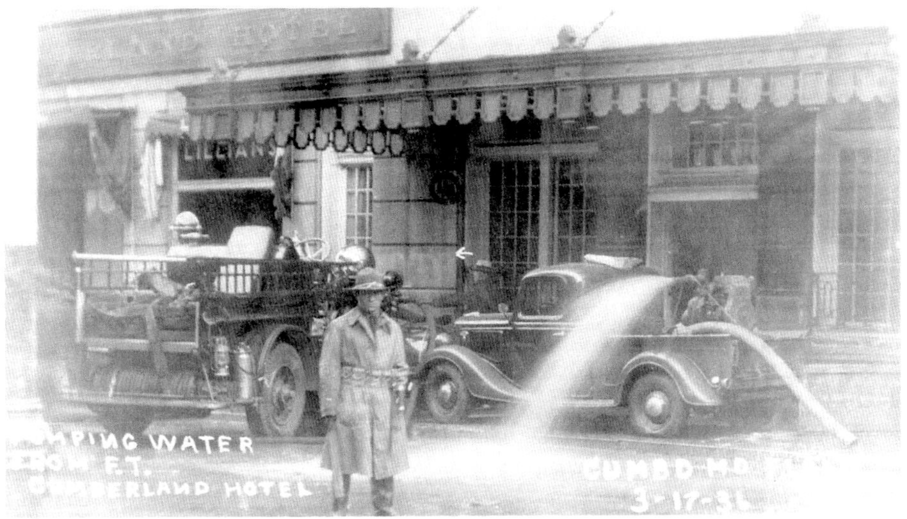

A National Guardsman stands his post on Baltimore Street while water is pumped from the Fort Cumberland Hotel in the flood's aftermath. Now a senior citizen housing facility known as the Cumberland Arms, the Fort Cumberland Hotel was built in 1916 and held its grand opening in 1918.

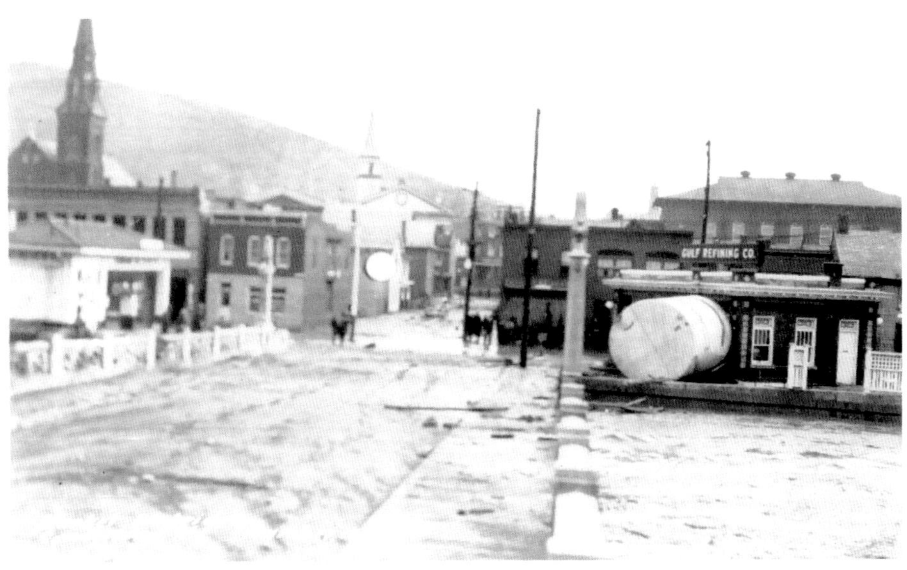

Water and debris from Wills Creek cover the Market Street Bridge. The spires from Centre Street Methodist, St. Patrick's and the Town Clock Church loom in the distance. *Photograph by Eleanor Gerkins.*

March 19, 1936

TO KELLY-SPRINGFIELD EMPLOYES:

Announcement will be made over Cumberland Radio Station WTBO at 6:00, 6:30 and 7:00 o'clock to-night as to the departments that will operate Friday, March 20th. Any employes in doubt can also telephone the plant (Cumberland 2850) after 5:00 o'clock tonight. All men not working tomorrow can obtain their pay checks at the gate house anytime between 8 a. m. and 4:30 p. m.

THE KELLY-SPRINGFIELD TIRE COMPANY

This notice from the March 19, 1936 edition of the *Cumberland Evening Times* urges employees to listen to WTBO radio for work-related announcements. *Courtesy the* Cumberland Times-News.

REPORT FIRES BY PHONE

CALL FIRE STATIONS BY TELEPHONE TO REPORT FIRES

SOUTH END 1405
WEST SIDE 1411
EAST SIDE 1407
CENTRAL 1481

The fire alarm service is out of order temporarily.

REID C. HOENICKA
Chief, Fire Department

On March 19, 1936, Cumberland citizens were told that the fire alarm system was out of order and to report fires by phone. *Courtesy the* Cumberland Times-News.

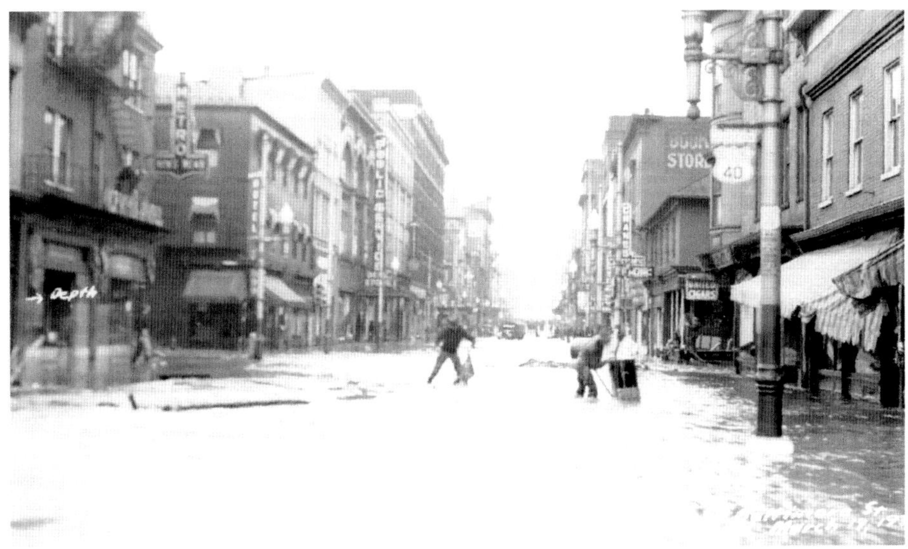

Floodwaters wreaked havoc on Baltimore Street, including at the Metro Store on the left, which was located in the basement of the old Olympia Hotel at the corner of Baltimore and North Mechanic Streets. *Photograph by Eleanor Gerkins.*

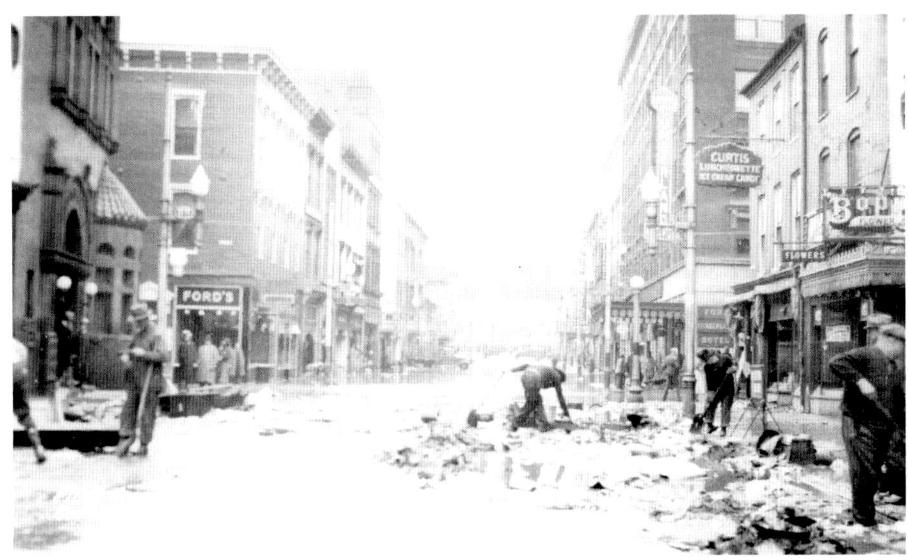

The Strand, Embassy, Liberty and Garden movie theatres were closed, with the Strand requiring extensive work prior to reopening as many of the furnishings were destroyed. However, the Maryland Theatre, located at 37 North Mechanic Street, suffered only slightly because of its high concrete and stone entrance on Mechanic Street. It reopened on March 21, with a Laurel and Hardy film entitled *Bohemian Girl*. The Maryland Theatre had opened in 1907 and was closed in 1963, and the building was razed in 1964. *Photograph by Eleanor Gerkins.*

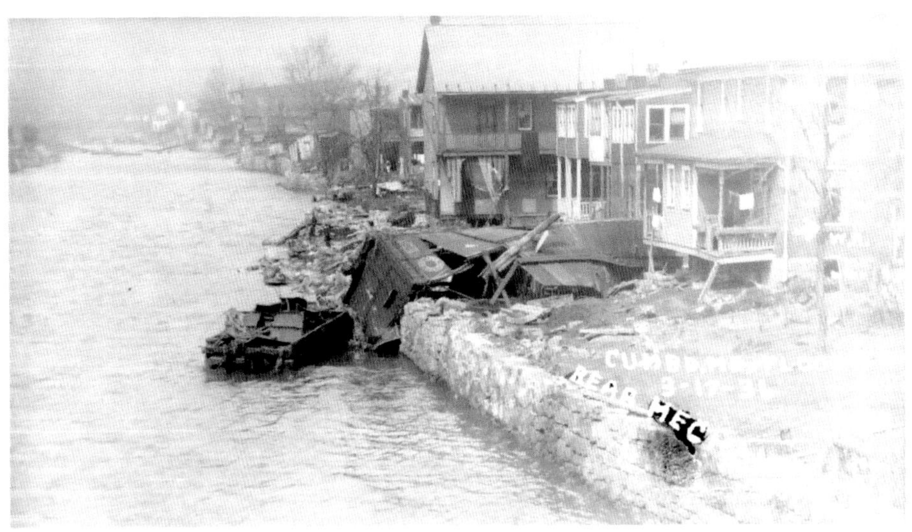

Smashed railroad freight cars were among the devastation found in the backyards of these North Mechanic Street homes along Wills Creek.

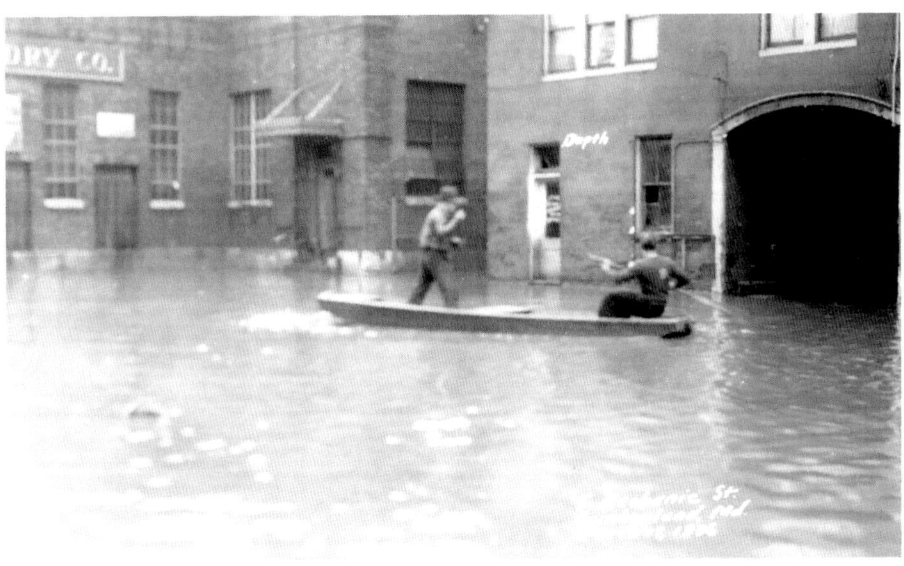

Two men in a boat traverse lower South Mechanic Street. The Crystal Laundry building, now Atlantic Broadband, is on the left. Note the word "Depth" written above the door in the middle. *Photograph by Eleanor Gerkins.*

SS. PETER AND PAUL TOURNEY POSTPONED

On account of the inability of a number of out-of-town teams to reach here because many of the roads leading into Cumberland are impassable due to flood waters, the SS. Peter and Paul fourth annual basketball tournament has been postponed.

The tourney was scheduled to start tonight and end Sunday afternoon. Promoters will announce new dates.

Impassable roads leading into Cumberland caused the cancellation of many events, as documented in this notice from the March 19, 1936 *Cumberland Evening Times*. *Courtesy the* Cumberland Times-News.

Darling Shop

Corner • of Baltimore • and • Centre • Streets

IS GLAD TO ANNOUNCE THAT THEIR STORE WILL BE COMPLETELY CLEANED

Ready for Business TOMORROW Saturday, March 21st.

Fortunately Our Entire Stock Was Removed To Safety Before The High Water and No Merchandise Was Damaged . . . .

The Darling Shop was located at the corner of Baltimore and Centre Streets on a site now occupied by the Downtown Dollar Store. As confirmed by this ad from the *Cumberland Daily News*, March 20, 1936, it would be open for business on Saturday. *Courtesy the* Cumberland Times-News.

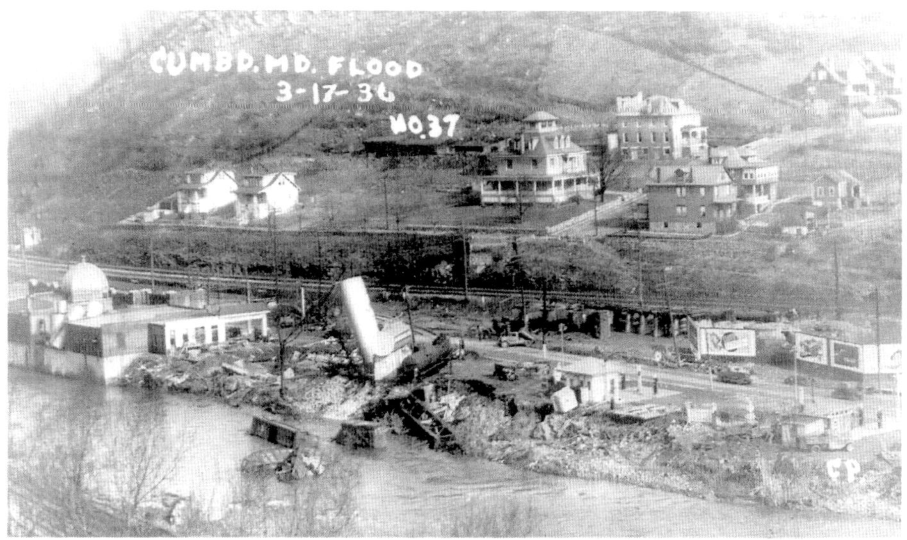

High ground was the place to be in the eastern end of the Narrows, where railroad cars were washed down Wills Creek. Shown on the left is the Richfield Service Station erected in 1919 by Vincent Buchholtz. It was razed in 1952 as part of the flood control construction project. The large house in the middle, with the "widow's walk," is located on Piedmont Avenue and was built in 1896. It is the former home of Anthony Zihlman, president of the Cumberland Glass Works.

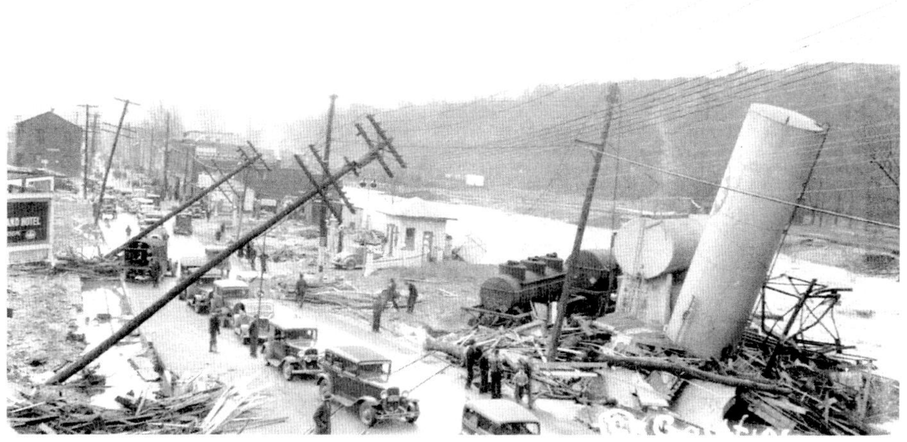

There is gridlock on North Mechanic Street at the Narrows entrance. The American Oil Company gasoline tank on the left leans perilously. *Goldfine Studio Photograph.*

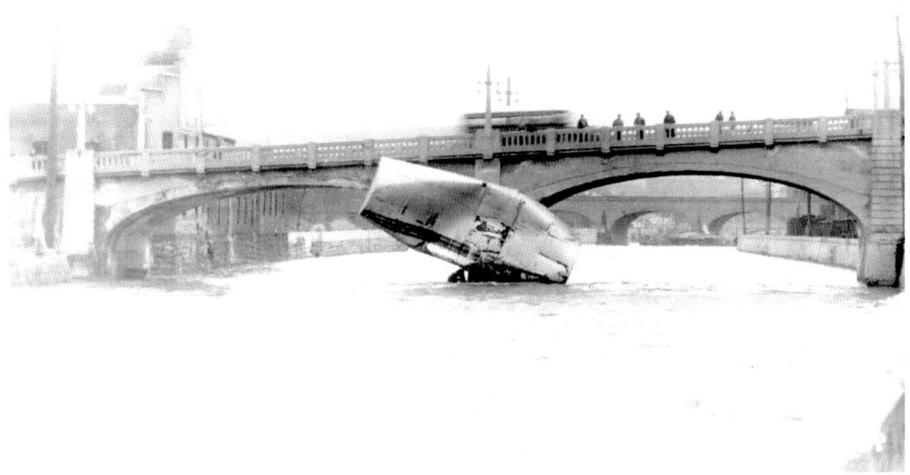

"We lost everything downstairs. This is a big gasoline tank which was right across Mechanic Street. If it ever would have bursted or caught fire, oh how terrible for all. Hope LeRoy, you, and Margaret and boys are all well and happy. Marge got her dress. Will write soon, Florence." As alluded to by the sender of this postcard, people were warned to stay away from the bridge. As seen here, folks walked out to observe any possible explosion.

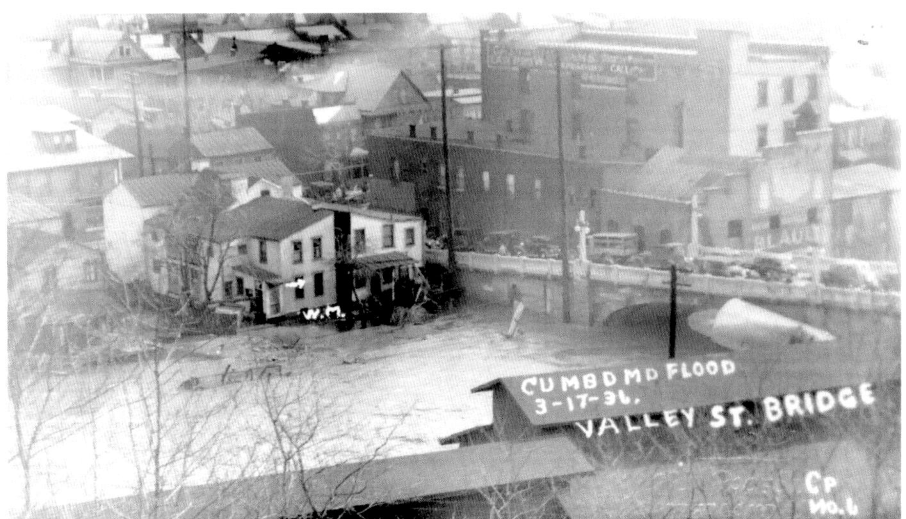

Automobile traffic crosses the Valley Street Bridge above the inundated backyards and homes along North Mechanic Street.

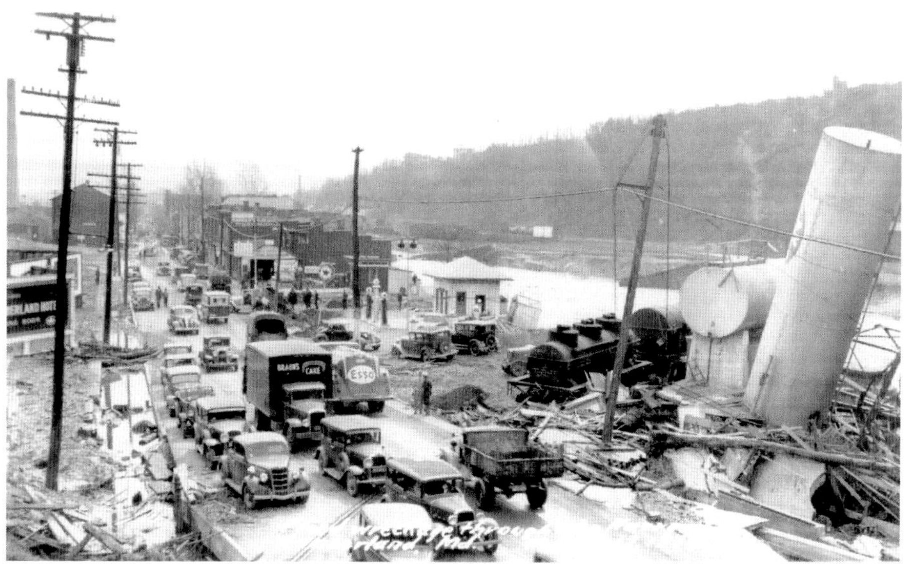

This photograph, taken from the same location as an earlier scene, shows the progress in cleaning up the North Mechanic Street Narrows entrance area. Note the now upright status of the telephone poles on the left, debris removal and the two-way traffic. *Photograph by Eleanor Gerkins.*

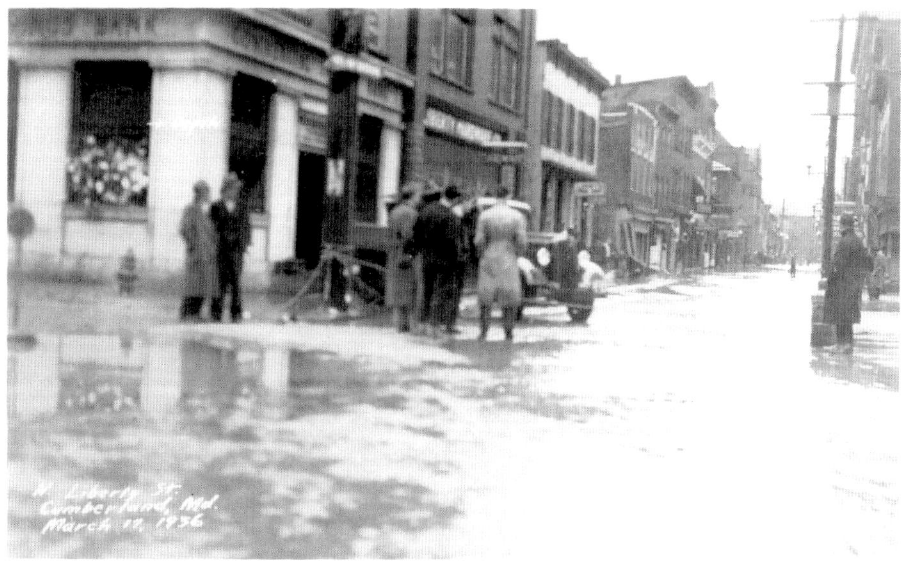

The waters begin to recede. The Commercial Savings Bank and Liberty Hardware Store, now Morgan Stanley and Passarell's Deli and Country Store, are depicted, respectively, in this North Liberty Street photograph.

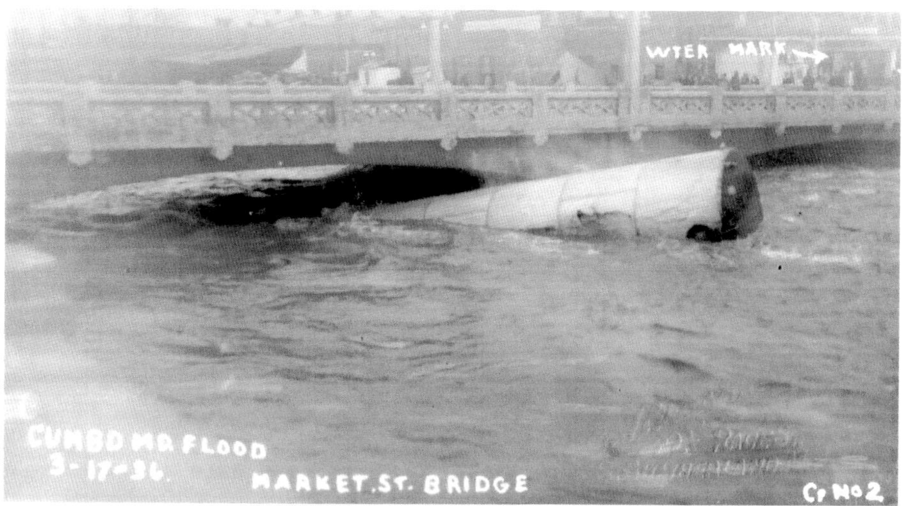

Though not at its height as indicated by the watermark and arrow, a torrent of water continues to flow under the Wills Creek Market Street Bridge. As seen in this E.E. Thrasher photograph, most of the onlookers seem to prefer to stand off to the side.

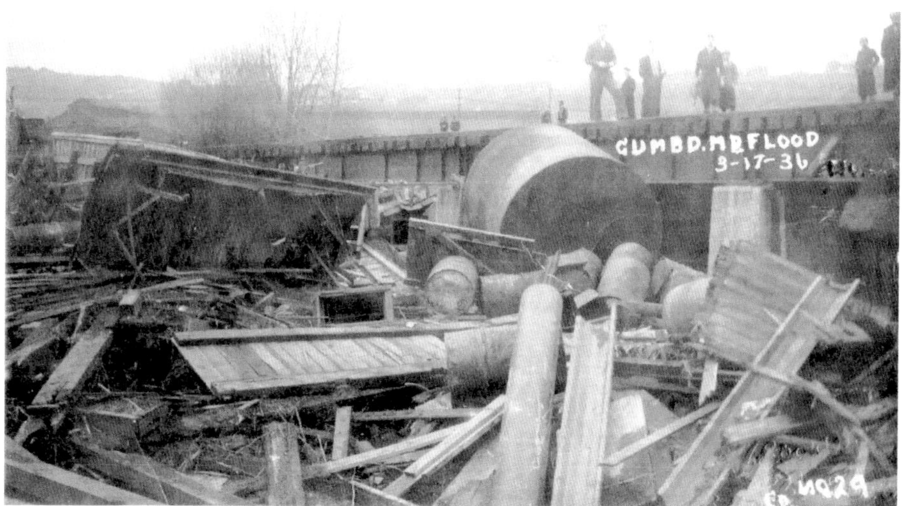

Another E.E. Thrasher scene depicts the accumulated wreckage washed up against one of the city's railroad bridges. The Thrasher photography studio was at this time located at 22 Race Street in South Cumberland. Sent on March 30, the postcard reads, "Dear Bill, I was in Cumberland on Friday. You never saw such a wreck as Baltimore and Mechanic Streets. Mabel."

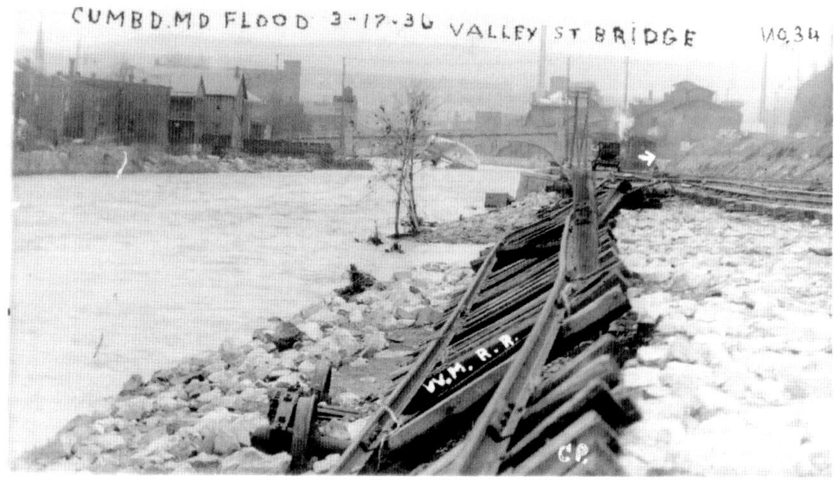

The sender of this E.E. Thrasher postcard writes, "We live just up the street a space from Valley Street Bridge. I never seen so much water and refuse come down the street. Like an ocean. I prayed all night long the bridge would still be here in the morning."

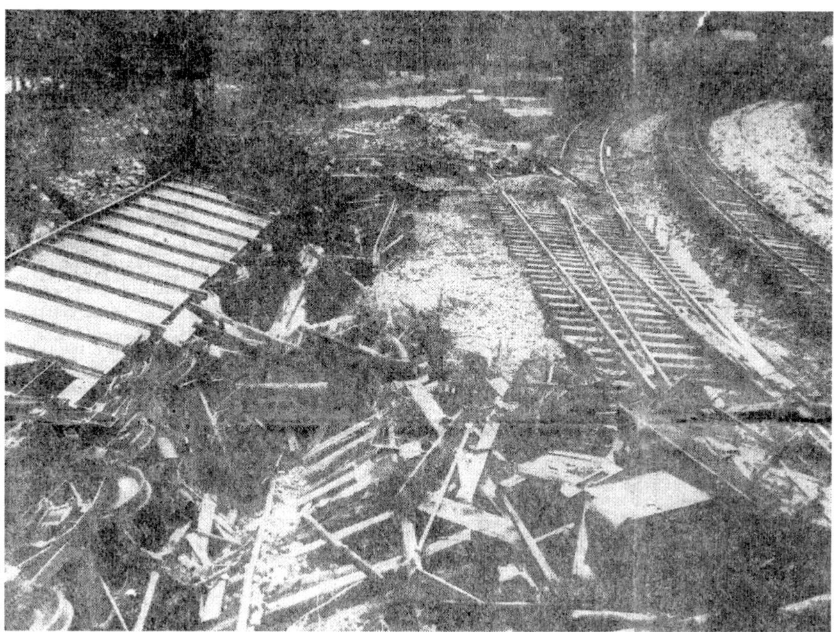

This Goldfine Studio photograph appeared in the *Cumberland Sunday Times* on March 29, 1936, and depicts torn-up railroad tracks, overturned cars, washed-out bridges and damaged roads in the Narrows. The Goldfine Photography Studio was located at 117 Baltimore Street, phone Cumberland-1865. *Courtesy the* Cumberland Times-News.

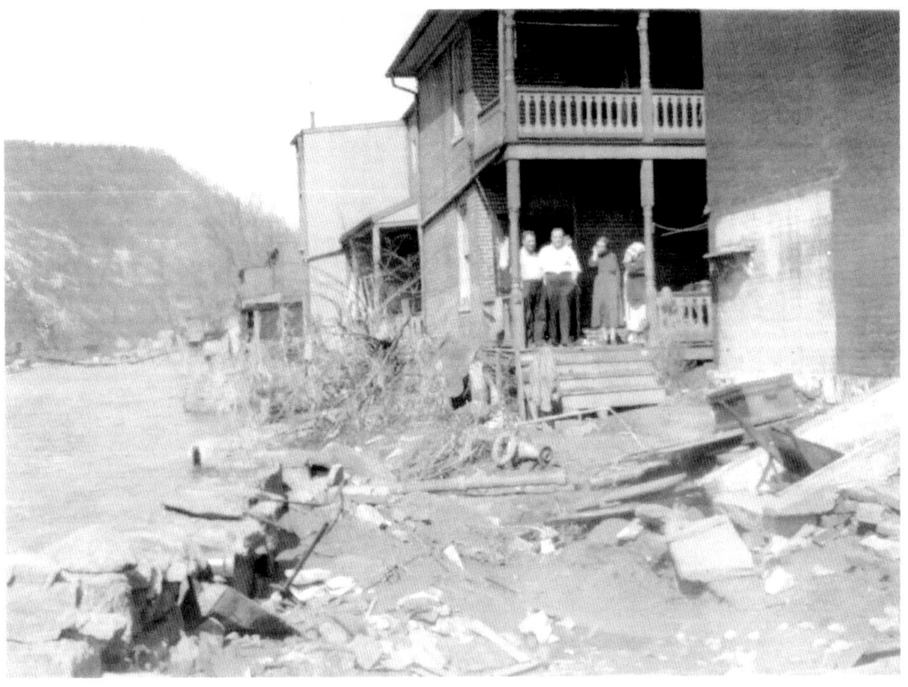

North Mechanic Street residents stand on their back porches along Wills Creek and inspect the damage wrought by the raging floodwaters.

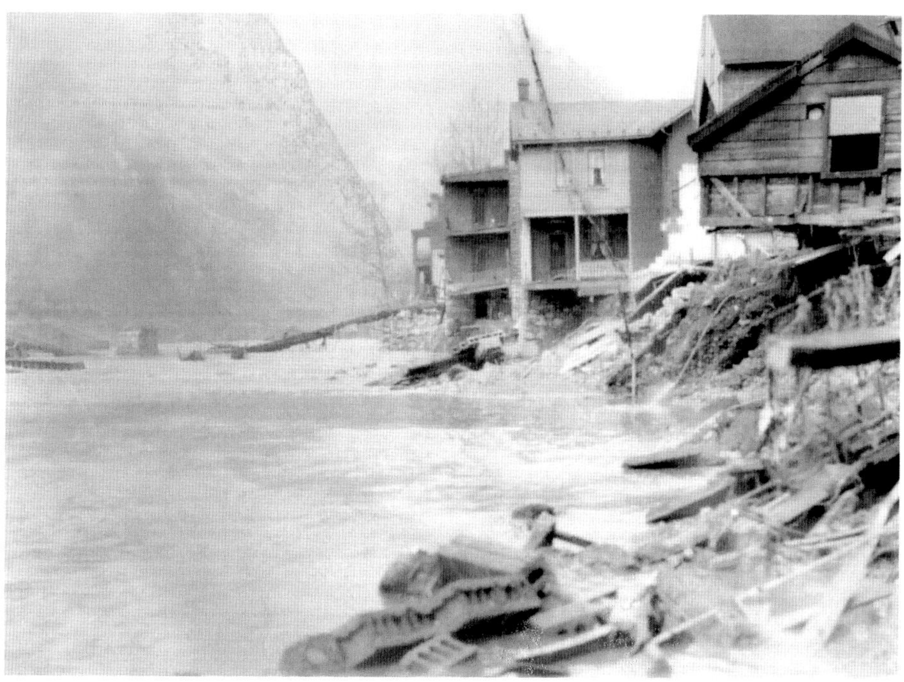

Entire homes and foundations were washed away or destroyed by the rushing floodwaters of Wills Creek.

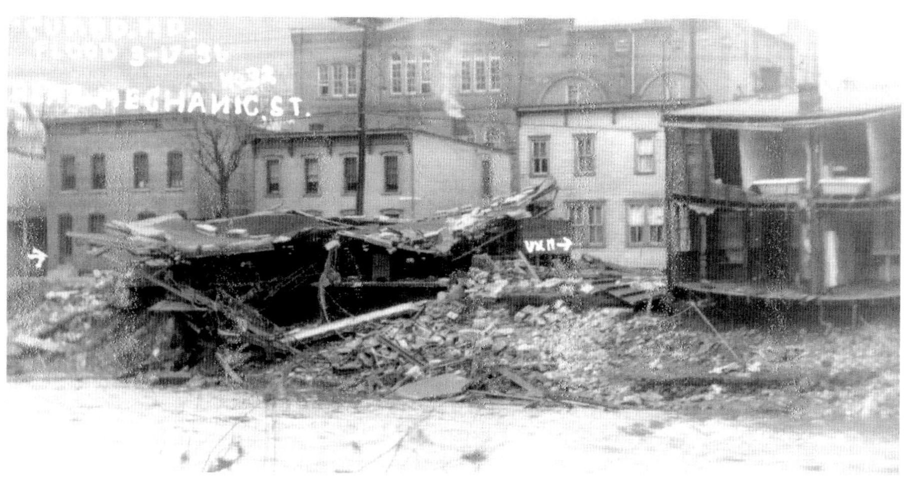

Notices were even published by the mayor and city council—in the public interest, of course—that the selling of intoxicating liquors in the city, including beer and wine, would be illegal until the flood emergency passed. This photograph shows the rear of Mechanic Street, looking north from Wills Creek. Note the bathtubs exposed on the second floor of the homes on the far right and the Cumberland Brewing Company building on North Centre Street in the distance.

Attention!

All Prescriptions formerly filled at Ford's Pharmacy, Center and Bedford Street and Ford's Baltimore Street Drug Store will be filled temporarily at Ford's Lee Street and Baltimore Avenue Stores.

Prescriptions Called for and Delivered

PHONE 183

Ford's Pharmacy made sure that people could still get their prescriptions filled at two of its four locations as seen in this March 20, 1936 *Cumberland Daily News* advertisement. *Courtesy the* Cumberland Times-News.

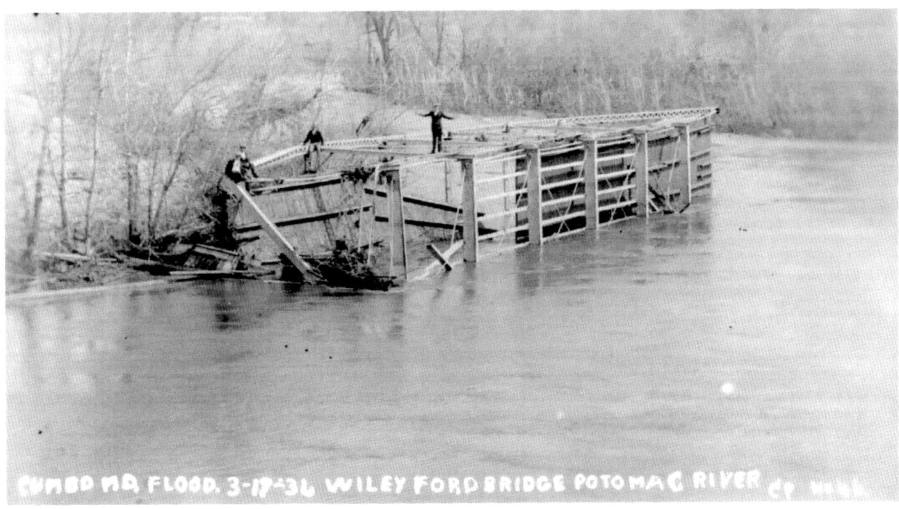

In the flood's aftermath, a span of the Wiley Ford Bridge lay in the North Branch of the Potomac River. *Courtesy U.S. Geological Survey.*

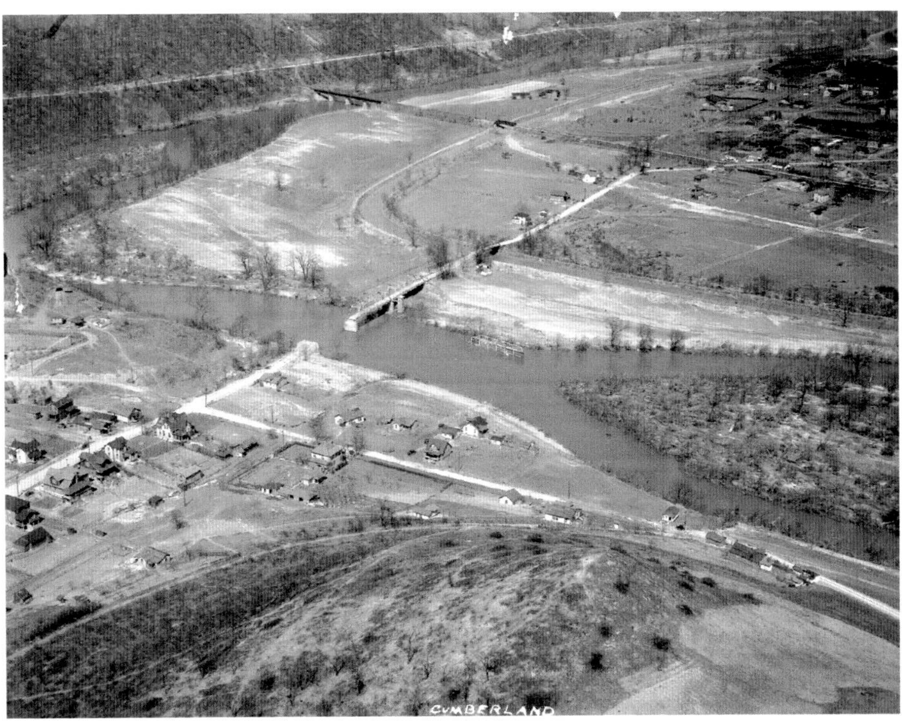

This aerial view shows the damaged Wiley Ford Bridge, which led into West Virginia at bottom, and the surrounding area in the aftermath of the St. Patrick's Day Flood of March 17, 1936. Also depicted is the C&O Canal just north of the bridge. *Courtesy U.S. Geological Survey.*

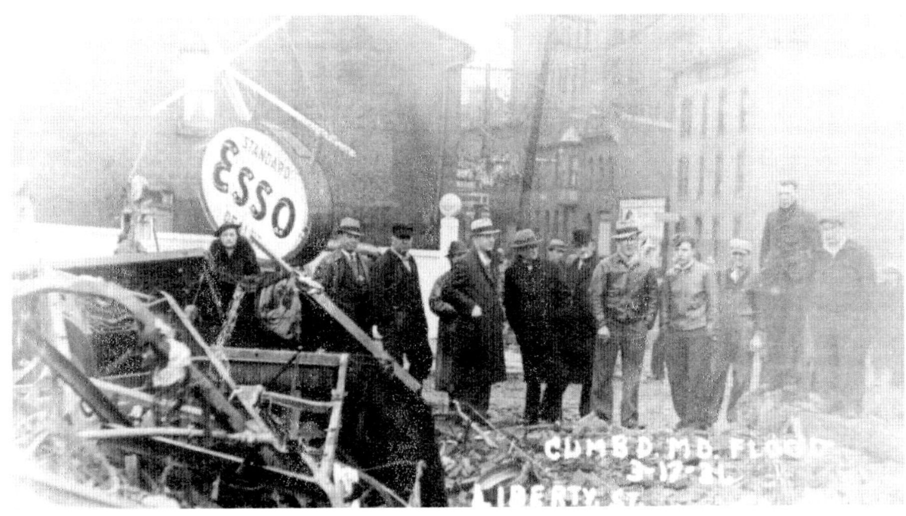

Crowds gather at the corner of South Liberty and Harrison Streets to inspect the accumulated damage.

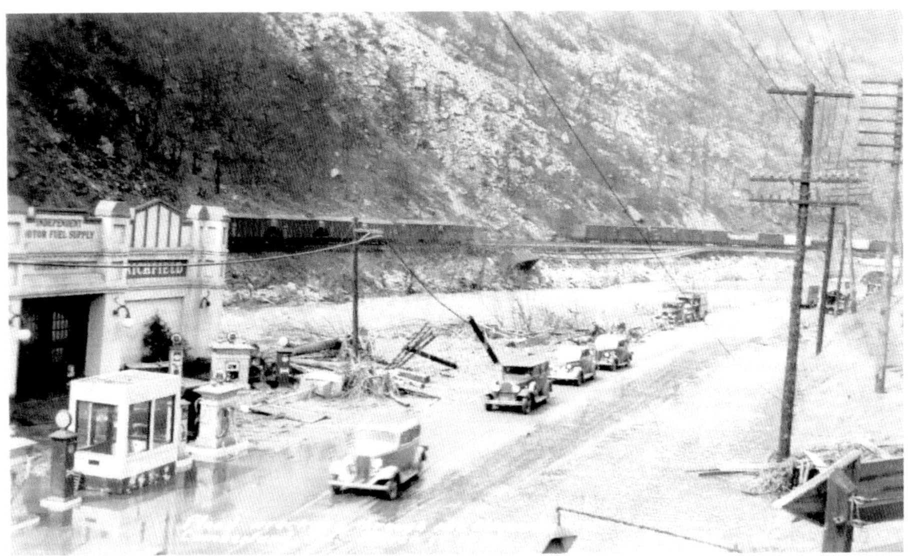

In the Narrows, flood wreckage included downed telephone poles and railroad tracks that had collapsed into Wills Creek. On the left is the Richfield Service Station, bulk oil plant and tire recapping center that was built in 1919. Razed in the 1950s during the construction of the Flood Control Project, it was located roughly where Route 40 crosses Wills Creek in the Narrows.

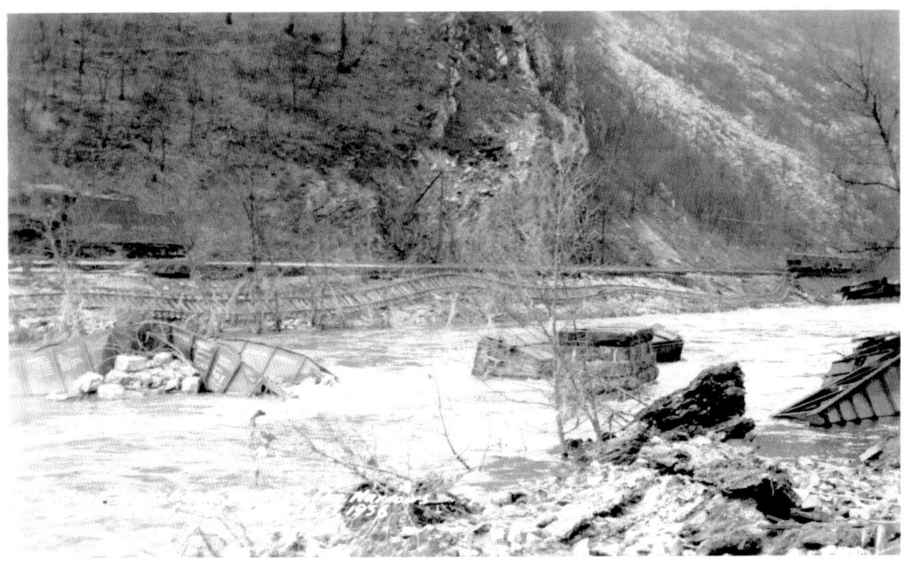

Washed-out Western Maryland Railroad tracks and boxcars adorned Wills Creek in the Narrows.

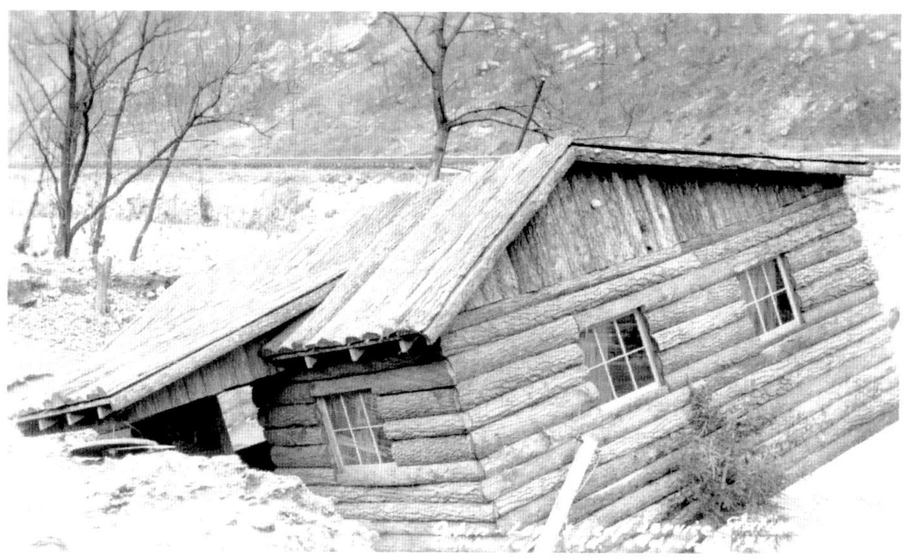

This log cabin, now destroyed, was located at the Lover's Leap Service Station in the Narrows. *Photograph by Eleanor Gerkins.*

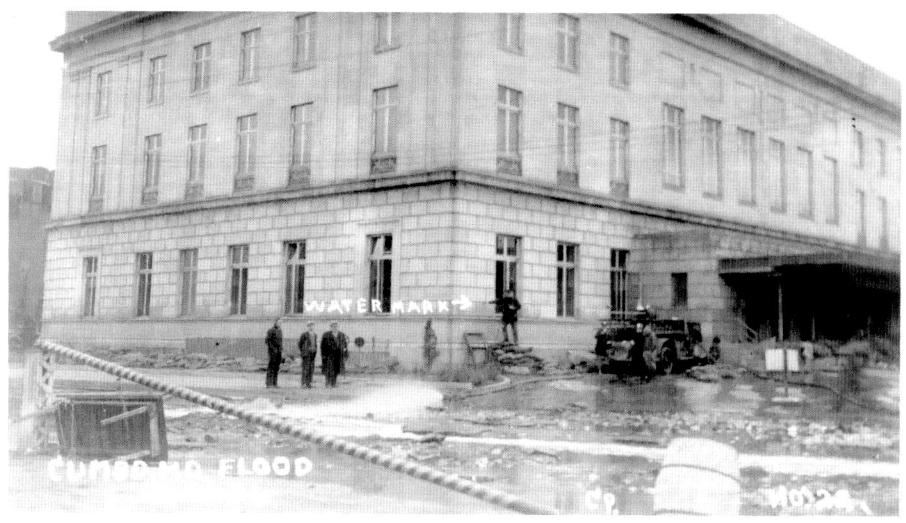

Note the gentleman standing on a pile of debris and the watermark white arrow showing the water level at this point on South Mechanic Street. The building is the former U.S. Post Office and federal courthouse, erected in 1932, on Pershing Street. *Courtesy U.S. Geological Survey.*

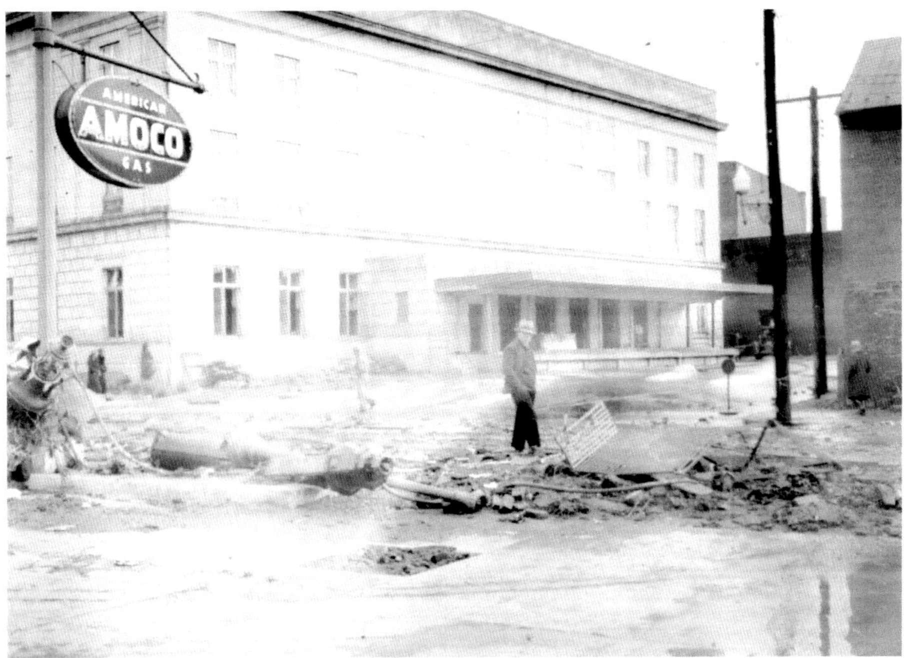

This South Mechanic Street image depicts the rear of the post office building. Note the heavy debris washed down the street in the torrent of water.

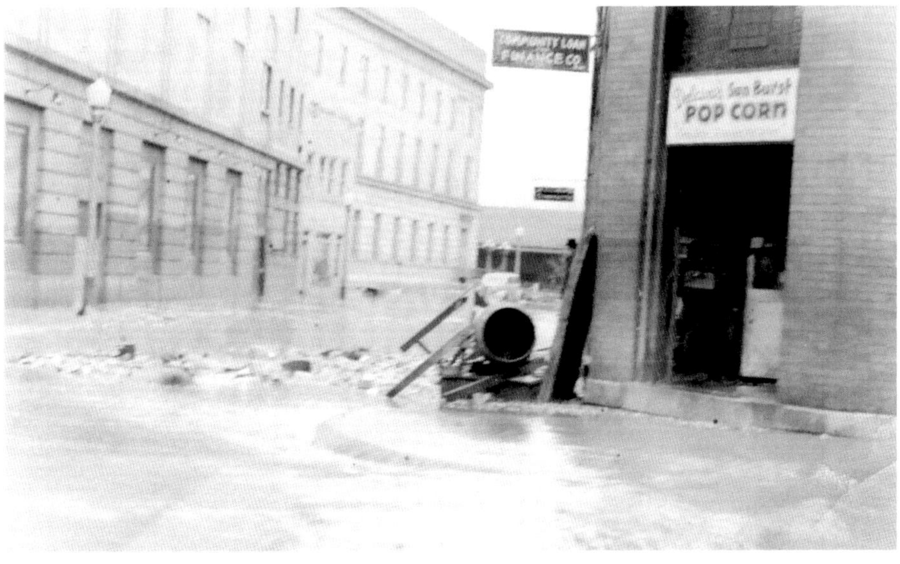

The Strand Theatre building is on the left, the post office is in the distance and what is now the Keller-Stonebraker Insurance office is on the right. Note the Community Loan Finance sign in this view of Pershing Street from South Liberty Street.

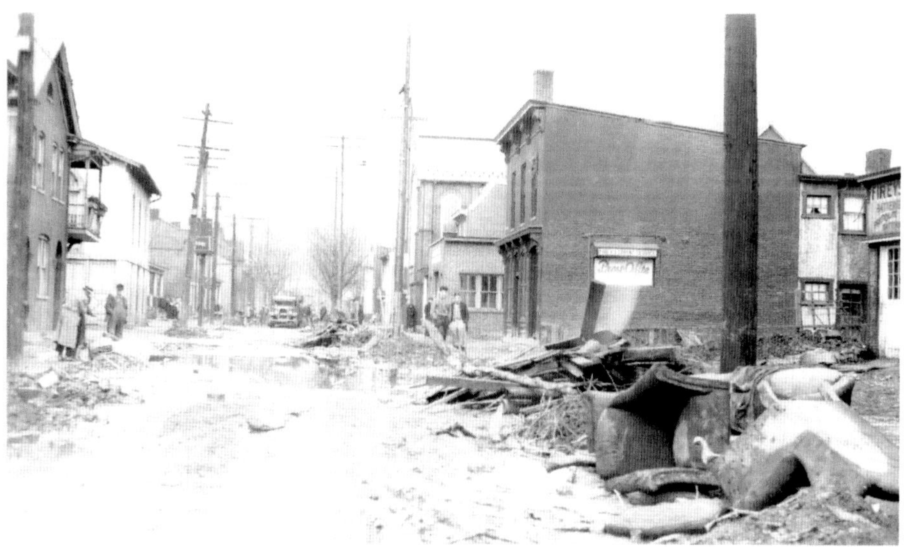

This scene is of North Mechanic Street, looking north from a point near the B&O Railroad viaduct. The Zion Church stands on the right in the background. *Photograph by Eleanor Gerkins.*

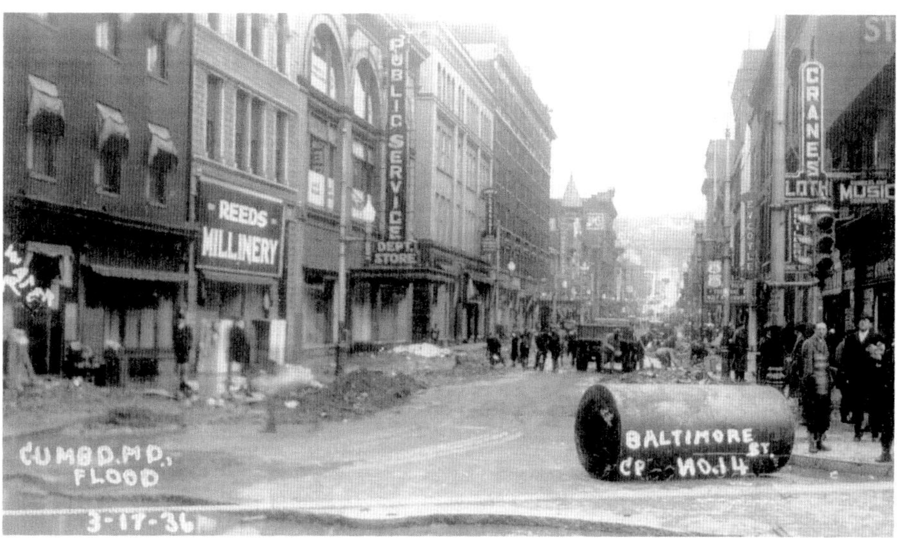

Cleanup is underway as can be seen from this image of Baltimore Street, looking east from Mechanic. Note the water level arrow on the left. The Reeds Millinery and Public Service Department Store buildings are now occupied by CBIZ, while Kauffman Music and Windsor Hall occupy what was once known as the E.V. Coyle Furniture Store on the right. *Courtesy Ora Mae Lewis.*

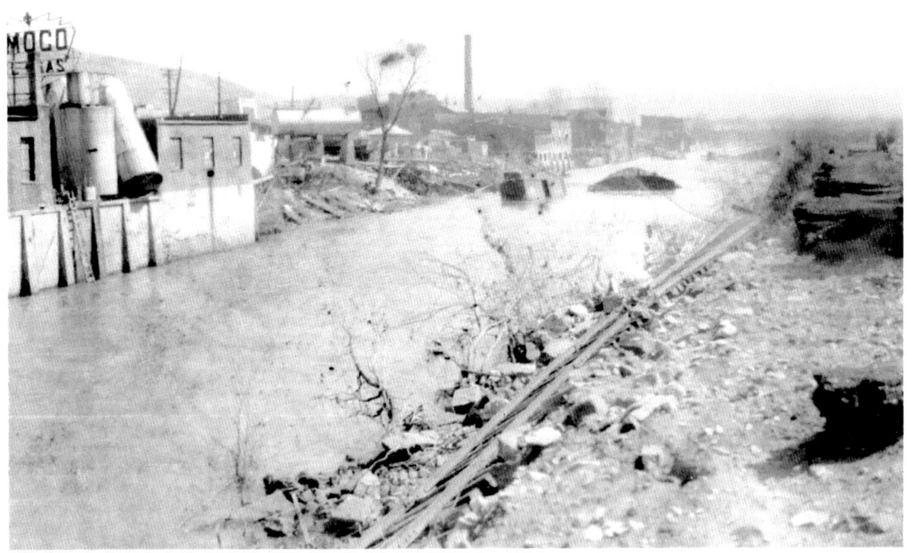

The devastation along Wills Creek, as seen in this photograph, was tremendous. Railroad boxcars were swept along in the raging waters.

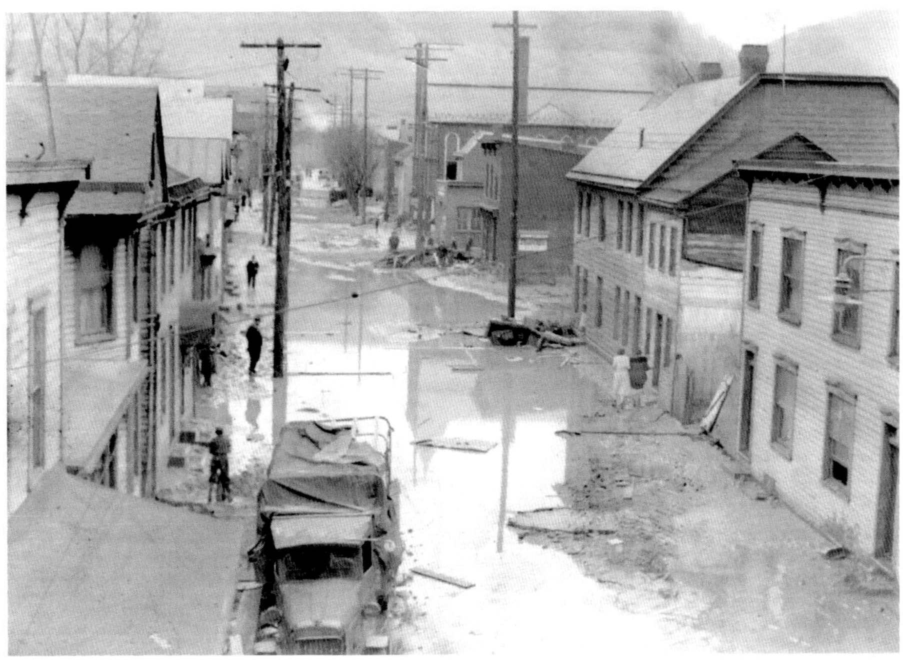

This view of North Mechanic Street, looking north from a photograph taken atop the B&O Railroad Viaduct, depicts the local citizenry viewing the damage and debris now visible from the receding waters.

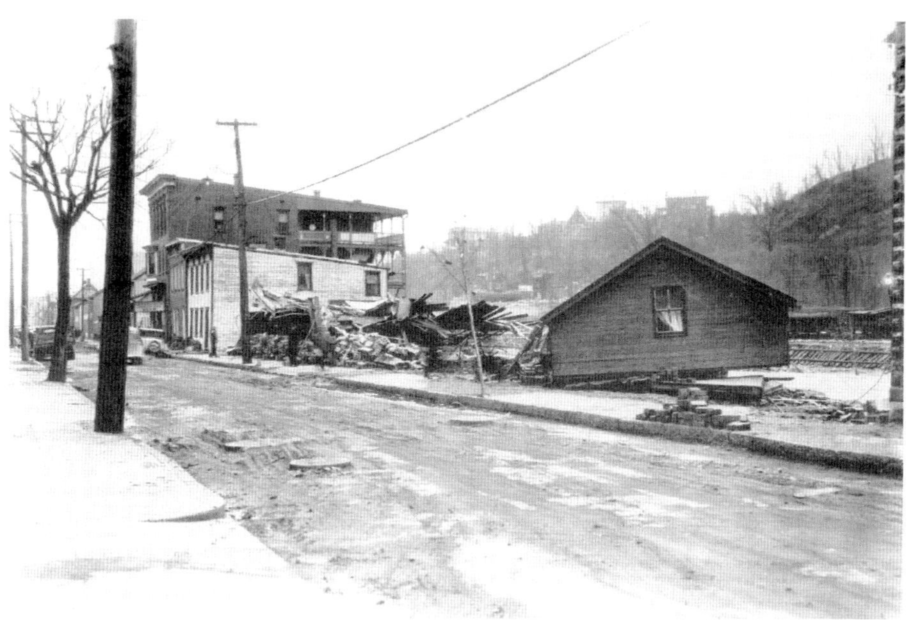

KAPLON'S

YOUNG MEN'S SHOP

115 BALTIMORE STREET

Wish to take this opportunity to thank all who aided us during the flood.

Your help was deeply appreciated

KAPLON'S ARE OPEN FOR BUSINESS AS USUAL

•

Above: Flood wreckage is dramatically portrayed in this photograph of North Mechanic Street. The second and third buildings from the right are presently occupied by Kline's Pawn Shop and Specialties. *Photograph by Eyerman Studios.*

Left: As shown here in the March 20, 1936 *Cumberland Daily News*, one could still buy a suit in Cumberland. *Courtesy* Cumberland Times-News.

NOTICE TO DEALERS SELLING INTOXICATING LIQUORS, WINES AND BEERS IN THE CITY OF CUMBERLAND

By order of the Mayor and City Council of Cumberland, Md., as a measure of public safety.

All business places selling intoxicating liquors, wines or beer are hereby notified and directed to close, beginning Saturday evening, March 21, 1936, at 9 o'clock p. m., and to continue to close their places of business at the same hour until the present emergency in Cumberland has ceased to exist. The police department of Cumberland has been directed to strictly enforce this order.

Signed

GEORGE W. LEGGE,

Mayor

Advertisement

The message is quite obvious in this notice, which appeared in the *Cumberland Daily News* on March 21, 1936. *Courtesy* Cumberland Times-News.

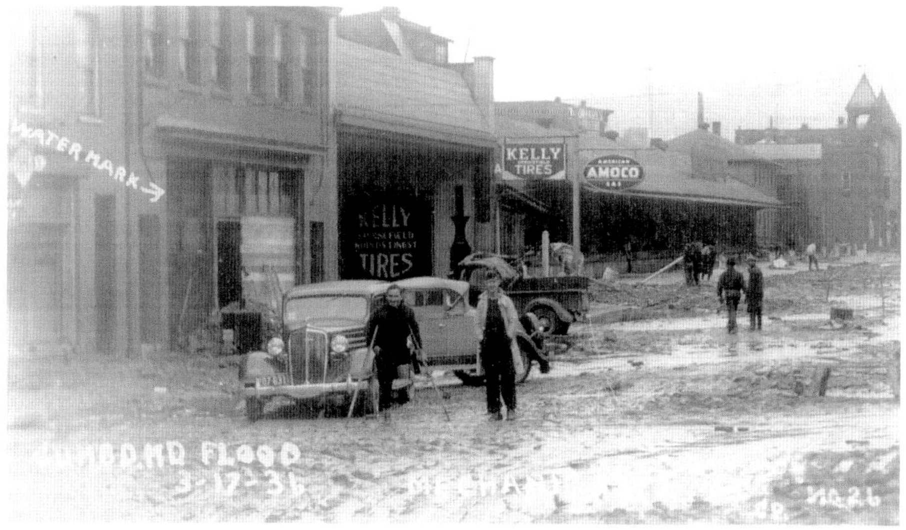

The Kelly-Springfield Tire Company Retail Store at 129 South Mechanic Street saw the water rise to a level exceeding fifteen feet, as seen in this E.E. Thrasher postcard. By the way, if you needed to call the Kelly store, you could just phone Cumberland-300. *Courtesy Ora Mae Lewis.*

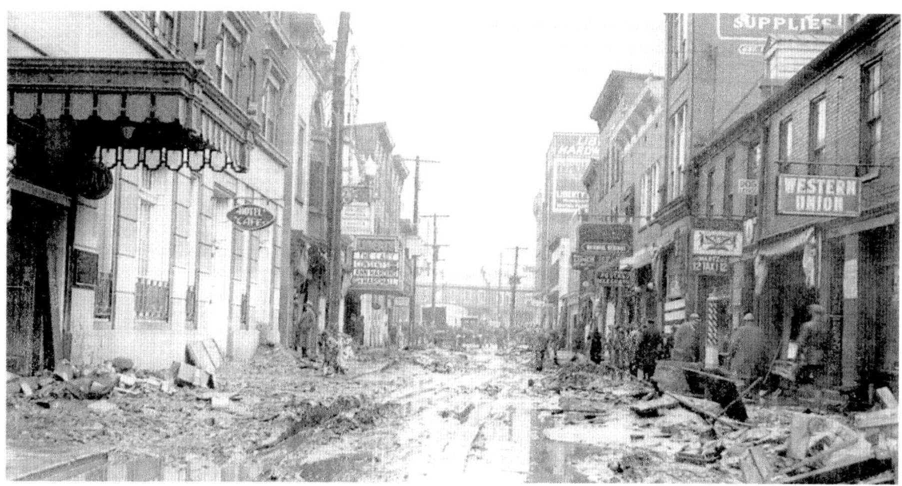

Many of the local businesses that existed at the time of the 1936 flood are vividly portrayed in this Goldfine Studio photograph of North Liberty Street. The Fort Cumberland Hotel, which was constructed in 1916 with its grand opening in 1918, is on the left, while the Liberty Movie Theatre marquee, advertising *The Lady Consents* with Ann Harding and Herbert Marshall, is visible farther down the street. The Liberty had opened in 1912. During the 1936 flood, the theatre's organ was swept away, and water rose almost to the balcony level. The theatre closed in 1955.

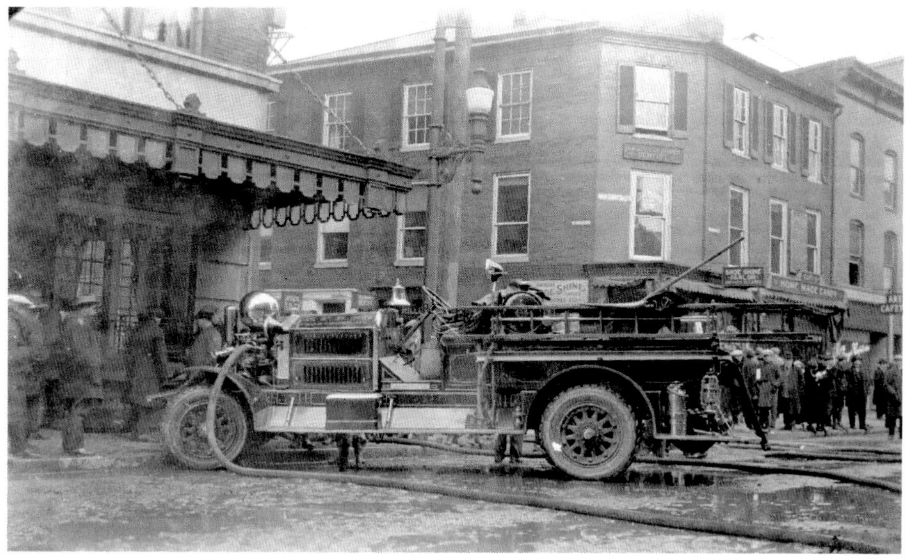

The Cumberland Fire Department was busy pumping out water from numerous establishments around the city. The building in the background once stood at the corner of North Liberty and Baltimore Streets. The site is now a parklet. Among the businesses located here was Curtis Home Made Candy at 72 Baltimore Street. *Photograph by James Edward Grabenstein.*

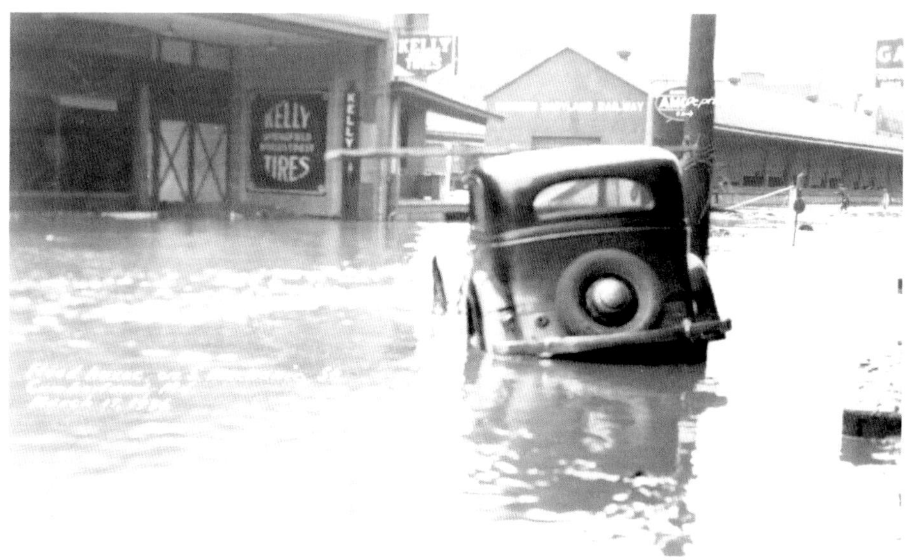

New tires from the Kelly-Springfield Tire Company retail store on South Mechanic Street are probably the least of this car owner's concerns at the moment. Note the Western Maryland Railroad warehouse in the background. *Photograph by Eleanor Gerkins.*

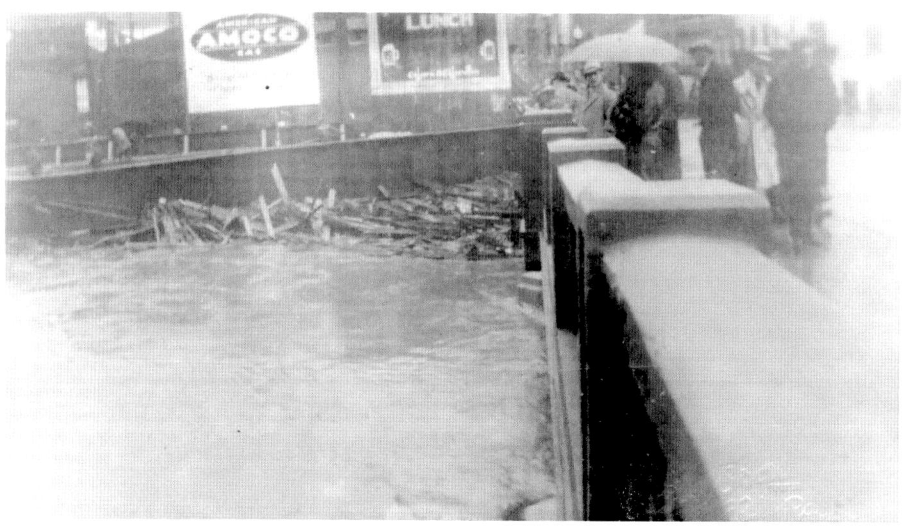

As the raging waters of Wills Creek lessen, spectators gather on the Baltimore Street Bridge to inspect the aftermath of the March 17 torrent. The back of this postcard, which was sent on May 8, simply reads, "Is everybody happy? Mort." *Photograph by E.E. Thrasher.*

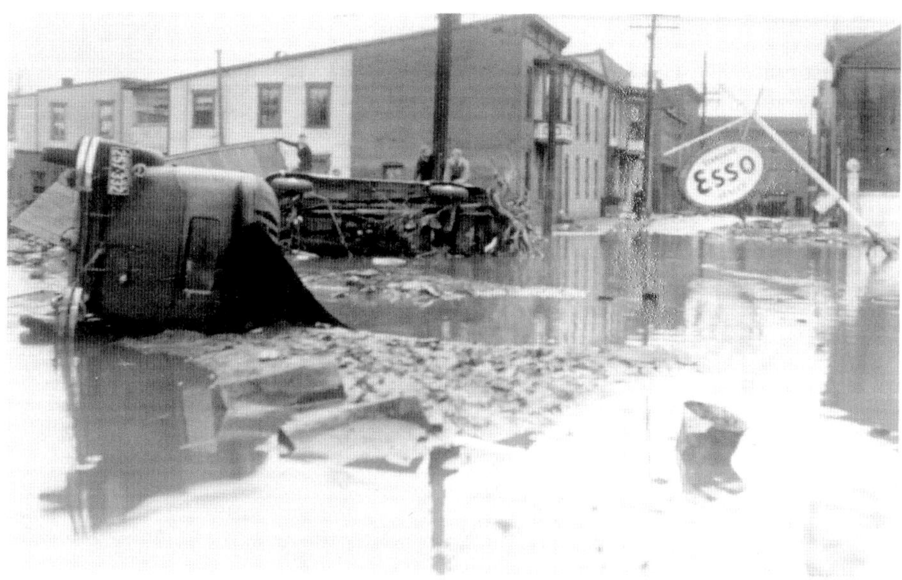

This is Harrison Street, looking west from South Centre. The area on the left would now be the site of the on-ramp for Interstate 68 West. *Photograph by Eyerman Studios.*

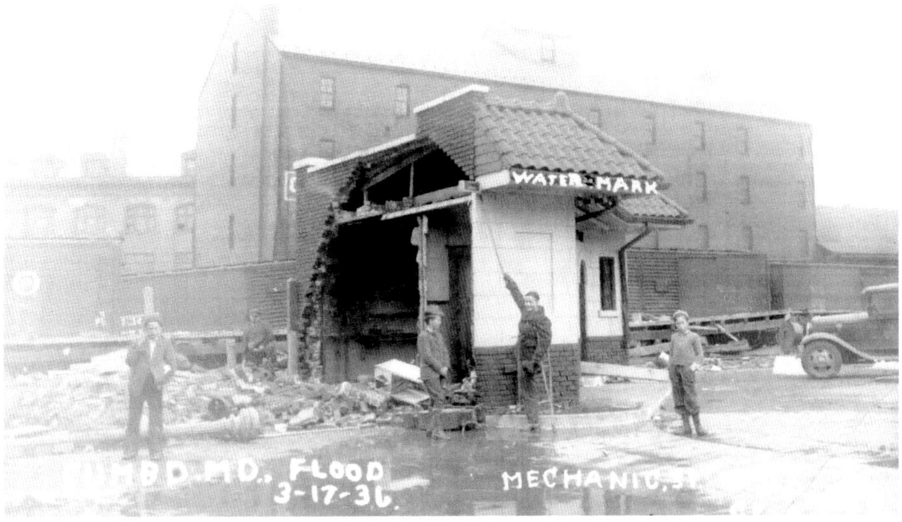

The back of this postcard, which depicts South Mechanic Street looking west, reads, "This is where we lived close. We sure had some flood. Also some mess. Florence." The building on the left is the Western Maryland Railway Station.

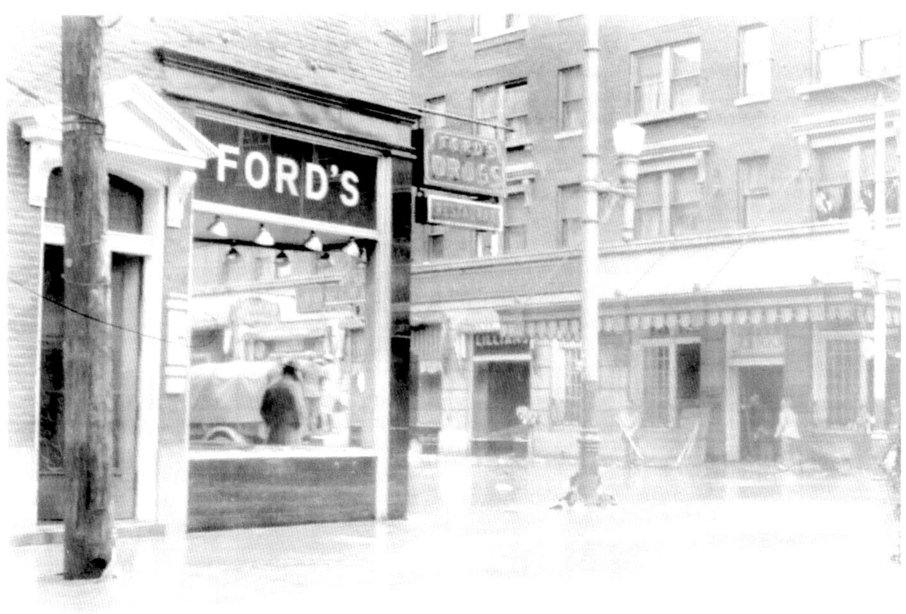

The Ford's Drug Store location at the corner of Baltimore and South Liberty Streets was unable to fill prescriptions immediately after the flood. Customers were directed to other Ford locations.

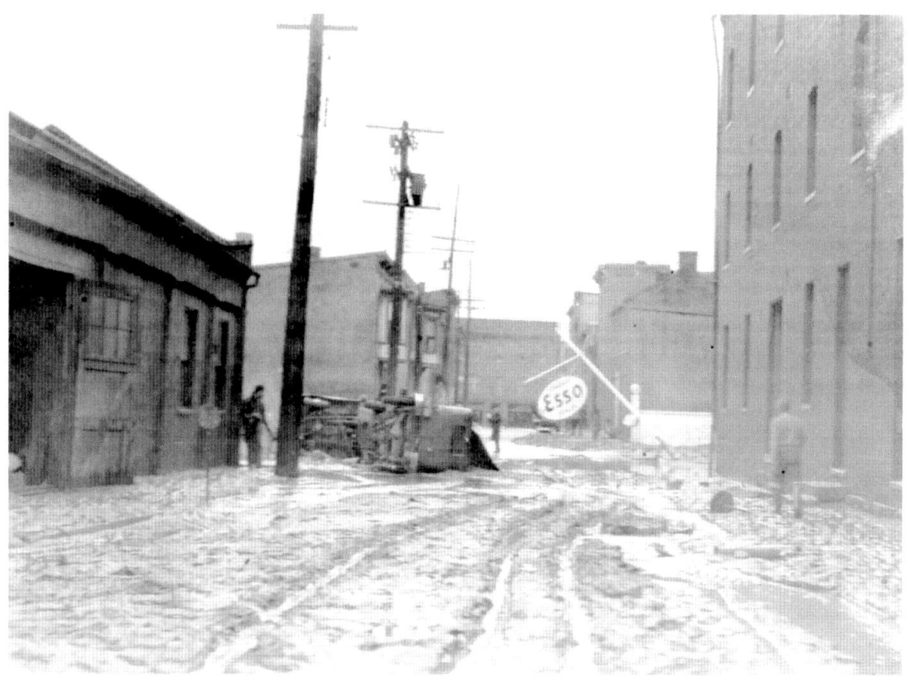

Note the degree of mud in this photograph of Harrison Street, looking west from Centre.

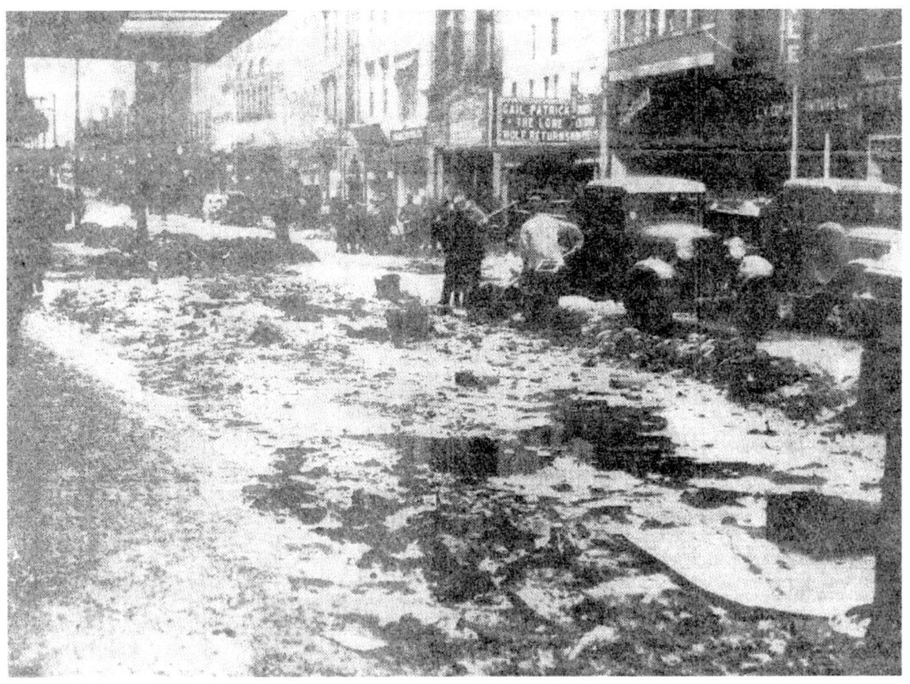

At the time this photograph was taken on March 18, 1936, and as noted in the caption when the photograph appeared in the *Cumberland Sunday Times* on March 29, every plate glass window on Baltimore Street in the block between Mechanic and Liberty Streets was broken. *Courtesy the* Cumberland Times-News.

NO SERVICES SUNDAY AT CENTRE ST. M. E.

There will be no services at Centre Street M. E. Church tomorrow because of damage done by the flood. The mud and debris washed into the lower floor was being removed today, but the heating system is out of order and not expected to be in operation before the first of next week.

If you were a member of Centre Street Methodist Church, this article in the March 21, 1936 *Cumberland Daily News* seemed to indicate that you were going to need to find another church for next day Sunday worship. *Courtesy the* Cumberland Times-News.

Events Briefly Noted

There will be no dance at Cumberland Country Club tonight. The bridge over Evitts Creek to the club grounds was washed out. Plans to repair flood damage will be decided at a meeting of club directors tomorrow.

Bad news. The dance at the Cumberland Country Club, as evidenced in this article from the *Cumberland Daily News*, March 21, 1936, has been cancelled due to the club's Evitts Creek Bridge being washed away. Too bad. I wasn't planning to attend anyway. *Courtesy the* Cumberland Times-News.

FREE DRINKING WATER

Clear, Sparkling, Pure water from our Ozone Machine. Our Ozone Machine will purify and remove all bacteria and sediment from the water. All Coca-Cola is being bottled from this source. . . . .

Bring your own container and get all the water you want free

Cumberland Coca-Cola Bottling Works, Inc.

315-317 S. Centre St.

Fortunately, the Cumberland Coca-Cola Bottling Works on Centre Street—thanks to its Ozone Machine as mentioned in this March 21, 1936 edition of the *Cumberland Daily News*—was providing purified free drinking water, with no bacteria. *Courtesy the* Cumberland Times-News.

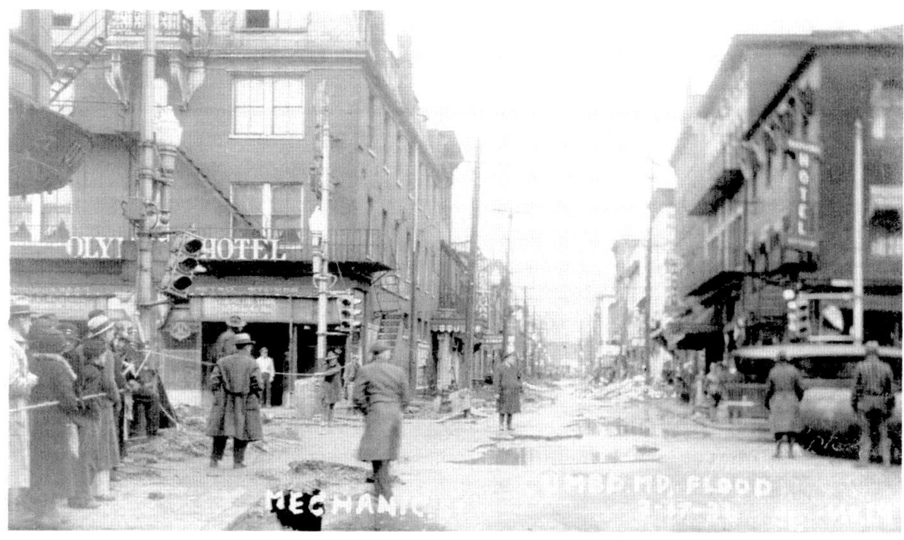

Immediately after the floodwaters receded, large areas of downtown Cumberland, as seen in this view of Mechanic Street at Baltimore looking north, were roped off to allow cleanup to begin. The Olympia Hotel's address was 8 North Mechanic Street, and its phone number was Cumberland-54. The site is now a parking lot. *Courtesy City of Cumberland.*

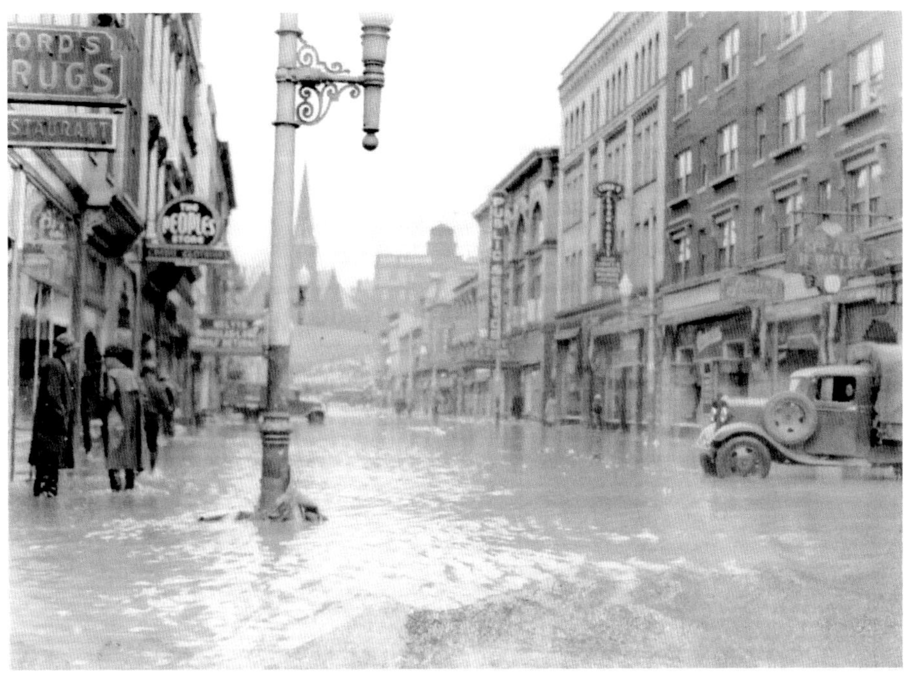

The deluge and torrent of water closed banks, movie theatres and businesses. The National Guard was called in to keep order. Buses, cars and even trains were stranded. With communications cut off, the city was isolated for the duration of the high water. Many hundreds spent the night in the State Armory Maryland National Guard on South Centre Street and were cared for by the Red Cross. It was estimated that the number of families washed out of their homes was about 1,200, close to 6,000 people.

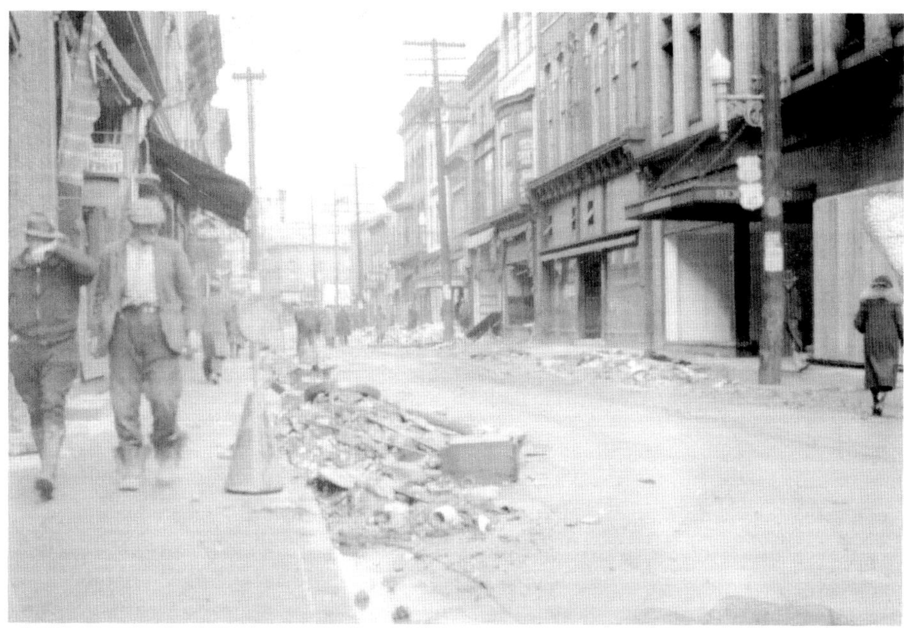

The flood had begun as a downpour. The heavy rainfall and melting snow caused much of downtown Cumberland to be underwater by mid-afternoon. The entire first floor of many homes and businesses was covered on Mechanic, Baltimore and Greene Streets, and in several areas the water rose to a level well over ten feet. This scene depicts North Centre looking north from Baltimore Street.

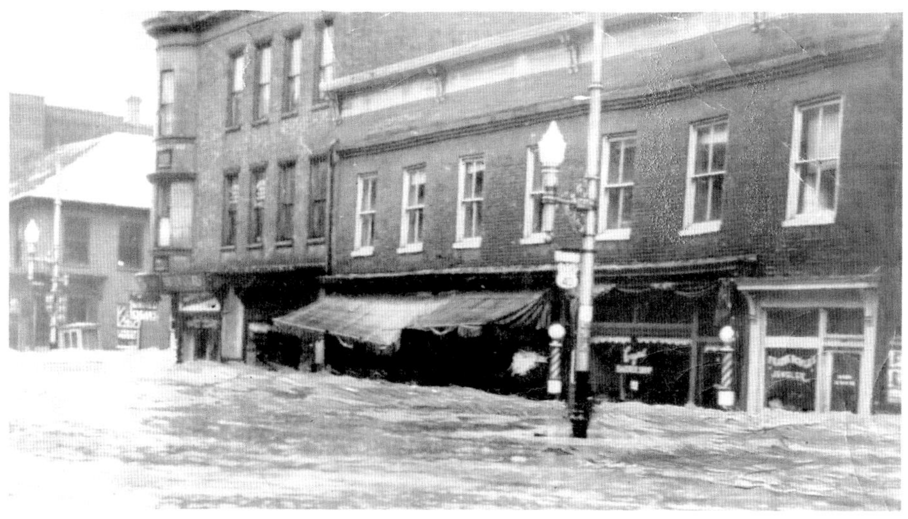

Even though the waters have already begun to recede, this Goldfine Studio photograph dramatizes the intensity of the flood. We are looking toward the corner of Baltimore and South Mechanic Streets from a point near the Western Maryland Railroad tracks.

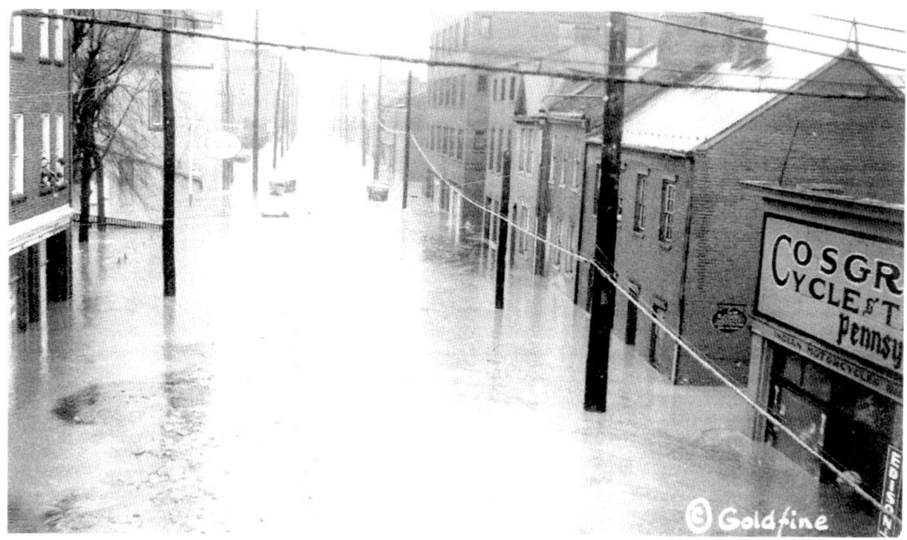

This Goldfine Studio image, taken atop the B&O Railroad Viaduct, is looking south on Centre Street. Note the Cosgrove Cycle & Tire Company on the right, featuring Indian Motorcycles. It is also interesting to note that the second building on the left, just beyond the Esso sign, is the old McKendree Methodist Episcopal Church, which was established in 1854 and served the African American community until the 1960s.

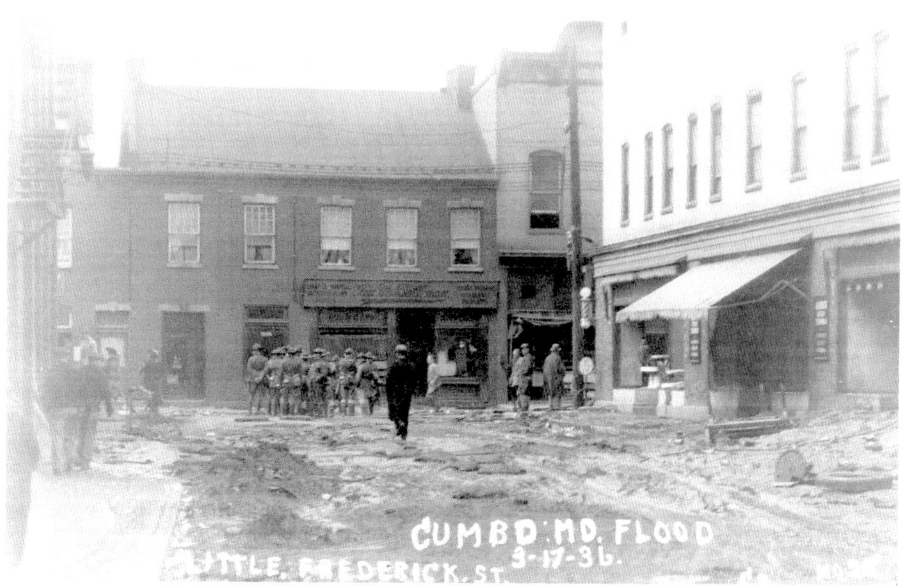

A group of what appear to be National Guardsmen—or perhaps state police or a combination of both—is seen in this E.E. Thrasher postcard depiction converging at the intersection of North Mechanic and Frederick Streets to receive their orders.

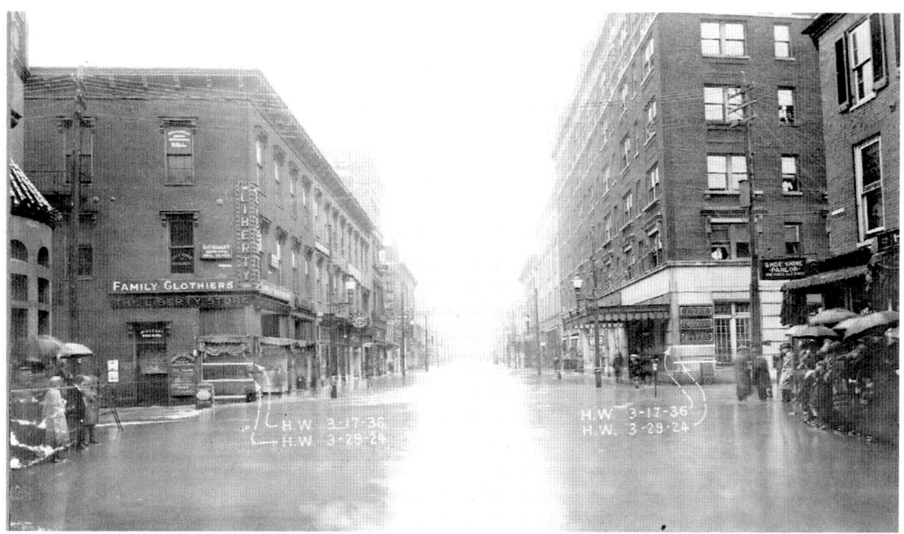

The intersection of Liberty and Baltimore Streets, looking west on Baltimore, is shown in this U.S. Army Corps of Engineers photograph. The scene is from the 1924 flood. The white lines indicate the height of water at this point from the floods of March 29, 1924, and March 17, 1936. On the left is the Liberty Store, ladies' and men's ready-to-wear clothing, which was located at the corner of Baltimore and South Liberty Streets.

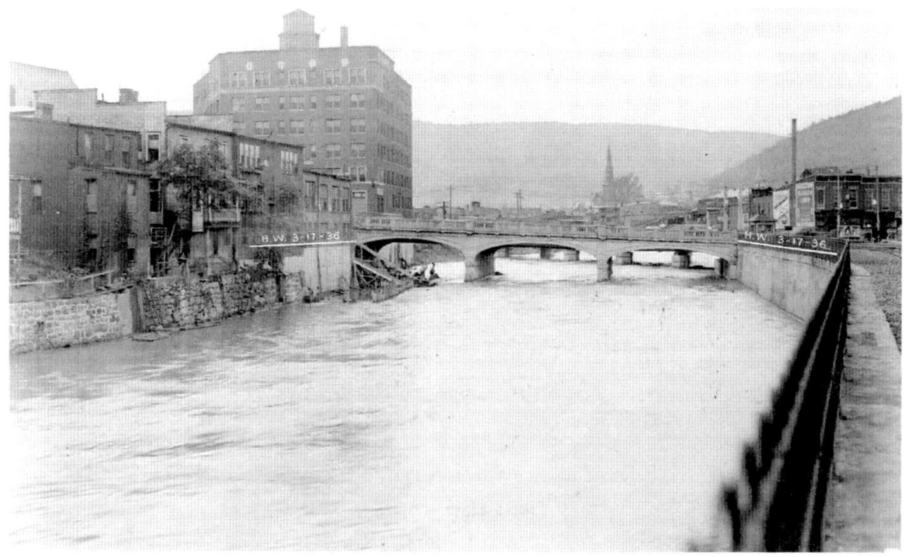

This Army Corps of Engineers photograph from 1940 shows Wills Creek, looking upstream toward the old Baltimore Street Bridge from the Western Maryland Railroad Depot. The crest of the overflowing water from the flood of 1936 is indicated by the white lines on both sides of the creek. The Algonquin Hotel looms on the left.

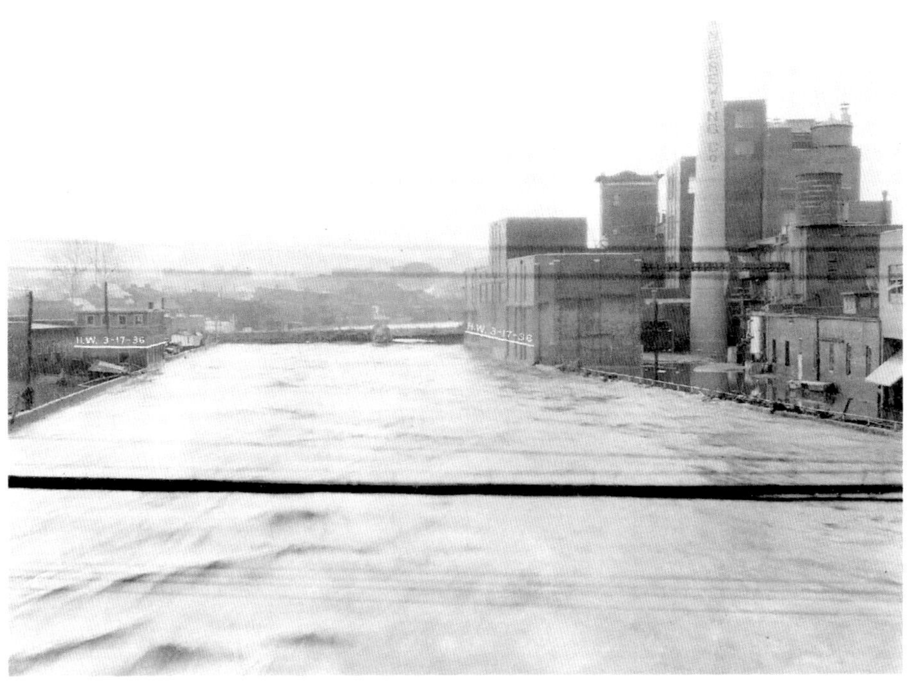

The torrent of Wills Creek had subsided somewhat at the time of this photograph, but the flow's crest is still indicated on both sides of the creek. In the distance is the Market Street bridge with the gasoline tank perched beneath it. This image also depicts the former German Brewing Company on the right. *Courtesy U.S. Army Corps of Engineers. Photograph by Eyerman Studios.*

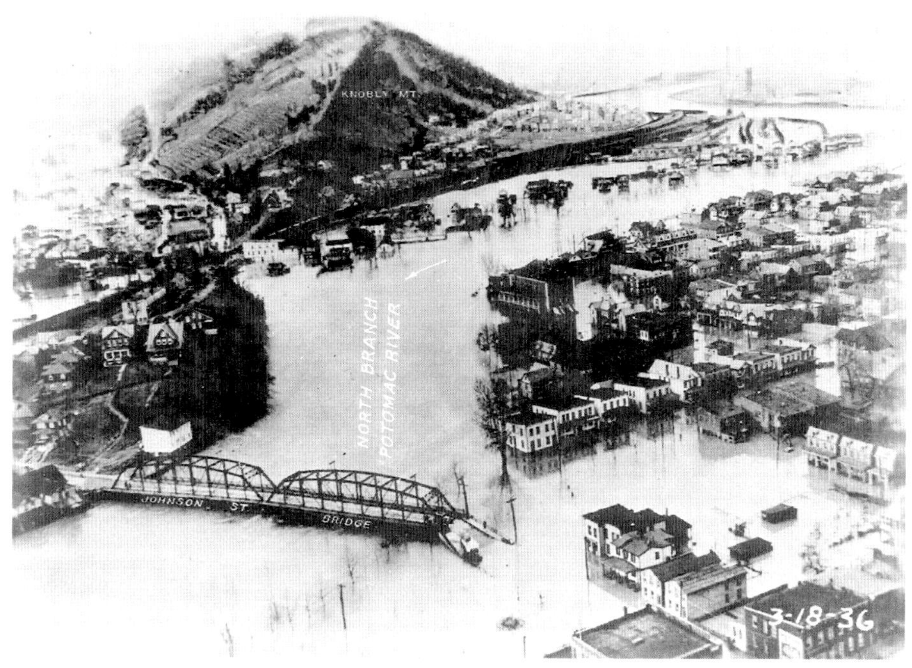

This photograph was taken on March 18, 1936, and appeared in a report published by the U.S. Army Corps of Engineers in 1940. On the left is Ridgeley, West Virginia, and on the right is a flooded Cumberland West Side. Note the inundated Johnson Street leading up to the bridge.

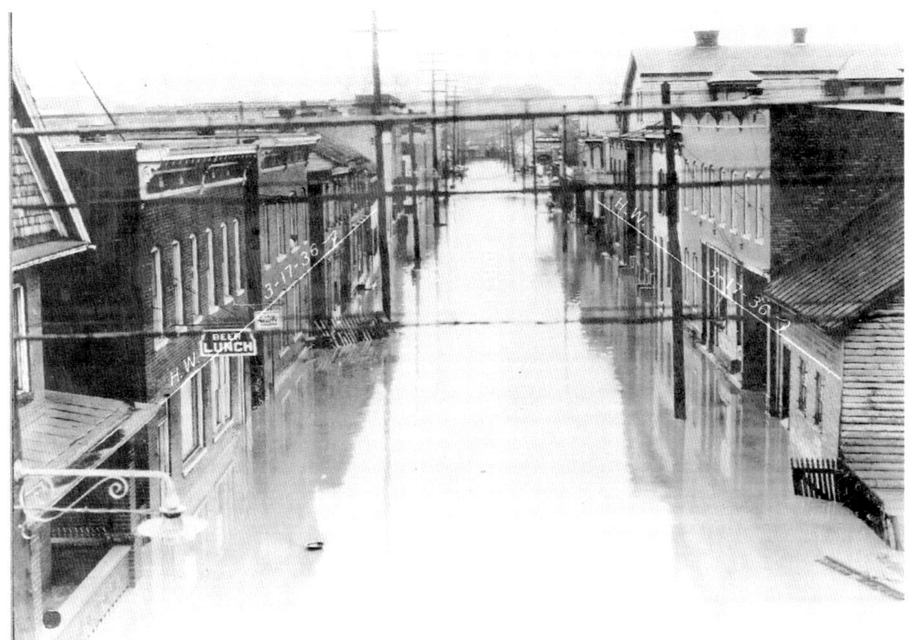

White lines on this image of North Mechanic Street, looking south from the B&O Viaduct, indicate how high the water rose at this point during the flood of 1936. The waters had receded greatly by the time of this photograph. *Courtesy U.S. Army Corps of Engineers. Photograph by Eyerman Studios.*

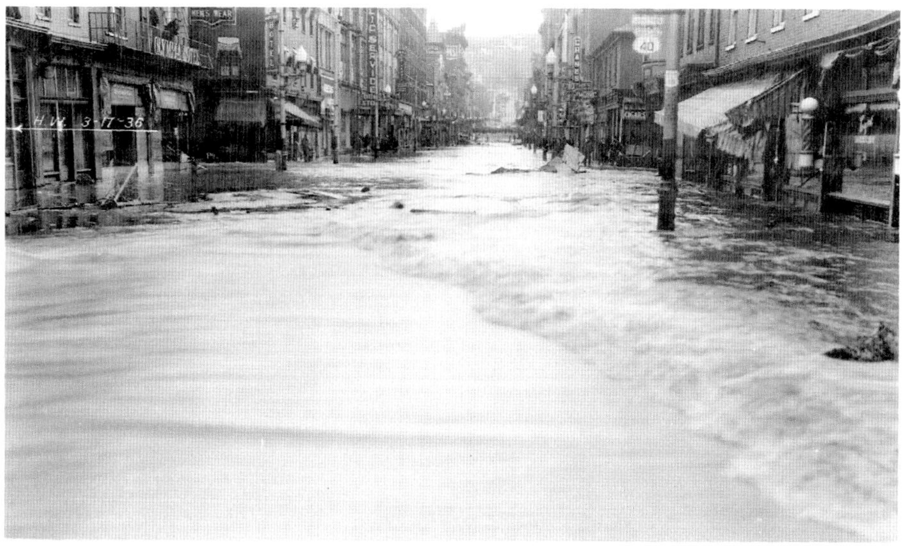

The 1940 report issued by the Corps included this 1936 image of Baltimore Street, looking east toward Mechanic from Canal Street. Again, waters had receded tremendously at the time of the photograph as indicated by the white line on the left showing the water level at its peak. *Courtesy U.S. Army Corps of Engineers. Photograph by Eyerman Studios.*

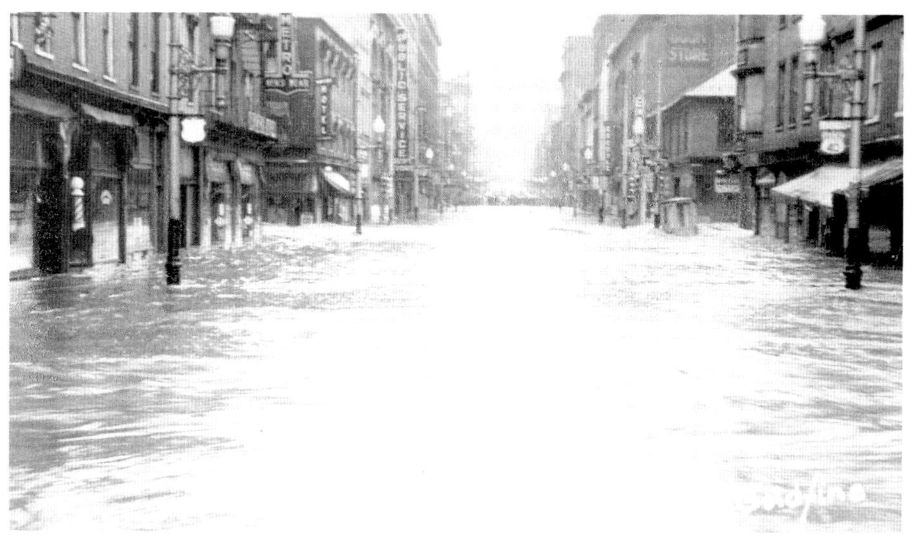

A final view of Baltimore Street, looking east, as captured by the Goldfine Studio. Shoe repair and barbershops were staples of Cumberland during this era, as evidenced by the signs and barber poles on both sides of the street and throughout the early flood photographs of this book.

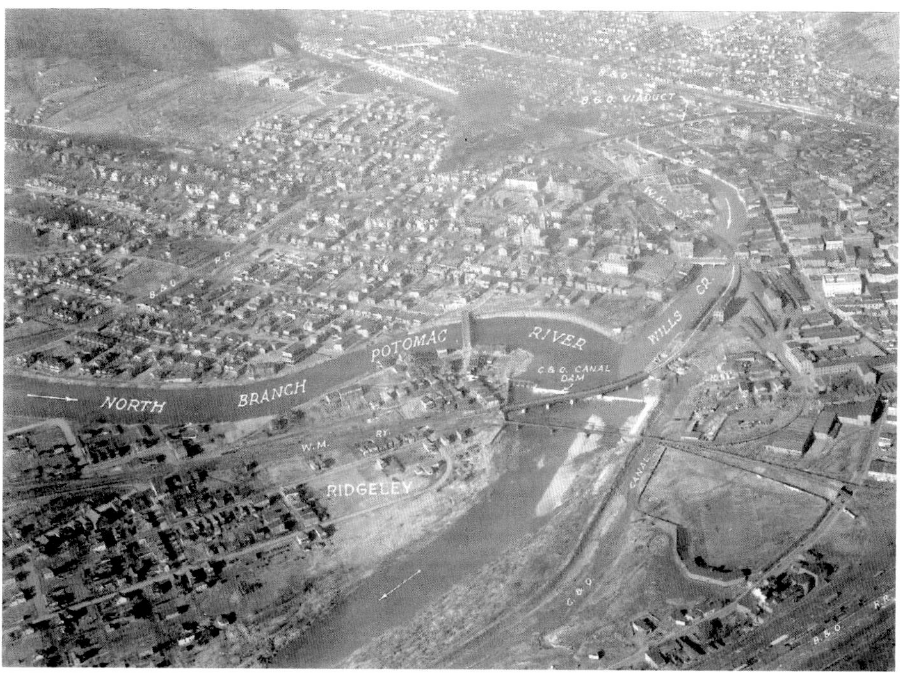

This U.S. Army Corps of Engineers aerial photograph from about 1940 provides some perspective: geographical and structural landmarks per the areas immediately adjacent to the North Branch of the Potomac River and Wills Creek, which were impacted by the flood.

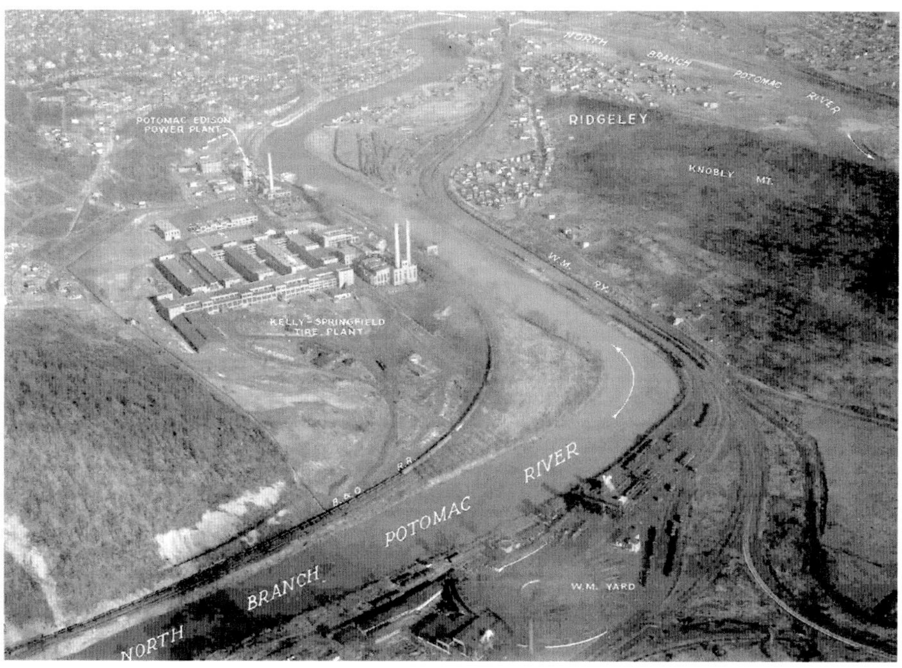

The former Kelly-Springfield Tire Plant, Western Maryland Railroad Yard, Ridgeley, West Virginia, North Branch and more are all identified in this aerial Corps photograph from about 1940.

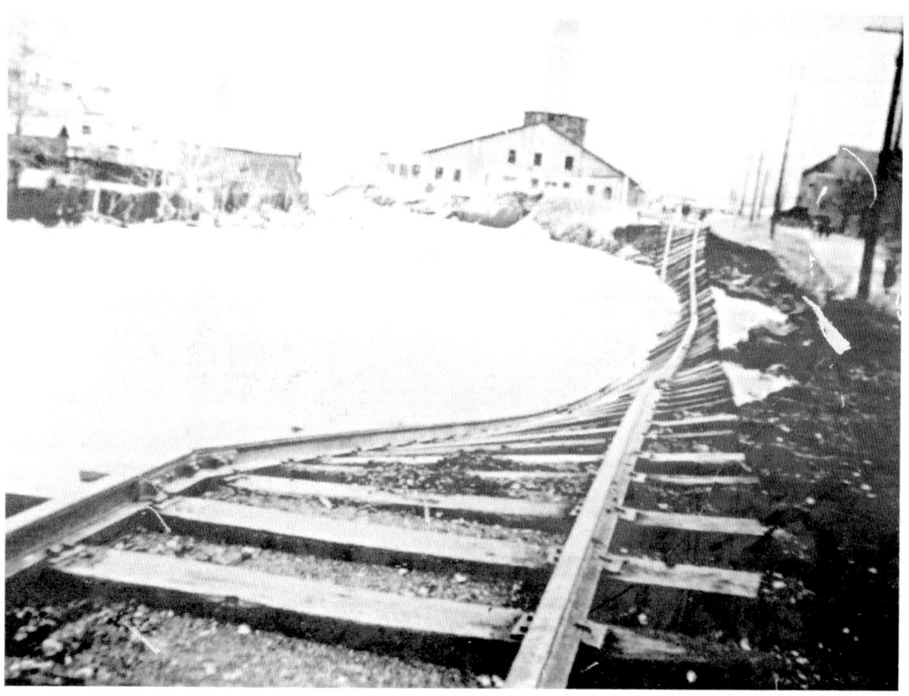

This Lonaconing scene from the March 1936 flood depicts railroad tracks washed into Georges Creek. The old glassworks on Railroad Street appears in the distance. *Courtesy George Ternent & Sons.*

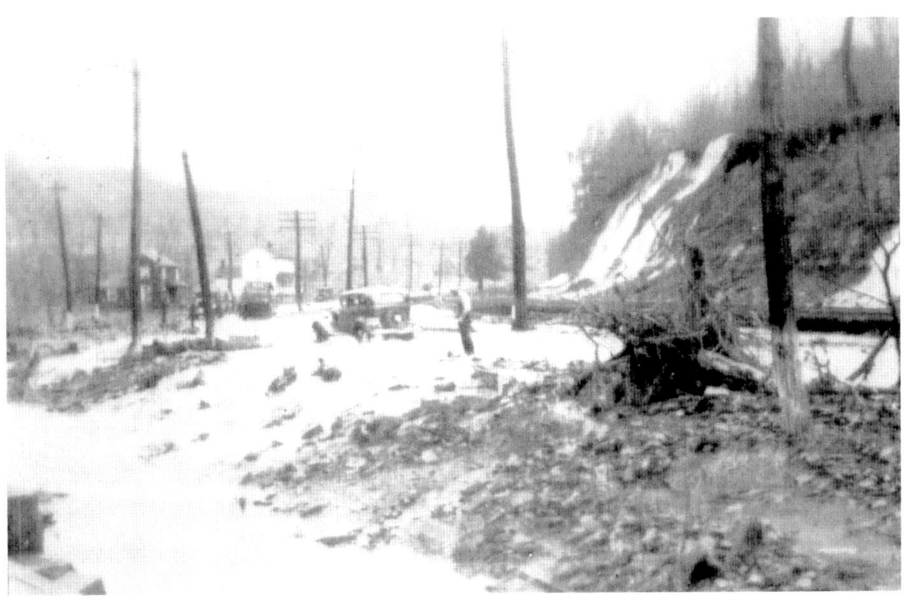

Many locations along Route 36 throughout Georges Creek were inundated and debris laden as a result of the 1936 deluge. The view in this image is from just north of Lonaconing. *Courtesy George Ternent & Sons.*

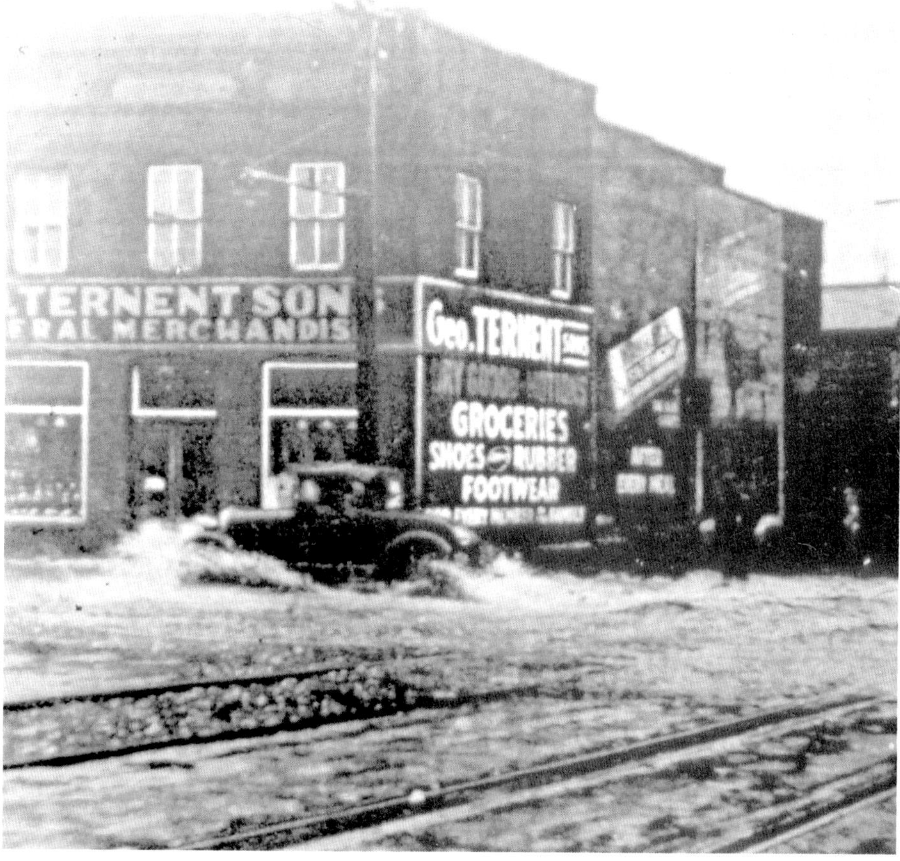

This view of Jackson Street in Lonaconing during the 1936 flood depicts the George Ternent & Sons General Merchandise Store. Established in 1885, the business has borne witness to numerous torrents but still exists today in this same location. *Courtesy George Ternent & Sons.*

Chapter 4

RECENT FLOODING EVENTS

Since 1942, and as alluded to in the introduction, we have continued to have a historical relationship with the catastrophic forces of flood and nature. Our vulnerability has remained with us despite our best efforts. Sometimes nature even fights back, as during the flood control construction project through downtown Cumberland. Along with the heavy rains and Potomac River swelling caused by Hurricane Hazel in October 1954, Wills Creek again experienced flooding in 1957, resulting in a rush of water that actually swept away some of the flood control construction equipment. In 1972, Hurricane Agnes devastated portions of the Chesapeake and Ohio Canal and Potomac River in a flood that is still remembered for the damage inflicted on the national historical park. Hyndman, Pennsylvania, has experienced terrible damage in recent years, and the flood of 1985 was devastating, particularly along the South Branch of the Potomac River Valley in nearby West Virginia, where the loss of property and life occurred. This flooding was so great that according to a friend I had lunch with a few days after the January 1996 flood, the water mark from 1985 was eight feet higher than in 1996, at least at his location on the South Branch at Millenson's, where he had "had" a camp. It was also these rains from Hurricane Juan in 1985 that resulted in the awarding of over $60,000 in federal funds for flood damage work to be undertaken in the Georges Creek region. Repairs to the creek's retaining walls; the removal of debris and silt bars blocking the stream channels, bridges and culverts; and Georges Creek channel restoration were all undertaken as part of the project.

More recently, in just a sixteen-month period, beginning in June 1995 and again in January and September 1996, our Western Maryland region was hit (no other word for it) by a series of devastating deluges, with each of these three flooding events being classified as a one-hundred-year flood. In June 1995, after several days of rain (up to five inches according to some estimates), a heavy torrent of runoff from the mountains and an overflowing of the Potomac River and Georges Creek resulted in almost $2 million worth of damage in Westernport. Dozens of homes (many located on surrounding hillsides), sidewalks, streets, storm drains and businesses were either damaged, destroyed, washed out or filled with mud and debris, including boulders resulting from rock slides. Fifteen volunteer fire departments were among the numerous public and private, paid and volunteer, human service and relief agencies that responded.

On January 6, 1996, a blizzard hit the region, dumping between two and three feet of snow throughout the area. Just two weeks later, a rapid snowmelt coupled with heavy rains on the evening of January 18, 1996, resulted in one of the worst flooding events in memory. Several roads, properties and residential areas in Cumberland were affected, including the West Side, which saw several cars abandoned at an inundated Greene Street underpass, and lower South Cumberland. This was mostly characterized by flooded basements, either from a swelling Potomac River or runoff from nearby hillsides. For Cumberland, though, this flood portrayed one example where the forces of nature were, for the most part, "controlled." It was the Cumberland Flood Control Construction Project, built during the 1950s, that is credited with saving downtown Cumberland and its adjacent neighborhoods from ruination. In addition to the channelization of Wills Creek, the three pumps were put into action to force storm water into Wills Creek and the Potomac River, thereby preventing a backup of water flooding the city.

Much of this storm water was from the higher elevations that would normally flow to Wills Creek and the Potomac River but could not discharge to the streams due to their high water levels. Though the pumping stations are routinely tested and kept in working order, this was the first time that they were truly put into action. At one point, Wills Creek had actually breached and covered a portion of Mechanic Street. Once the pumps were turned on, "It was like pulling a plug on your bathtub the way the water went down so fast from the street," stated Cumberland fire chief Russell Livengood. Water had come within five feet of the Baltimore Street Bridge, and according to the city engineer, John DiFonzo, this was the "flood of record for Wills Creek," with a flow exceeding the 1936 disaster.

Other areas of the county—including the Narrows, LaVale, Georges Creek, Locust Grove, Winchester Road, the Route 220 corridor, Cresaptown, Mount Savage and more—were not so lucky. Rising torrents of water resulted in residential evacuations from Locust Grove,

Corriganville, along Evitts Creek, as well as in Pekin, Moscow, Barton and other locations within Georges Creek. Dozens of people were evacuated to the LaVale Fire Hall, where food, shelter and other assistance awaited. The Motor City area along Route 36 was basically submerged, with automobile dealerships and other businesses heavily damaged and about twenty people being stranded by the high water at Gabriel's Department Store for almost ten hours. Locals in Lonaconing state that it was the worst flooding in that community since 1936, and town officials in Westernport cited over a dozen homes experiencing damage.

As if all of this was not enough, just a few months later, on September 6, 1996, a six-inch heavy rainfall over a twenty-four-hour period brought by Tropical Storm Fran and the resulting torrents again struck the area. Though Cumberland was largely spared, Georges Creek was devastated. In Lonaconing, homes were uplifted from foundations, and a wall of water, three feet high, smashed through the front door of the town hall on Jackson Street. An annex to the nearby Republican Club, which housed a bowling alley, was crumpled and left hanging in Georges Creek. Though the flood's aftermath left debris piled almost four feet high on the street, the George Ternent & Sons Store on Jackson Street, through experience, suffered minimal damage by sandbagging and other preparations. The impact on Westernport was truly disastrous, no better characterized than in the damage or total destruction of numerous homes along Front Street adjacent to Georges Creek. Over two dozen of these houses were later acquired and razed, with the site now being home to Creekside Park. Fourteen miles of CSX railroad line through Georges Creek, used for the hauling of coal, were damaged, washed out and closed, as were six public schools throughout the county from Oldtown to Westernport for a week or more. Damage to Allegany County's bridges, public roads and utilities exceeded $6 million. (As an aside, my choice for the name of Creekside Park would have been "Hardscrabble." Hardscrabble was the original name of the community that was to become known as Westernport. "Hardscrabble" is defined as a hard piece of ground to farm or a hard place to live or make a living. I felt that name would have been appropriate for this park site.)

These 1996 floods resulted in two presidential disaster declarations and the formation of the Western Maryland Flood Mitigation Task Force. The purpose of the task force was to recommend and implement measures to be taken to reduce the risk to life and property from future flooding in the region. Millions of dollars were secured over the next several years for an array of flood mitigation, restoration, infrastructure repair projects and studies.

Moving into the twenty-first century, on September 12, 2000, a sudden storm and cloudburst Monday night dropped almost six inches of rain. Drainage systems were overwhelmed with runoff from Haystack Mountain. Within Cumberland, most of the damage centered on Cumberland's west side, the Dingle, Braddock Road and Fayette Street areas in particular. At least 32 structures were reported to have major damage, 141 suffered minor damage and 3 were destroyed. Automobiles were washed away or practically submerged, as witnessed at the Greene Street underpass, or simply abandoned with the drivers seeking high ground on Washington Street. Many homes and businesses were deluged, and in the words of National Weather Service observer Tim Thomas, "In my thirty-five years with the National Weather Service, I've never seen places flooded that were flooded here tonight." Even Interstate 68 was closed for a period of time, with almost three feet of water in the vicinity of the "Moose Curve." At nearby Geatz's Restaurant on Paca Street, water reached the ceiling in the downstairs Rascal's Nightclub, while upstairs kitchen equipment floated through the restaurant.

Less than a year later, in early June 2001, heavy rains and the resulting runoff again struck. This time the areas affected were primarily along Route 220, as well as in Westernport, where almost five inches of rain fell within twenty-four hours, flooding basements, damaging streets and inundating portions of Main Street with water three feet deep. Once again, within less than a year, heavy rainfall just east of Cumberland on Monday evening, May 27, 2002, hit the Baltimore Pike area. A wall of rushing water estimated at three feet high and almost sixty feet wide closed Interstate 68 and Route 144. Twenty homes were heavily damaged, with dozens of others suffering minor damage, while about a dozen bridges were also affected to one degree or another.

Finally, for the time being, in September 2004 a series of storms and resulting deluges again wreaked havoc. On September 7 and 8, the remnants of Hurricane Frances brought significant rainfall in the amount of about seven inches. A landslide occurred in Westernport. Mount Savage and LaVale experienced flooding from Jennings Run and Braddock Run, respectively. The communities along Georges Creek and even Frostburg were affected by runoff and overflow from nearby tributaries, which required debris removal afterward. By most accounts, things could have been worse. And they soon were. In Mount Savage, it was the remnants of Hurricane Ivan that brought the Friday night, September 17, 2004 downpour that, by some estimates, ranged anywhere from six to ten inches.

Rock slides and runoff dumped into the streets and poured into an already swollen Jennings Run. Some evacuation occurred. Over one hundred homes and businesses experienced flooding to one degree or another. Between twenty-seven and thirty-five homes experienced serious damage. Along Station Master Road, some homes had water reaching six to seven feet in basements, and behind the Mount Savage Fire Hall, eight to ten feet of a rock-filled gabion retaining wall, stream bank, guardrail, road and parking lot were washed away. As noted by an eyewitness, the gabion flood wall and guardrail had come down within three minutes. Up until September 2004, a little over two hundred properties had been acquired and razed through an Allegany County program targeting properties located in flood-prone areas. Most of these buyouts occurred in the aftermath of the 1996 floods, which decimated Locust Grove and ravaged Georges Creek. This total was expected to rise following the September 2004 floods by the planned acquisition of at least seven homes along Jennings Run.

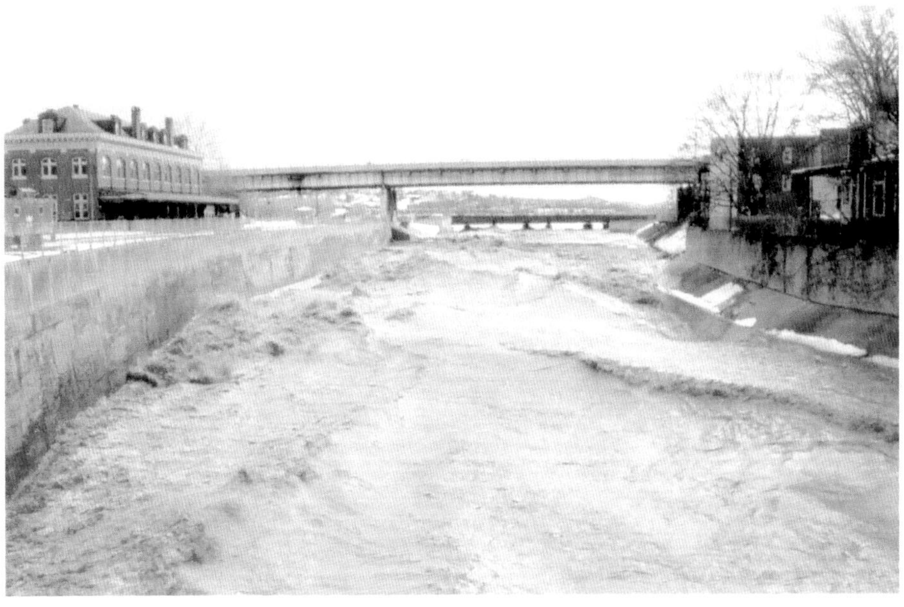

A blizzard in early January 1996 dumped over two feet of snow throughout the region. A heavy rainfall during the evening of January 18, coupled with a rapid snowmelt, proved the right combination for the next day's devastation. This photograph was taken by Paul Detrick on January 19, 1996. The view is looking south from the Baltimore Street Bridge and portrays a raging Wills Creek. The Western Maryland Railroad Station appears on the left. *Courtesy City of Cumberland.*

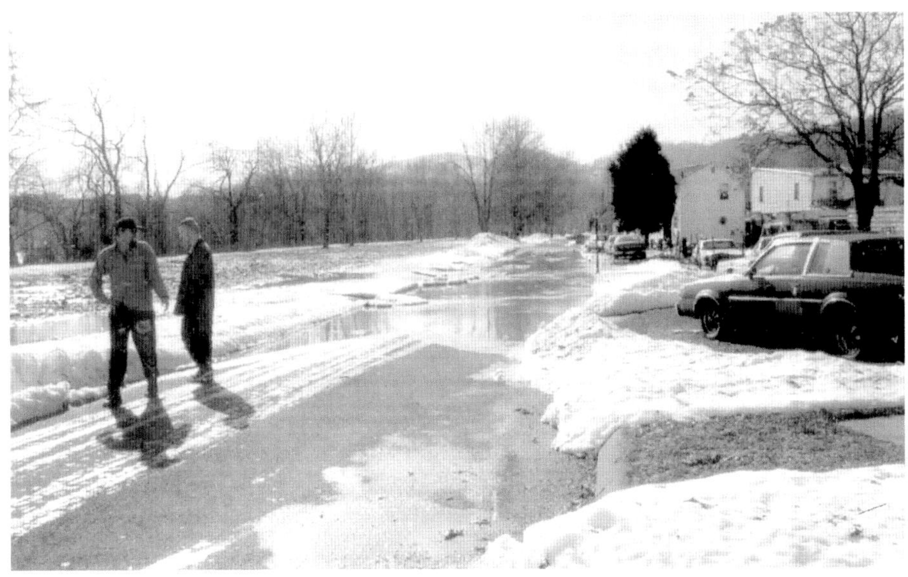

Portions of South Cumberland, particularly those areas along the Potomac River and Chesapeake and Ohio Canal towpath, depicted on the left, were also flooded. This photograph of Candoc Lane was taken on January 19, 1996. *Courtesy City of Cumberland.*

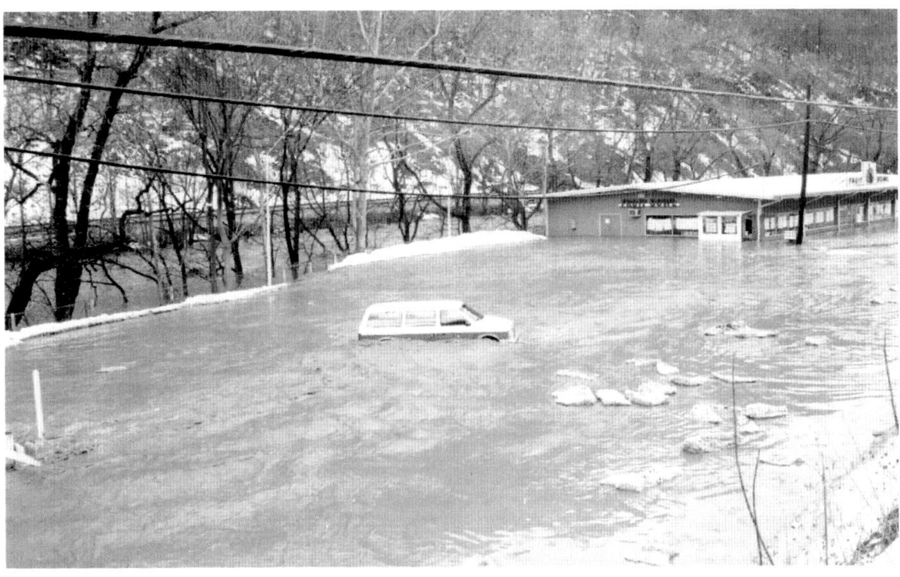

With Wills Creek overflowing its banks, the flood of 1996 awarded the Narrows and adjacent areas with some of the region's most dramatic flood scenes. The Fruit Bowl appears on the left, while the only vehicle in the parking lot is an almost totally submerged pickup truck. Sandbags "litter" an inundated Alternate Route U.S. 40, the National Road, in the foreground. *Courtesy Babb Motor Sales.*

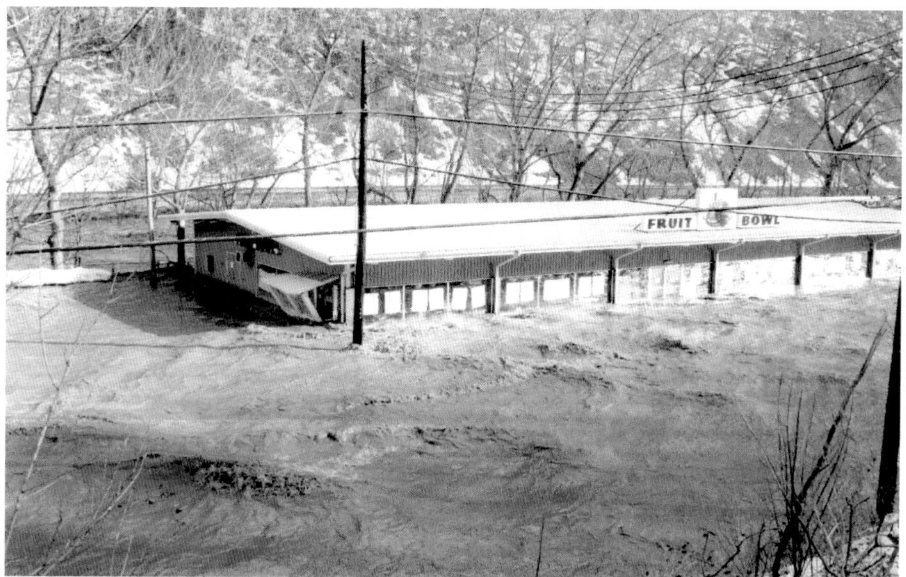

This close-up view of the Fruit Bowl in the Narrows, taken from across Route 40 atop the railroad tracks, clearly shows the raging torrent of water resulting during the flood of 1996 and a swelling Wills Creek. By some estimates, water reached a height of nearly five feet on Route 40. *Courtesy Babb Motor Sales.*

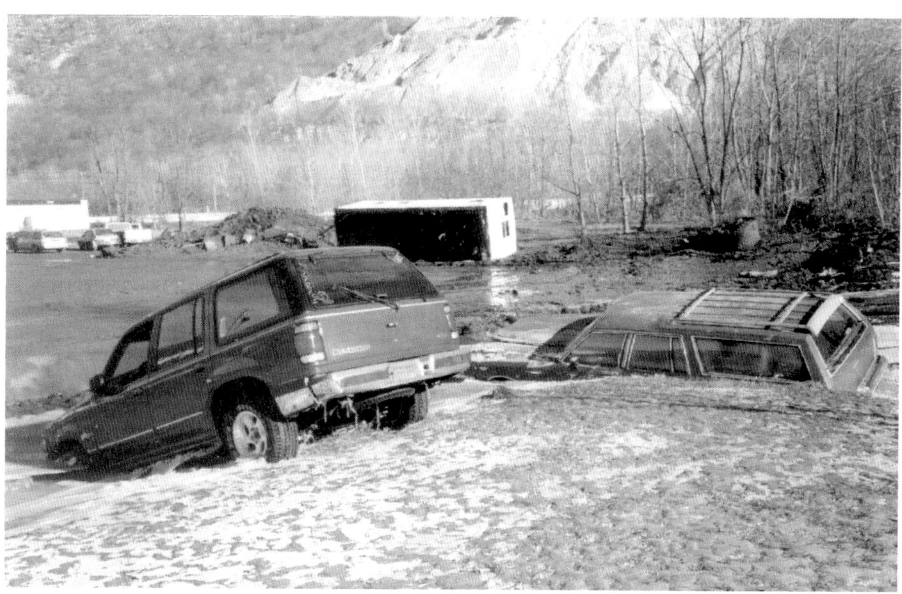

These automobiles, as photographed on January 20, 1996, were among several buried in the muck and mire behind Shaffer Ford along Mount Savage Road, Route 36, Motor City, in the aftermath of the 1996 flooding event. *Feldstein Photograph.*

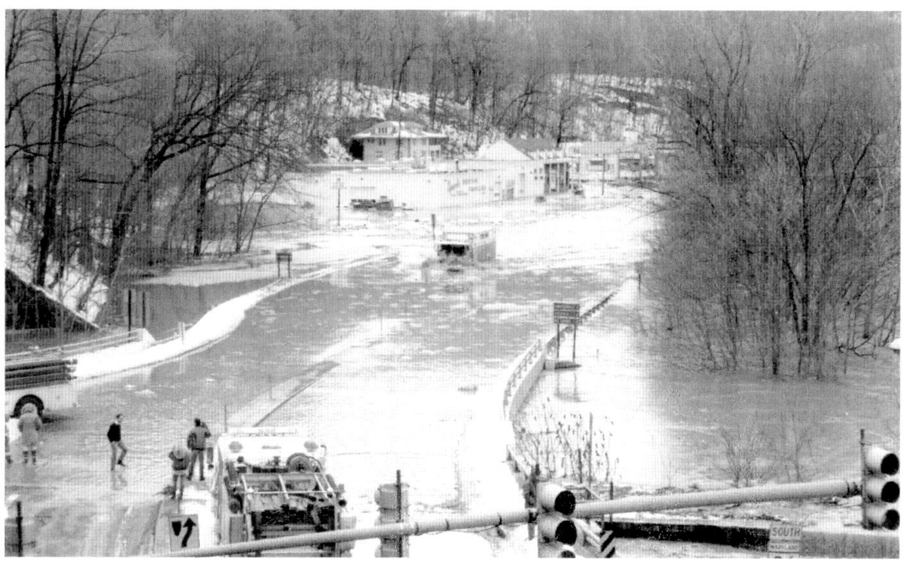

This 1996 flood scene portrays the inundated bridge that crosses Wills Creek at the intersection of Alternate Route U.S. 40 and State Route 36. In the background is Spoerl's, now Timbrook's, Automobile dealership. *Courtesy Babb Motor Sales.*

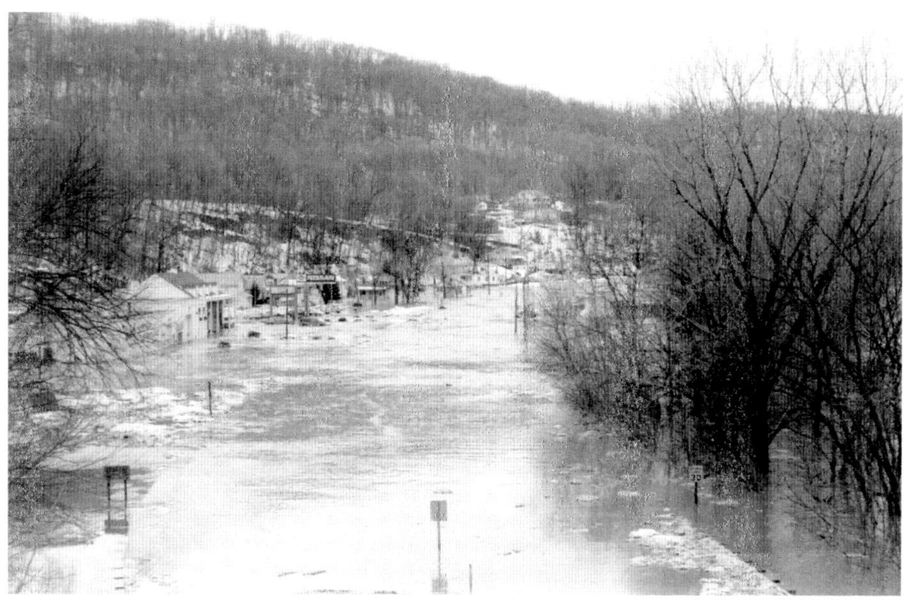

Looking farther north along a completely submerged Route 36, the Mount Savage Road, the scale and scope of an overflowing Wills Creek is obvious. About a mile down the road, customers and employees were stranded in the former Gabriel's Department Store building. *Courtesy Babb Motor Sales.*

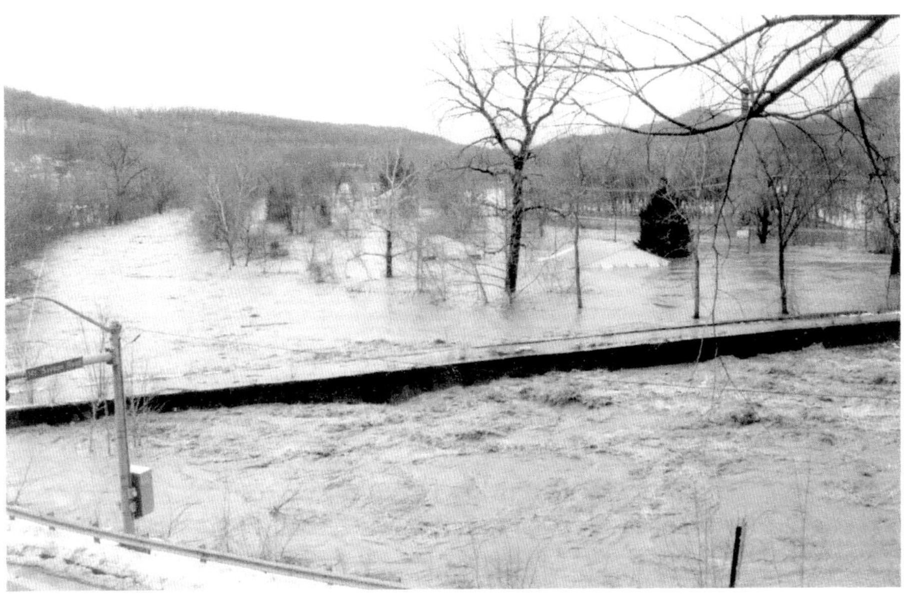

A raging Wills Creek practically covers the old brick Maryland Mining Company Railroad Bridge. The building on the right, with the water up to the roofline, is Wayne Babb's Motor Sales on Locust Grove Road. To its left, barely visible in the middle of this photograph, is another Babb's building. This one was swept away shortly after this photograph was taken. Many of the homes in Locust Grove were inundated, utterly destroyed or severely damaged, and others were later razed. This photograph was taken from the safety of the old Western Maryland Railway tracks across Alternate Route U.S. 40. *Courtesy Babb Motor Sales.*

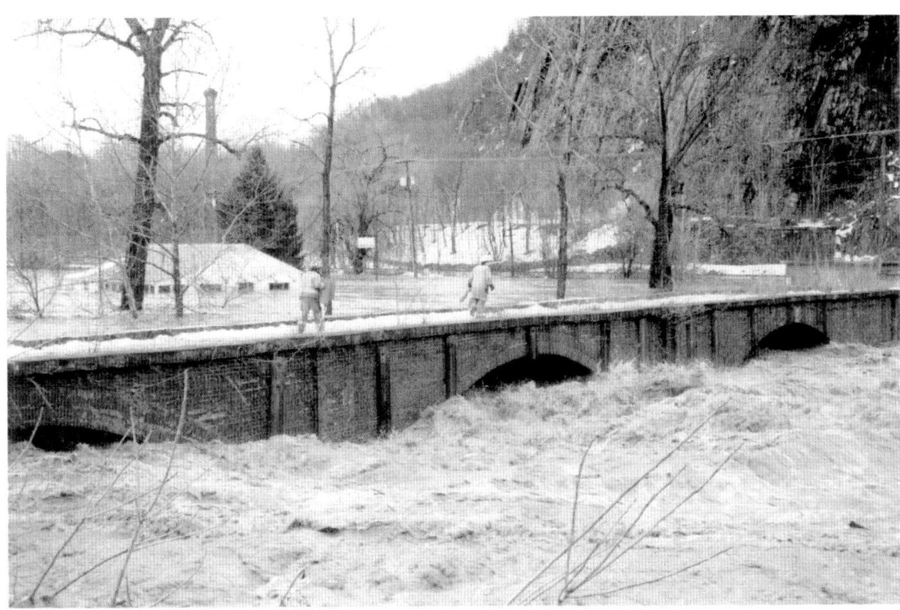

Firemen traverse the old Maryland Mining Company Bridge across Wills Creek. Though still a torrent, the waters have begun to recede somewhat. In the background on the left is the Babb Motor Sales building and beyond that the smokestack from a paper company that once existed at Locust Grove long ago. Wills Mountain is on the right. *Courtesy Babb Motor Sales.*

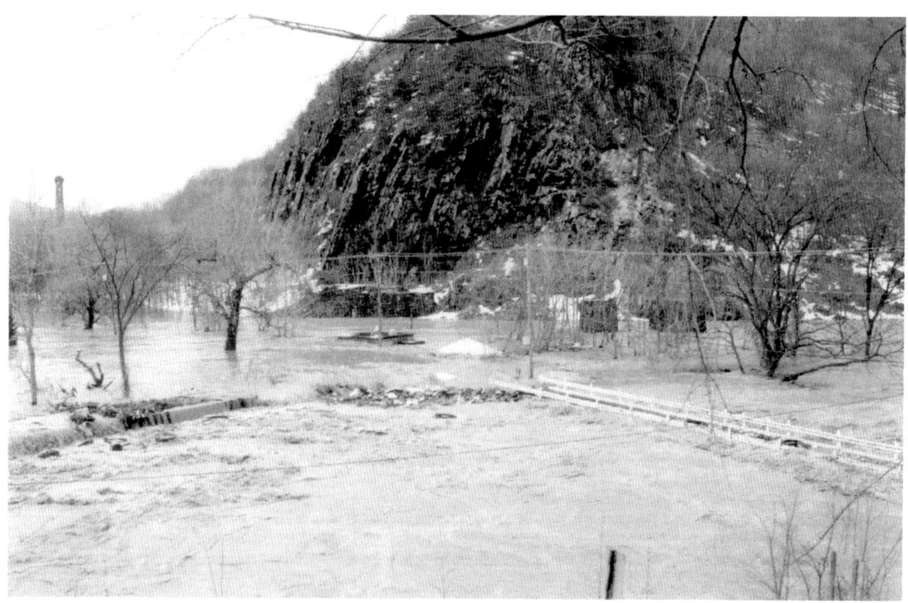

With what is known as the Devil's Backbone of Wills Mountain in the background, this 1996 flood depiction clearly displays the battered brick Maryland Mining Company Bridge on the left and a submerged Locust Grove Bridge on the right. *Courtesy Babb Motor Sales.*

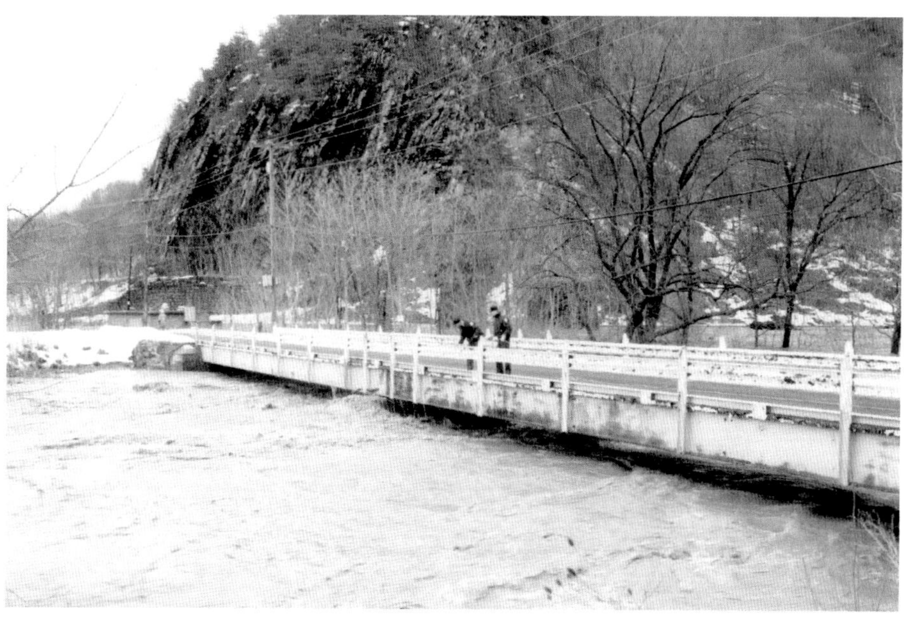

As a raging Wills Creek begins to ease, people walk out upon the Locust Grove Bridge for a closer view of the still rushing torrent of water. *Courtesy Babb Motor Sales.*

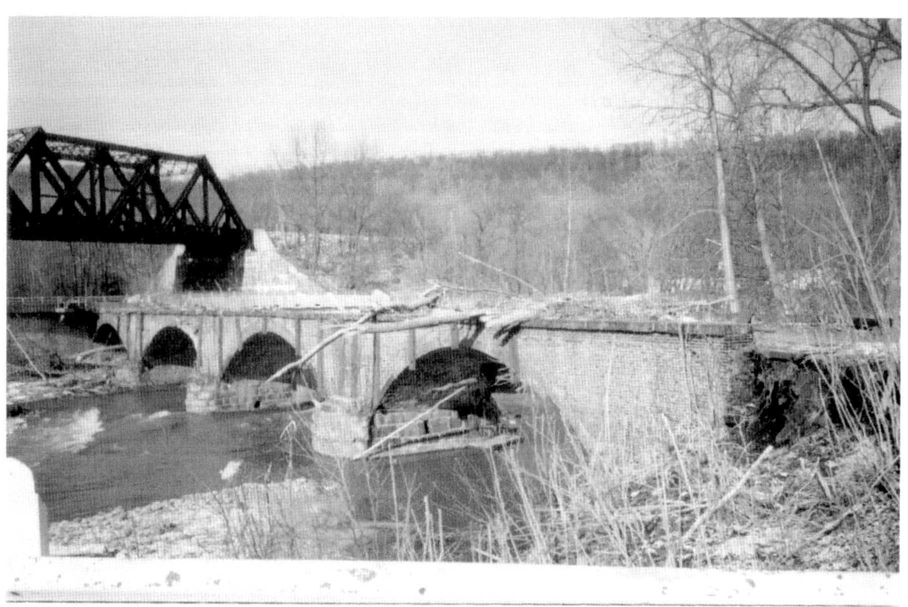

Taken on March 3, 1996, well after the flood, this photograph shows debris still piled up on the old Maryland Mining Company Bridge. The bridge had been constructed across Wills Creek during the years 1845–46. The two-hundred-foot bridge featured four elliptical brick arches resting on three stone piers and stone abutments. The bridge was felt to have caused much of the backup of Wills Creek, resulting in the flooding of the Motor City area and Locust Grove. It was eventually razed in January 1998 as part of the Wills Creek flood mitigation effort. *Feldstein Photograph.*

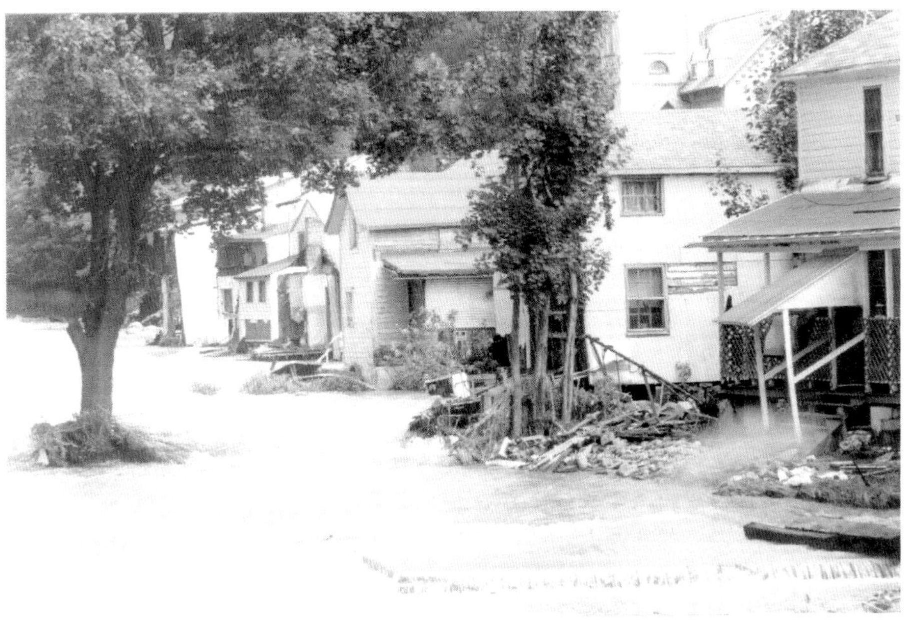

Heavy rainfall from Tropical Storm Fran on September 6, 1996, was responsible for severe flooding throughout the region, particularly within the Georges Creek Valley. This photograph depicts the numerous wooden frame homes along Front Street in Westernport and directly in harm's way of the adjacent Georges Creek. Over a half dozen homes were destroyed in the flood, and many more were severely damaged. Twenty-seven homes on Front Street were eventually acquired and razed with the site now the home of Creekside Park. Rising waters also flooded Main Street to a level of three feet in places, leaving behind mud and debris. *Photograph by Mark Middleton.*

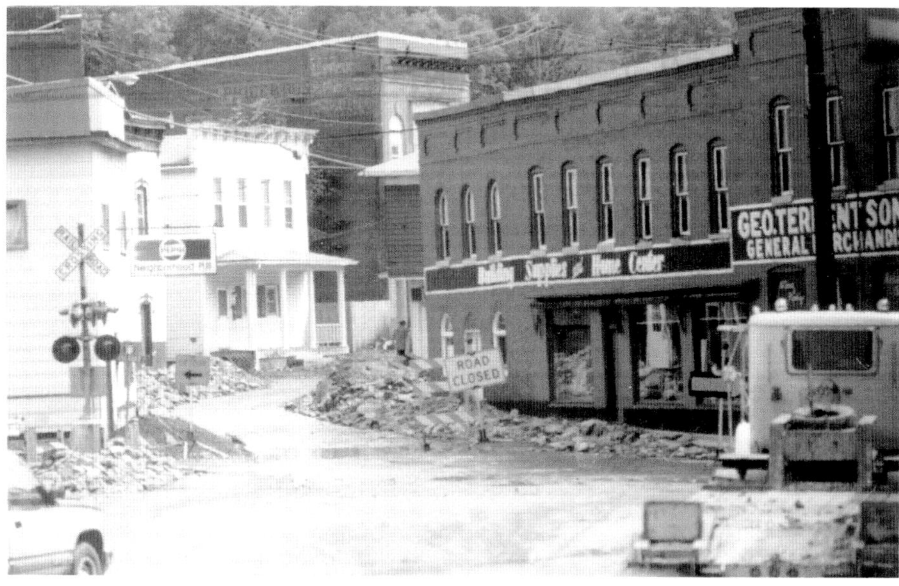

The mayor of Lonaconing said that water ran from Jackson Run down Union Street like a river. This is a debris- and boulder-littered Jackson Street in the aftermath of the flood of September 6, 1996. Note the Ternent store on the right, which is also depicted in a 1936 Lonaconing flood scene. *Photograph by Mark Middleton.*

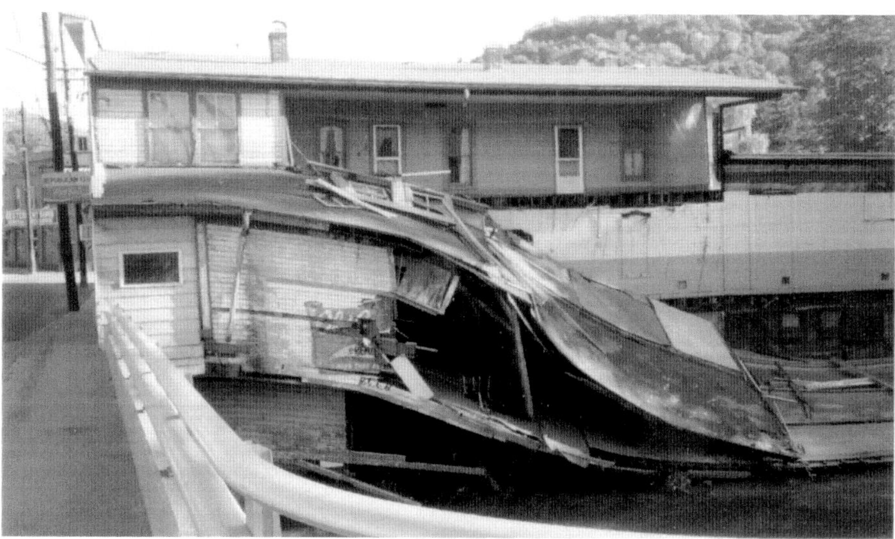

The Republican Club structure on Union Street in Lonaconing suffered major damage from the September 6 flood, as seen in this photograph taken on October 6, 1996. A bowling alley annex to the club collapsed with the bowling lane, as seen here, falling into the creek. Water service remained out for two days along Georges Creek in the communities of Barton and Midland, as well as Lonaconing. *Feldstein Photograph.*

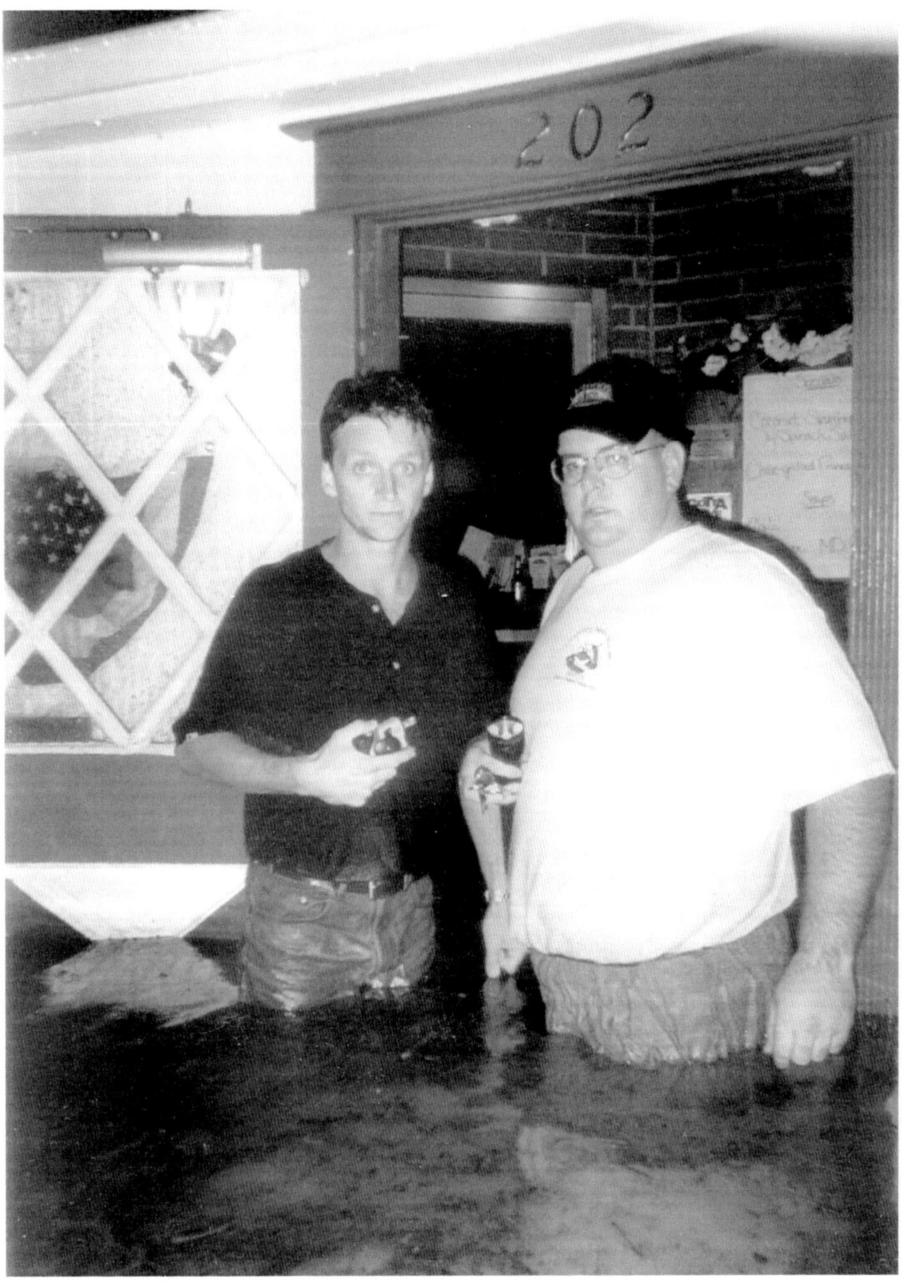

Among the hardest hit areas within Cumberland during the flooding event of September 2000 was Paca Street, on the city's West Side, and Geatz's Restaurant. Shown here, with water practically up to their waists, are Eric Geatz on the left and Sean Franklin on the right. Although the restaurant's computers were destroyed and over four patrons and staff lost their cars, Eric and Sean were proud to note that all of the beer had been saved. *Photograph by Brenda Geatz.*

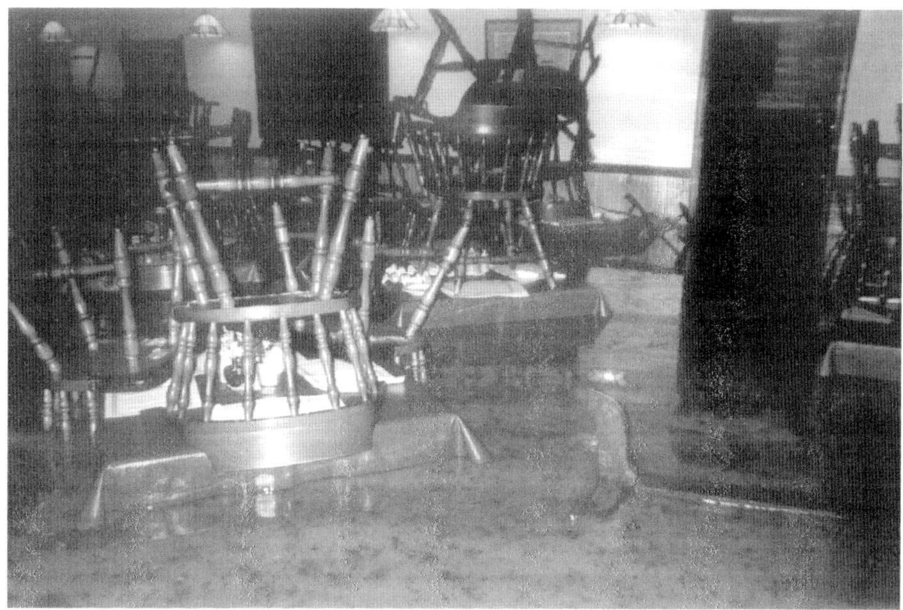

This is Geatz's Restaurant as it appeared on September 11, 2000. Water rose to the tabletops. Customers, however, remained at the restaurant until the last possible moment and continued to eat crabs, even as the water rose to a level of two feet. One gentleman, sitting at the bar, had a prosthetic leg that popped out in the rising waters and floated away. He finished his beer. Oddly enough, it was determined afterward that the electricity had been on the entire time. *Photograph by Brenda Geatz.*

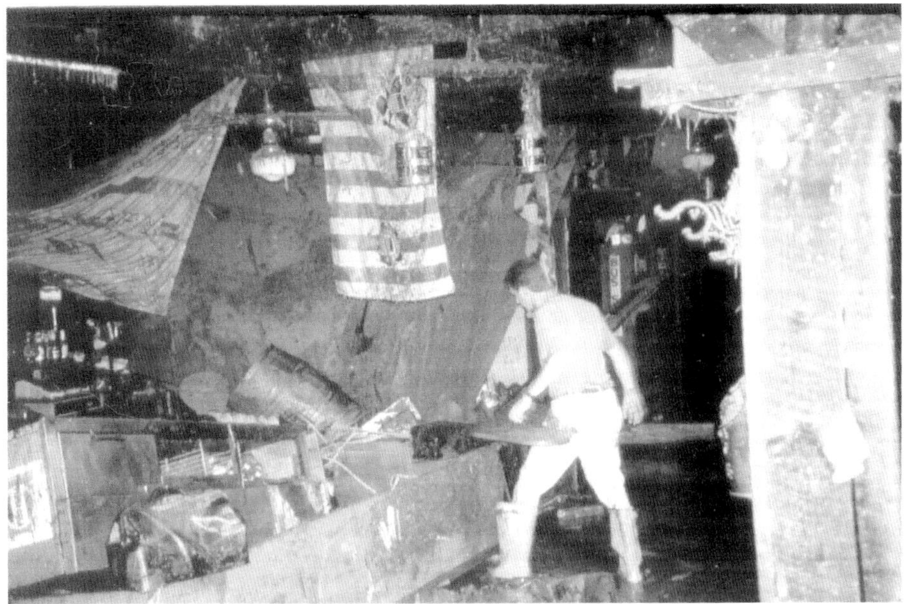

This photograph, taken on September 14, 2000, depicts Eric Geatz as he begins to clean the basement room of Geatz's. The cellar, now known as Geatz's Underground, was totally submerged, taking almost three days for the water to recede. *Photograph by Brenda Geatz.*

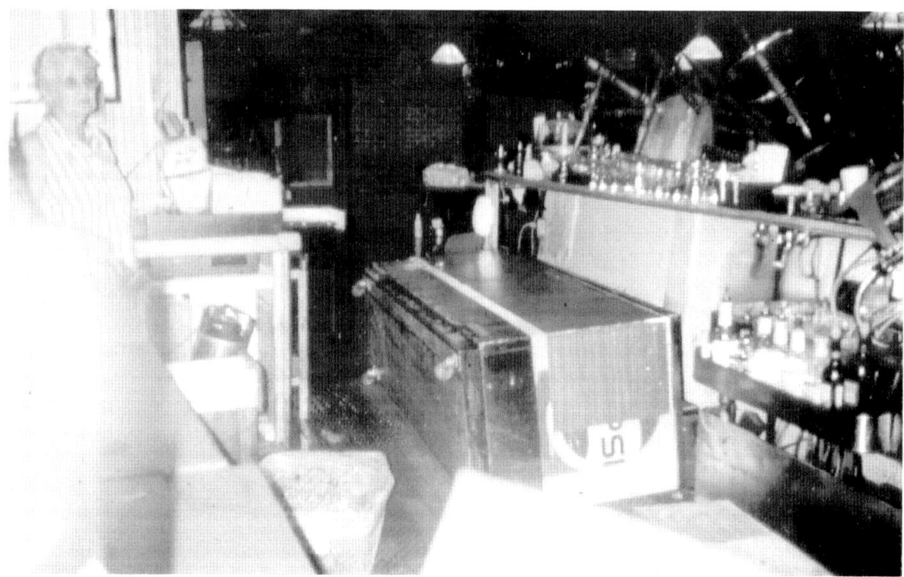

Joan "Sis" Geatz inspects the damage done to the bar area in the aftermath of the September 2000 flood event. The water, which was negotiated by customers and waitresses alike, at one point reached a height of almost four feet in the parking lot outside the restaurant. *Photograph by Brenda Geatz.*

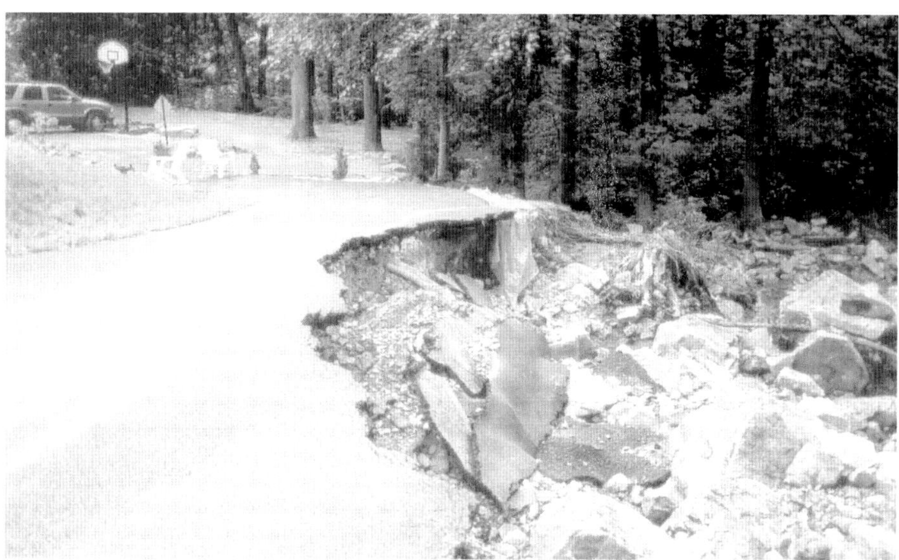

Runoff from the mountains in September 2000 also resulted in significant damage and flooding, particularly from Haystack Mountain on Cumberland's West Side. This photograph from McDonald Terrace vividly portrays the destruction vented on a driveway from the runoff. *Courtesy City of Cumberland.*

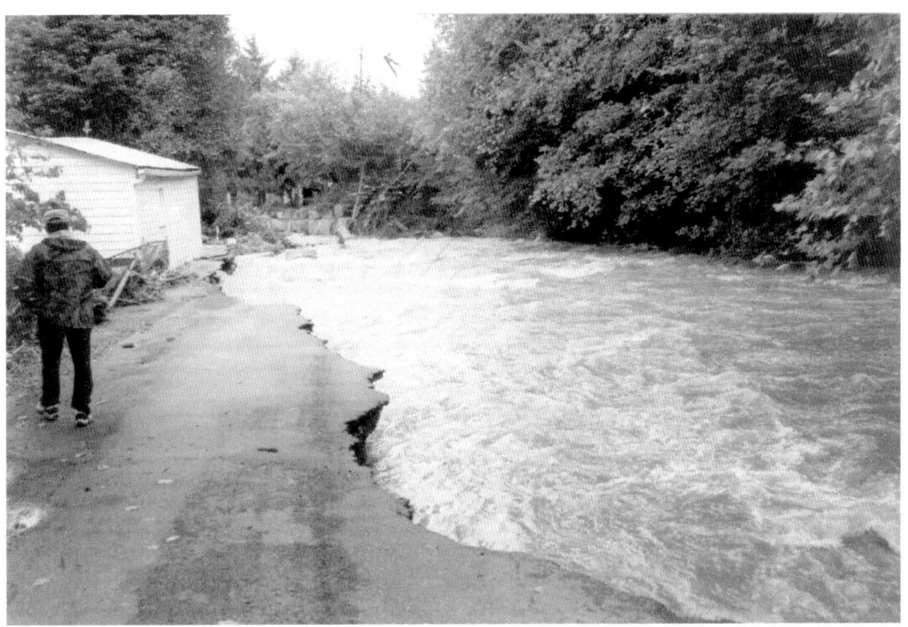

In September 2004, heavy rains caused a series of flooding events and overflow from Jennings Run into the adjacent community of Mount Savage, northwest of Cumberland along Route 36. This photograph from September 17, 2004, depicts Station Master Road in Mount Savage. Floodwaters from the adjacent Jennings Run have washed out the road. *Photograph by Cora B. Carter.*

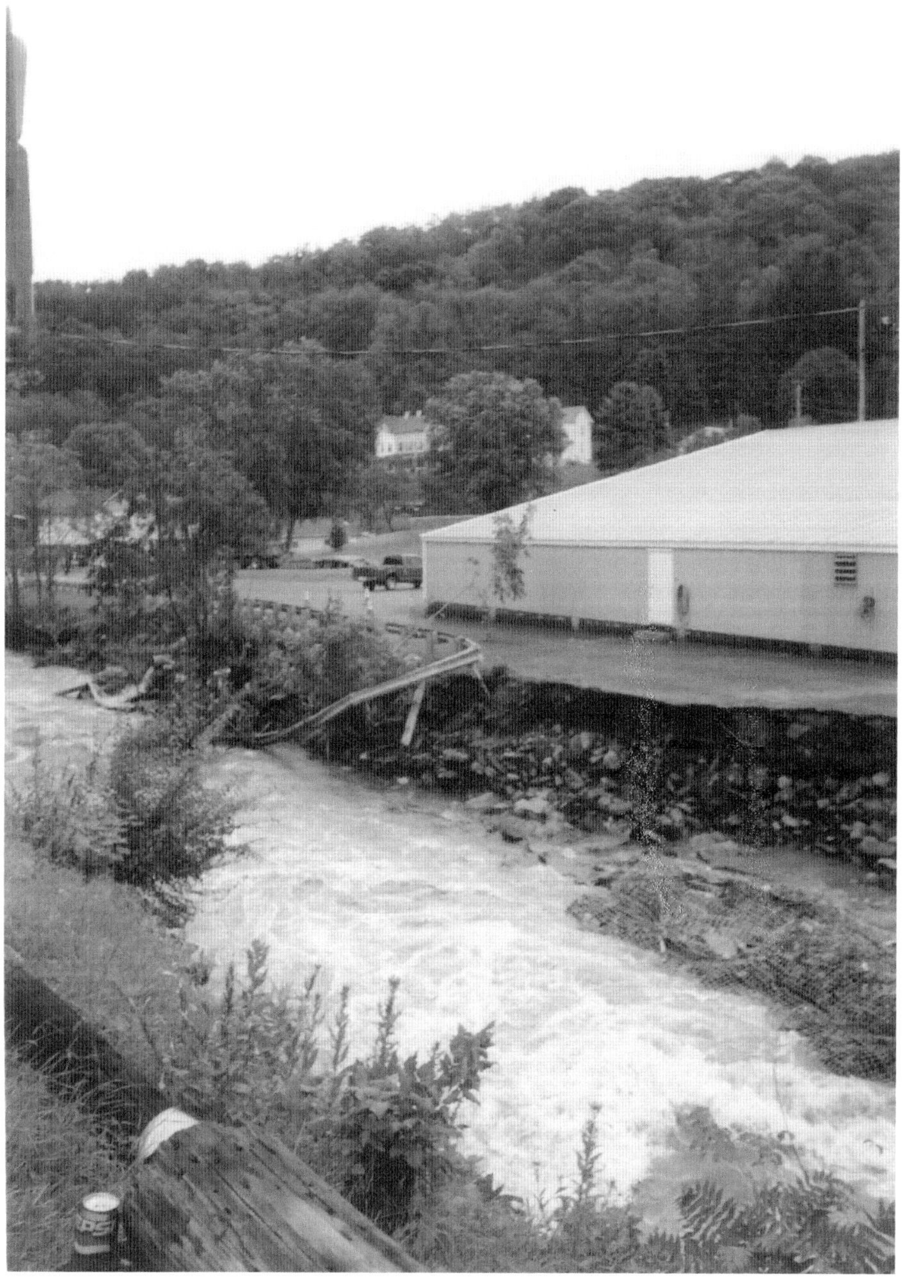

Taken on September 18, 2004, this photograph depicts a receding Jennings Run, but only after the havoc and destruction wrought on the guardrails and parking area in the rear of the Mount Savage Volunteer Fire Department. *Photograph by Portia Blank.*

Chapter 5

FIGHTING BACK THE WATERS

The Cumberland, Maryland–Ridgeley, West Virginia Flood Control Construction Project, 1949–1959

In 1936, the U.S. Senate approved the first of several appropriations for a flood control construction project to include not only the North Branch of the Potomac River, but also Wills Creek. Levees, retaining walls, channel clearing and channel deepening were included. The Army Corps of Engineers had even already begun to design plans by 1940. However, with the advent of World War II, all work obviously ceased for the duration.

Many people laid the groundwork for the Flood Control Construction Project or saw it through to completion. Cumberland mayors George W. Legge and Thomas Koon, Congressman David J. Lewis and the U.S. senators from Maryland and West Virginia all pushed for federal funds for flood control protection under Franklin Delano Roosevelt's administration. Construction work took place during the terms of office of Cumberland mayors Thomas S. Post (1944–52); Roy W. Eves (1952–58); and J. Edwin Keech (1958–62). The U.S. Army Corps of Engineers had been involved from 1924 in working with the City of Cumberland in planning for its flood protection. It was during the administration of Mayor Roy W. Eves, with C.Z. Nuzum as the city engineer, that four bridges were constructed over Wills Creek and the Potomac River. These were the Valley Street Bridge in 1954–55, the Market Street Bridge in 1956, the Baltimore Street Bridge in 1957–58 and the Blue Bridge (over the Potomac River) in 1955. J. Glenn Beall Sr., who served in the U.S. House of Representatives from 1943 to 1953 and the U.S. Senate from 1953 to 1965, along with other federal representatives, continued to help secure construction funds and also worked to fund other flood control protection measures along the Potomac River, such as the Savage River Dam in Garrett County, which went into operation in 1952.

The following narrative is reprinted from a report entitled "Cumberland, Maryland–Ridgeley, West Virginia Flood Protection Project," which was published by the U.S. Army Corps of Engineers in 1959. It should be further noted that all of the photographs in this chapter, unless otherwise indicated, were provided courtesy of the City of Cumberland's Engineering Department.

LOCAL FLOOD PROTECTION PROJECT
CUMBERLAND, MARYLAND–RIDGELEY, WEST VIRGINIA
Constructed by the U.S. Army Corps of Engineers
1949–1959

The local flood protection project for Cumberland was conceived when the flood of March 1924 inflicted $4,000,000 in damages to the City. Again in 1936 the City experienced a loss in excess of $2,000,000 in property damages due to a flood. The Flood Control Acts of 1936, 1938 and 1946 provide the authority for the project which now protects Cumberland, Maryland, and its neighboring community, Ridgeley, West Virginia.

Project features include improved channels in Wills Creek and the North Branch, levees, floodwalls, and an extensive modification of sewer and storm water drainage facilities and other utilities in Cumberland and Ridgeley. Three pumping stations with a combined capacity of 166,000 gallons per minute were constructed to remove storm drainage from behind the levees and walls during times of flood. One highway and one railroad bridge were removed, 3 highway and 2 railroad bridges were reconstructed or modified and interchange tracks between the Western Maryland Railway and the Baltimore and Ohio Railroad were relocated. A total of fifty (50) Cumberland and seventy (70) Ridgeley buildings were either razed or relocated.

The old Chesapeake & Ohio Canal feeder dam located on the North Branch just below the mouth of Wills Creek was removed and a new dam constructed 600 feet upstream on the North Branch. The new dam serves the primary purpose of furnishing water for the Potomac Edison Company, the Kelly Springfield Tire Company and other industries located in West Cumberland. Piers on the dam serve as the foundation for a new interstate highway bridge connecting Cumberland with Ridgeley, West Virginia.

A major problem of planning and design was the provision of facilities to pass a major flood through Wills Creek where urban development had encroached on the flood plain. As finally constructed the concrete channel in Wills Creek will pass a flood flow of 50,000 cubic feet per second, or

131% of the maximum flow recorded in March 1936. The Wills Creek improvement may be viewed from bridges crossing the creek on Baltimore Street, Market Street, Valley Street, and Route 40.

On the North Branch upstream of the mouth of Wills Creek, levees and floodwalls on both banks were constructed to confine a flood flow of 93,000 cubic feet per second. Downstream from the mouth of Wills Creek the North Branch channel was straightened widened and deepened and levees and slope protection constructed. This channel will safely pass a flood volume of 113,000 cubic feet per second or 128% of the maximum flow recorded in 1936. These channels may be seen from the new bridge crossing the North Branch into Ridgeley and from Riverside Park at the mouth of Wills Creek.

Construction was started in March 1949 and the work was completed in May 1959. The total cost of the completed project was $18,500,000 of which the local community contributed $2,900,000 (construction costs totaled $16,990,000 and real estate costs totaled $1,510,000). Since it was necessary that levees and walls be constructed on both banks of the North Branch and since the Town of Ridgeley was unable to finance its share of local costs, Cumberland assumed the total cost of lands, easements and rights-of-way and for the modifications of utilities and interior drainage for Ridgeley as well as for Cumberland. In addition, the City of Cumberland has assumed the responsibility for maintaining and operating the completed works both in Cumberland and Ridgeley. Maintenance of the channels is a Federal responsibility.

It is estimated that a recurrence of the 1936 flood under present conditions of development and without the flood protection features would cause damages in excess of 8 million dollars.

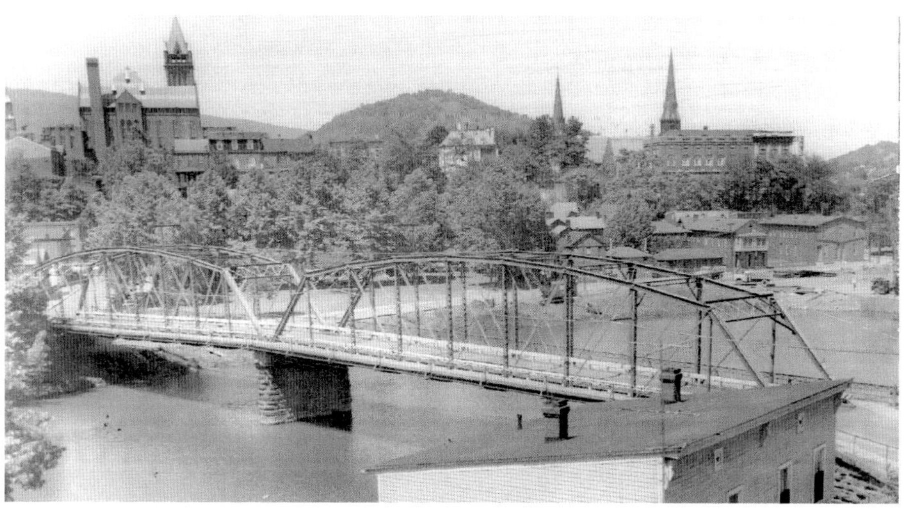

This is the old Johnson Street Bridge, which crossed the Potomac River, as viewed from the northeast and West Virginia side. Shown on the left is the Allegany County Courthouse, which was erected on Washington Street during the years 1893–94. *Corps photograph taken March 27, 1953.*

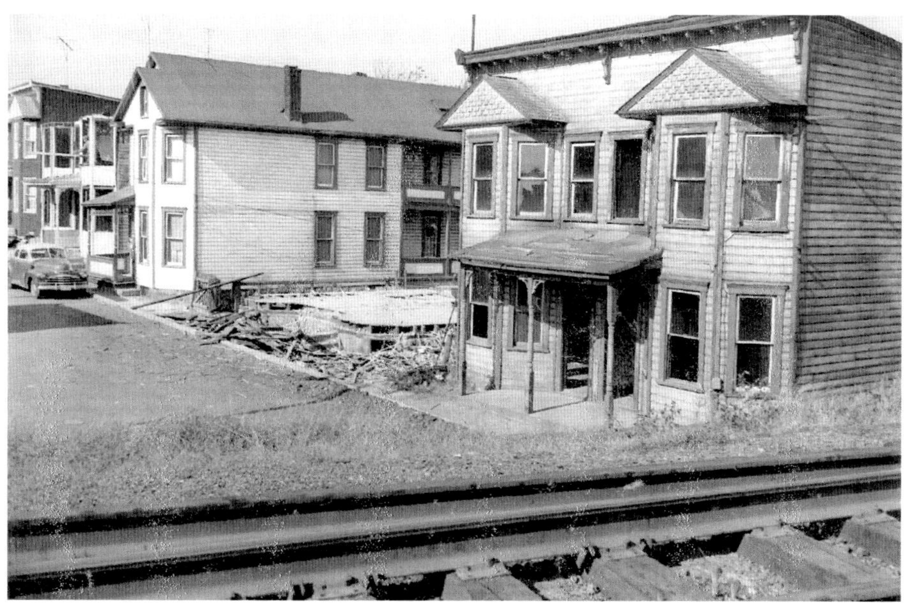

This scene depicts houses being vacated and demolished along John Street in Ridgeley. The center home had not yet been vacated. *Corps photograph taken October 21, 1955.*

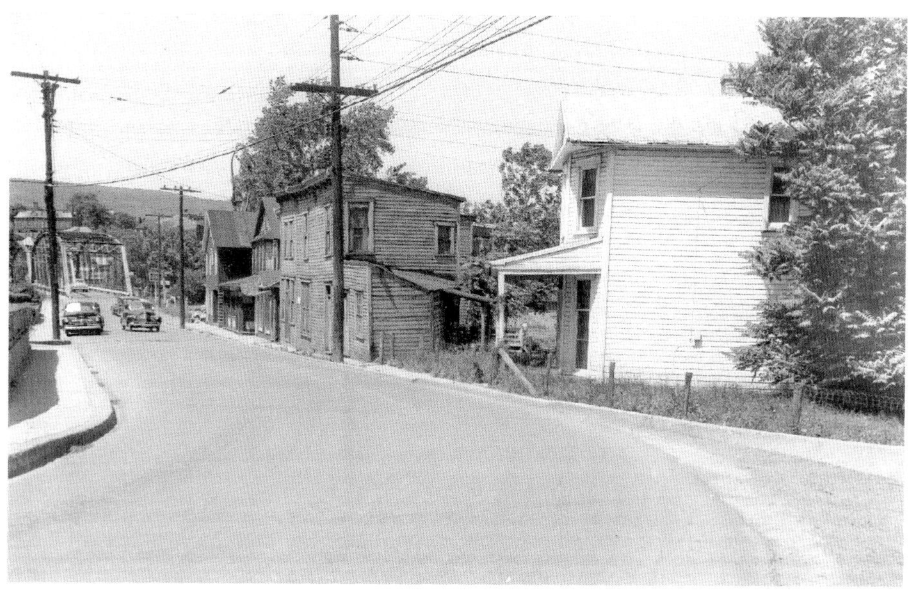

Here is Route 28 from John Street in Ridgeley, West Virginia. We are looking toward the Johnson Street Bridge. This row of homes will soon be removed. *Corps photograph taken May 28, 1953.*

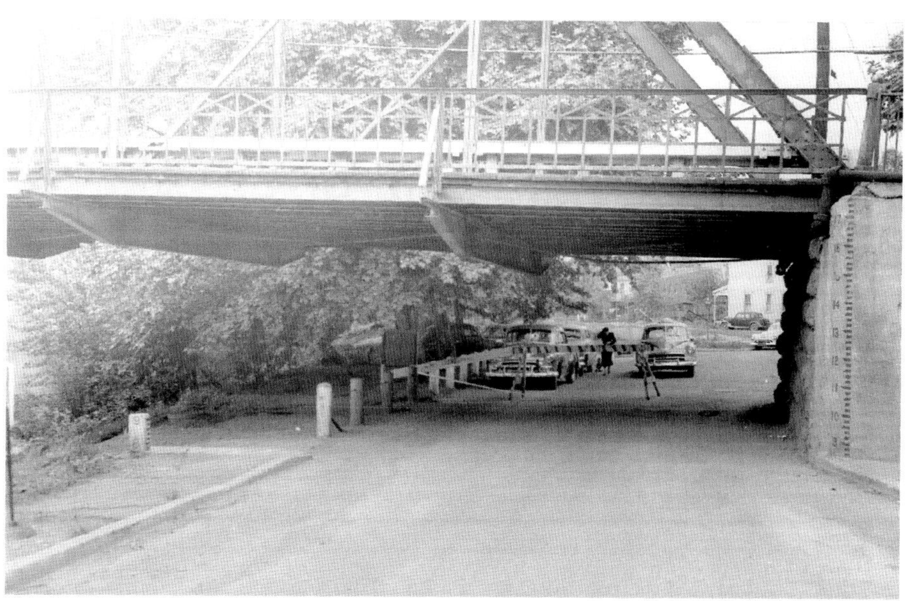

We are looking west from the Maryland side beneath the Johnson Street Bridge abutment. Note the old stream gauge on the bridge's center pier on the right. *Corps photograph taken May 29, 1953.*

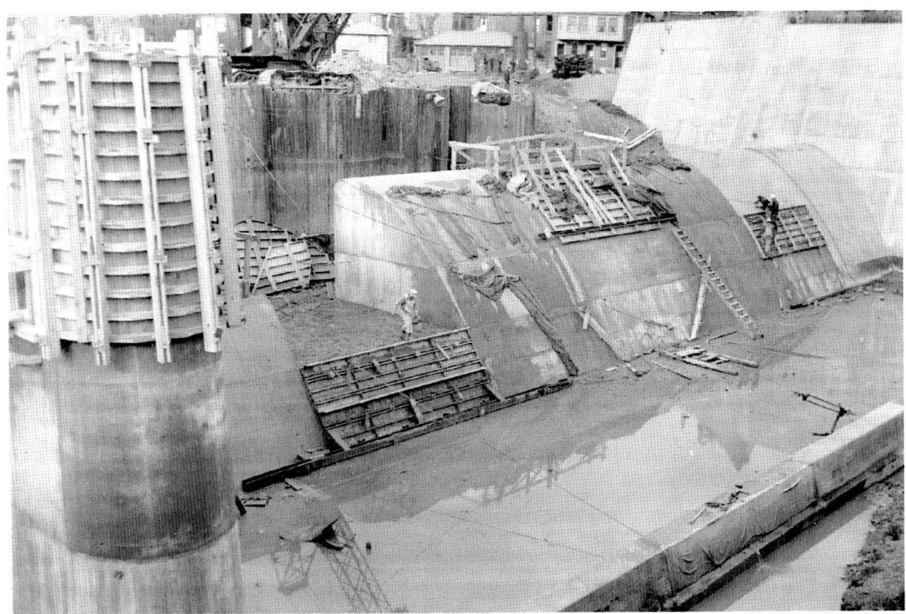

This is the downstream face of the Potomac River dam from center pier to its Cumberland abutment. The stilling basin appears in front. *Corps photograph taken December 29, 1953.*

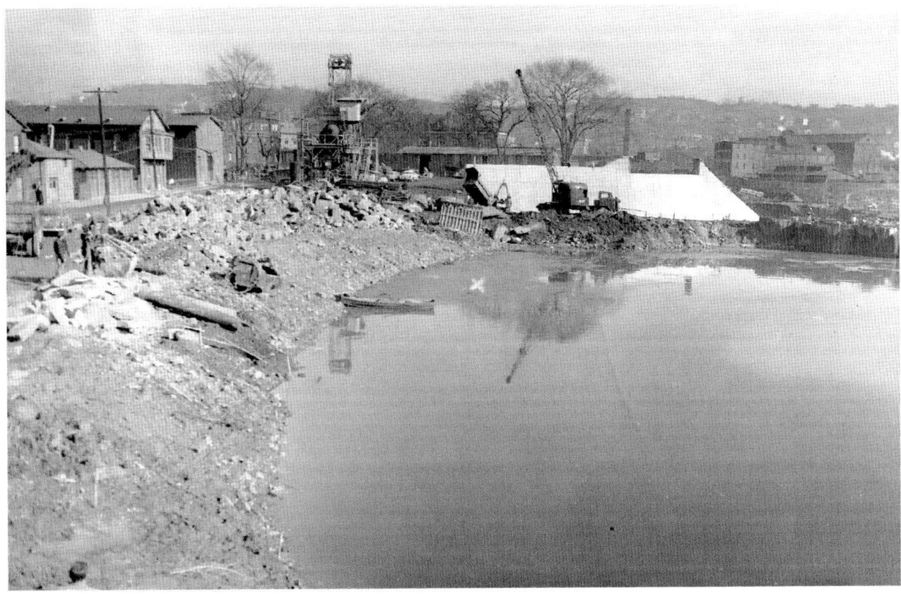

We are looking from the old Johnson Street Bridge toward the dam site on the Maryland side. An "x" shows the spot where eight-year-old Walter E. Smith Jr. broke through the ice and drowned about 4:50 p.m. on January 19. *Corps photograph taken January 26, 1954.*

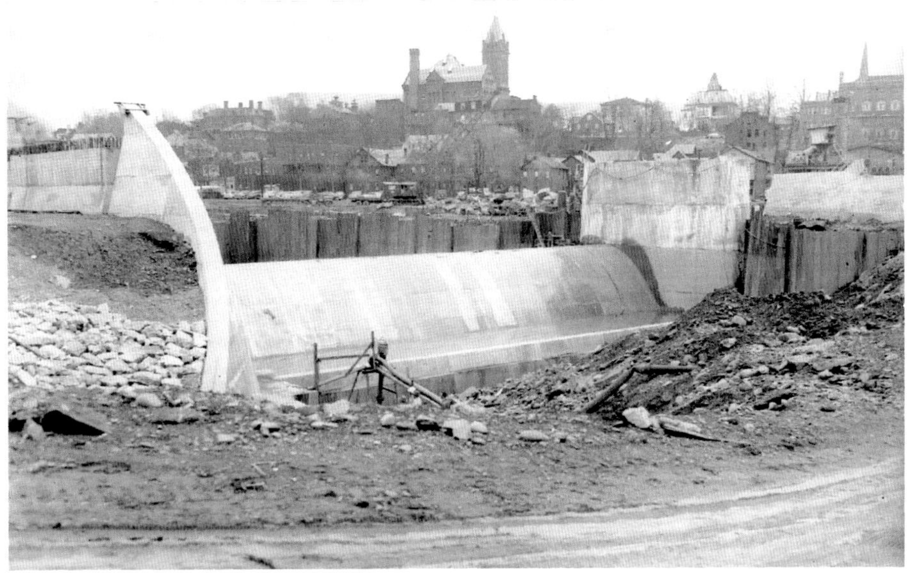

Here is the Ridgeley half of the completed dam, looking toward the center pier. *Corps photograph taken April 15, 1954.*

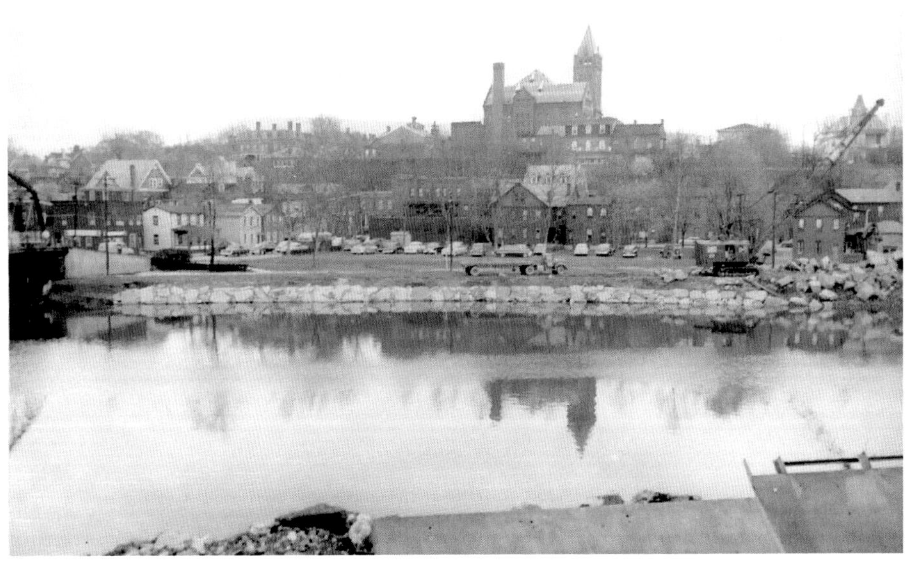

This view looks across the stream from atop the Ridgeley abutment toward Cumberland. Note the derrick-placed riprap on the left bank. *Corps photograph taken April 15, 1954.*

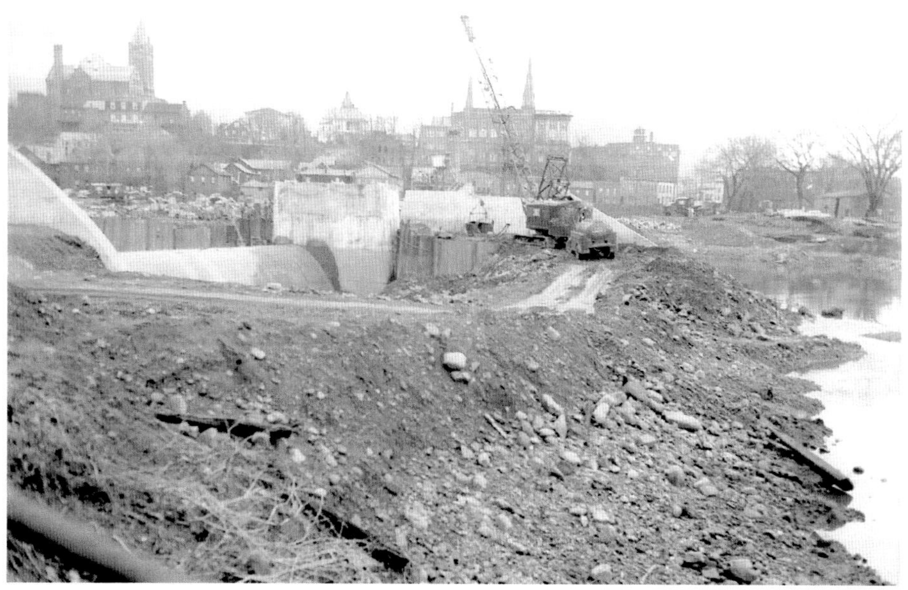

The Earthen Coffer Dam in front of the Ridgeley, West Virginia half of the completed dam is depicted here. It is in the process of being removed. Note Greene Street in the distance. *Corps photograph taken April 16, 1954.*

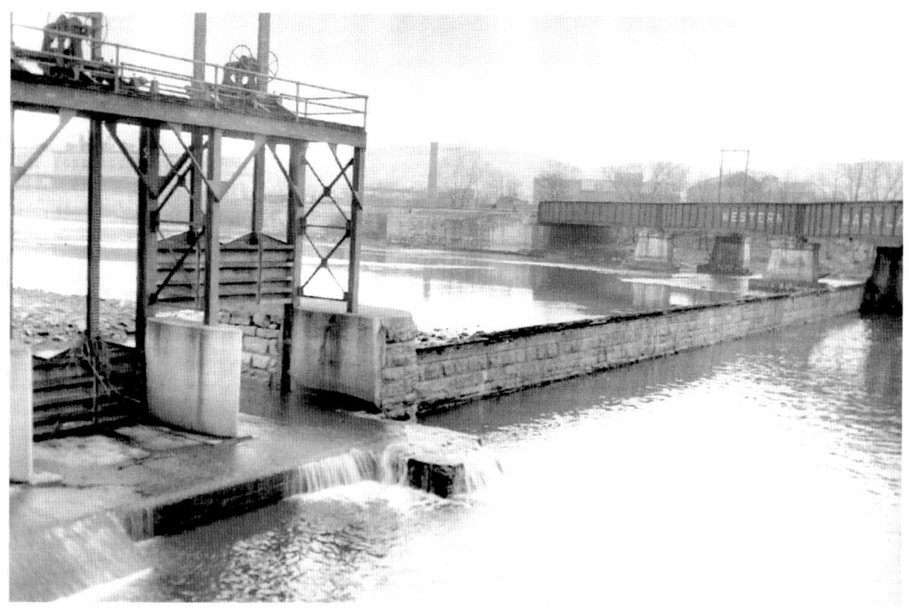

Shown here is the downstream face of the old dam from the Ridgeley side gates looking toward the Western Maryland Railroad Bridge. *Corps photograph taken April 16, 1954.*

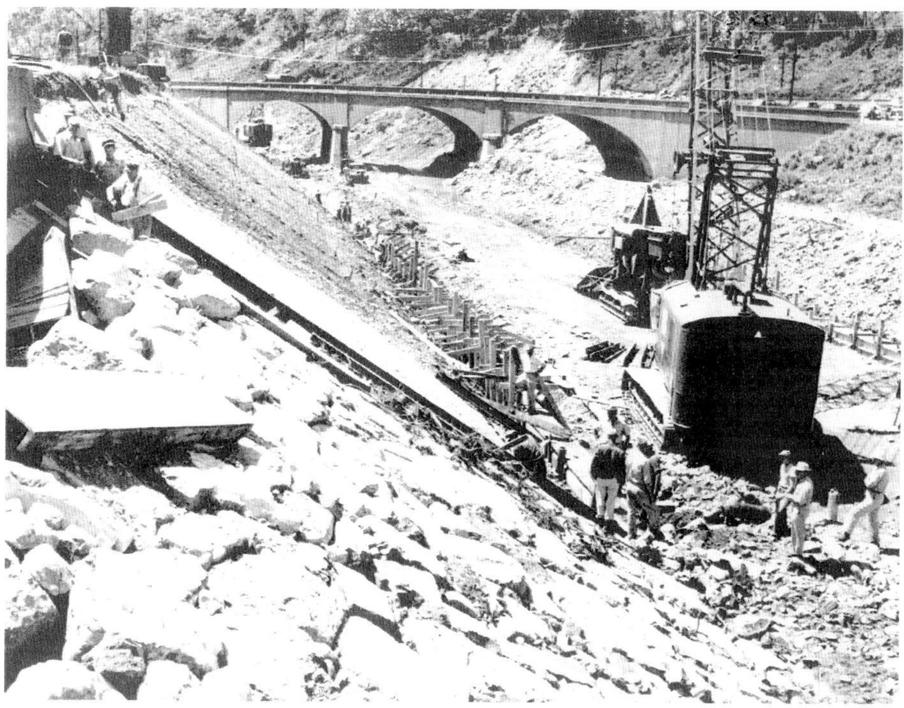

The view in this early 1950s photograph looks upstream and depicts flood control construction work in the Narrows. The Route 40 Bridge in the background, which crosses Wills Creek, was constructed in 1932. Cumberland Times *photograph courtesy the City of Cumberland.*

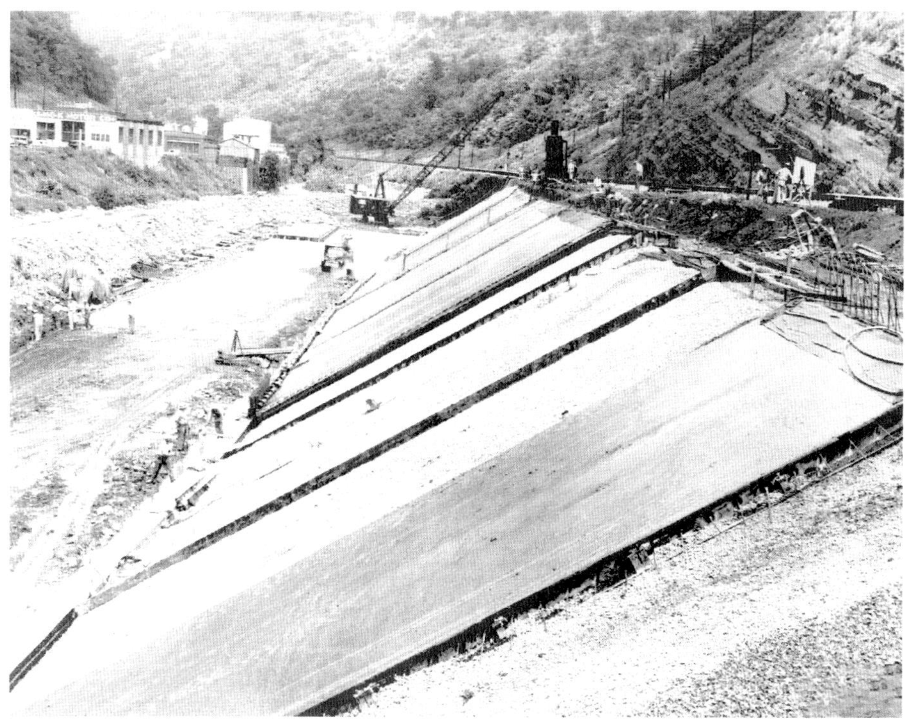

The building on the left is now the site of Kline's Restaurant and Lover's Leap Lounge. This early 1950s view looks upstream along Wills Creek and depicts work on the flood control construction project through the Narrows. Cumberland Times *photograph courtesy the City of Cumberland.*

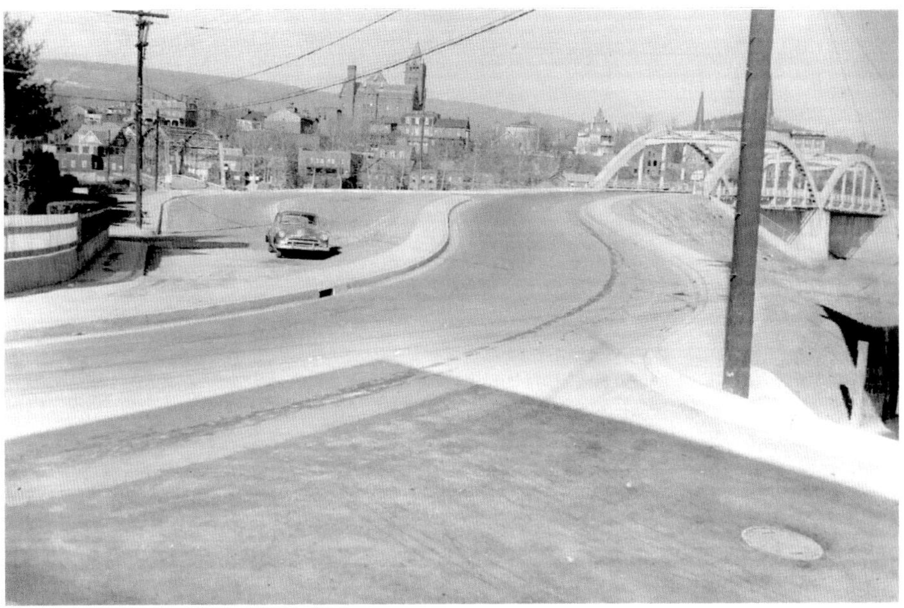

The approach over the dam to the new bridge connecting Cumberland, in the background, is completed. Based on news reports, the Potomac River span, now known as the Blue Bridge, was formally dedicated on October 11, 1955, and opened to general traffic on October 25. A plaque on the bridge formally refers to it as "George Washington's Crossing." Note the location of the old Johnson Street Bridge on the left. *Corps photograph taken December 2, 1955.*

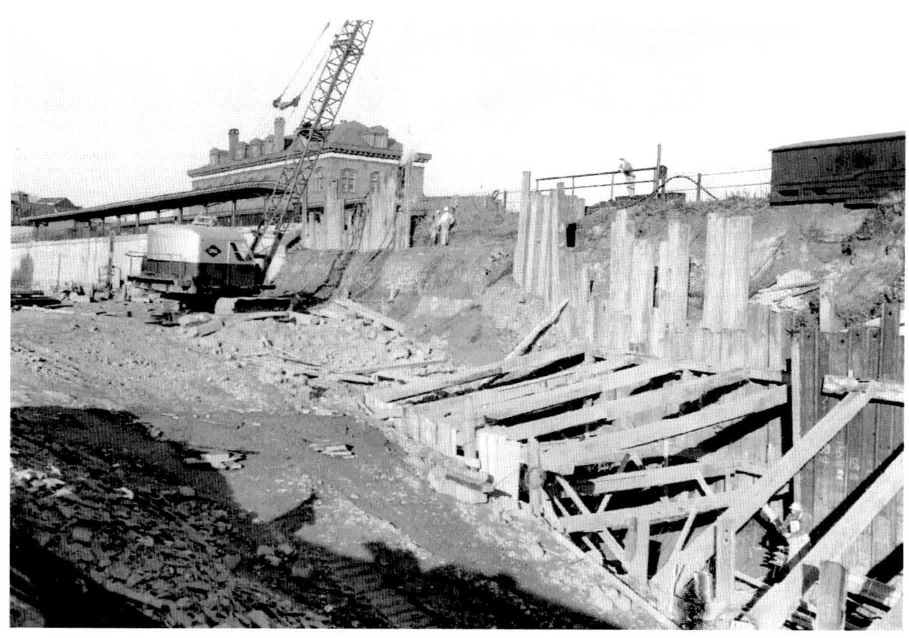

Sheet piling is being driven behind the old wall between the Western Maryland Railway tracks and Wills Creek. The wall is to be removed. The Western Maryland had been extended to Cumberland by 1906. The Western Maryland Railway Station, depicted in the background, opened in 1913. *Corps photograph taken November 6, 1956.*

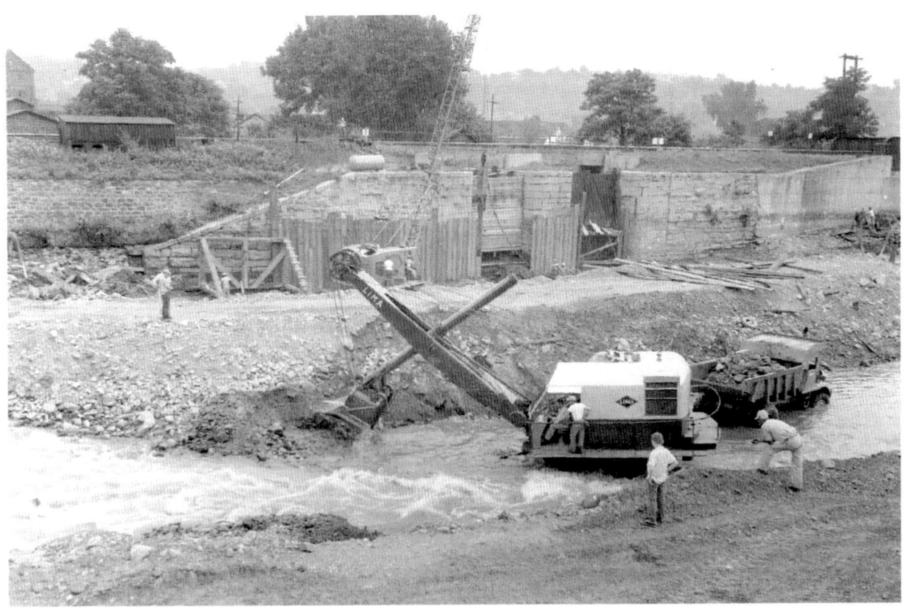

We are looking across Wills Creek from what was described as the old Riverside Park. This view shows the contractor driving steel piling along the outlet of the old Chesapeake and Ohio Canal. On July 4, 1828, President John Quincy Adams broke ground in Georgetown for the 184.5-mile Chesapeake and Ohio Canal. It was completed and opened to Cumberland on October 10, 1850. Two major floods in 1924 devastated the canal, and it ceased operations permanently that same year. In 1971, the Chesapeake and Ohio Canal was named a National Historical Park. *Corps photograph taken July 26, 1956.*

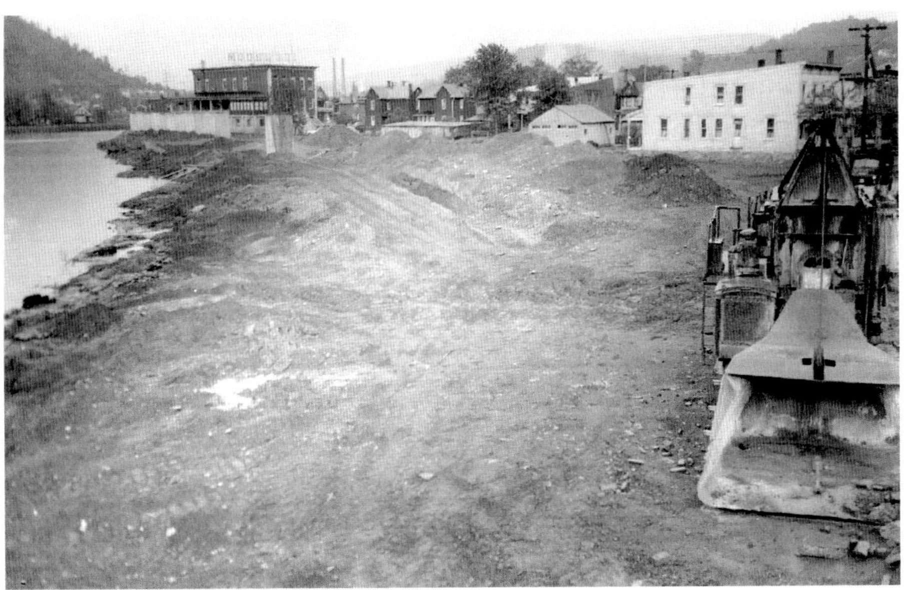

We are looking southwest from the old Johnson Street Bridge upstream to the lower end of the flood wall. Note the manhole extended to the top of the future levee and the former Moose Lodge, now the Biederlack Blanket Outlet, in the background. *Corps photograph taken May 15, 1956.*

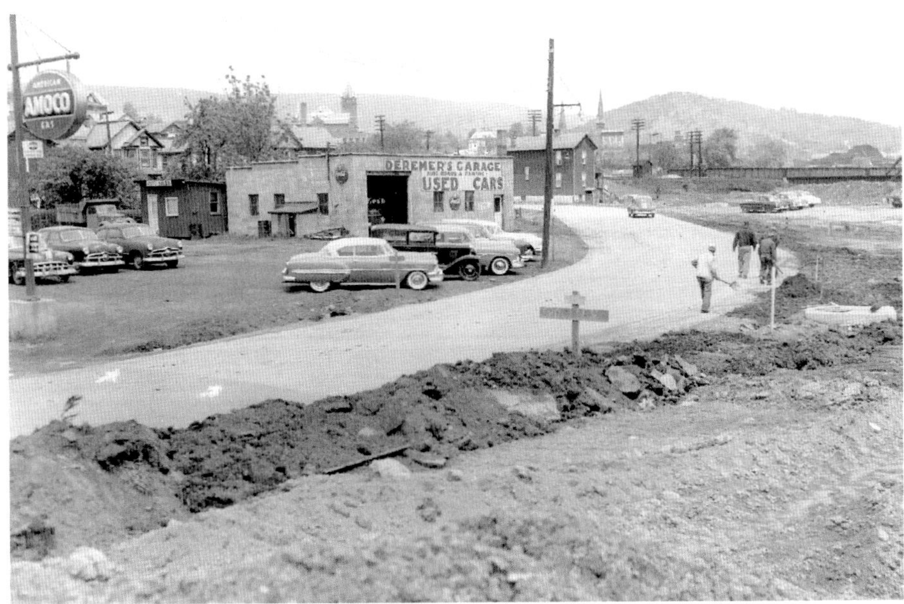

This scene portrays the relocation of Potomac Street, West Virginia Route 28, in Ridgeley. *Corps photograph taken May 16, 1956.*

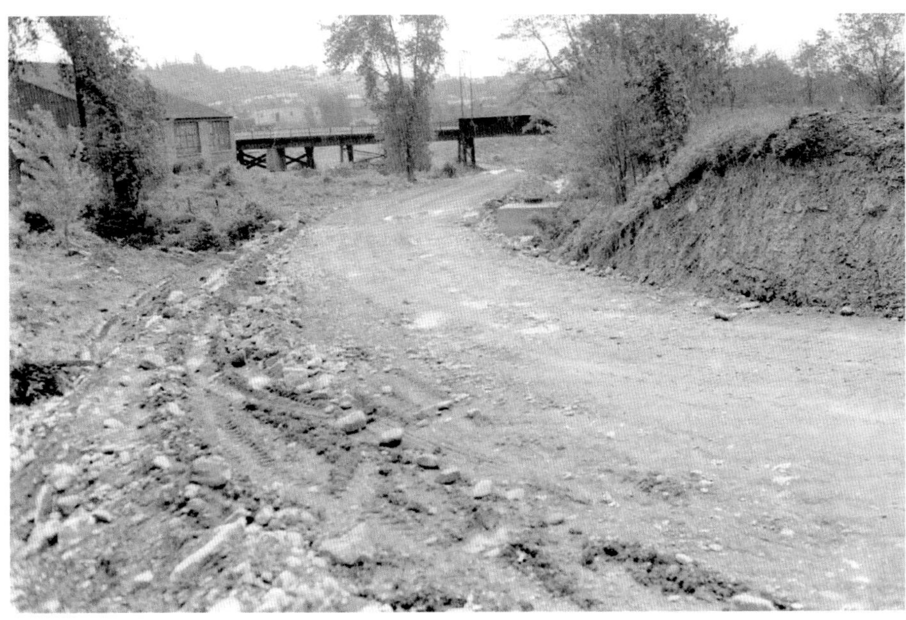

Here is the haul road in the old C&O Canal bed running through the Mill Race Pumping Station site and beneath the Western Maryland Interchange Railroad Bridge to the spoil area beyond. This view is south from a point near where the haul road comes out of the canal bank to pass under the Western Maryland mainline bridge. *Corps photograph taken May 16, 1956.*

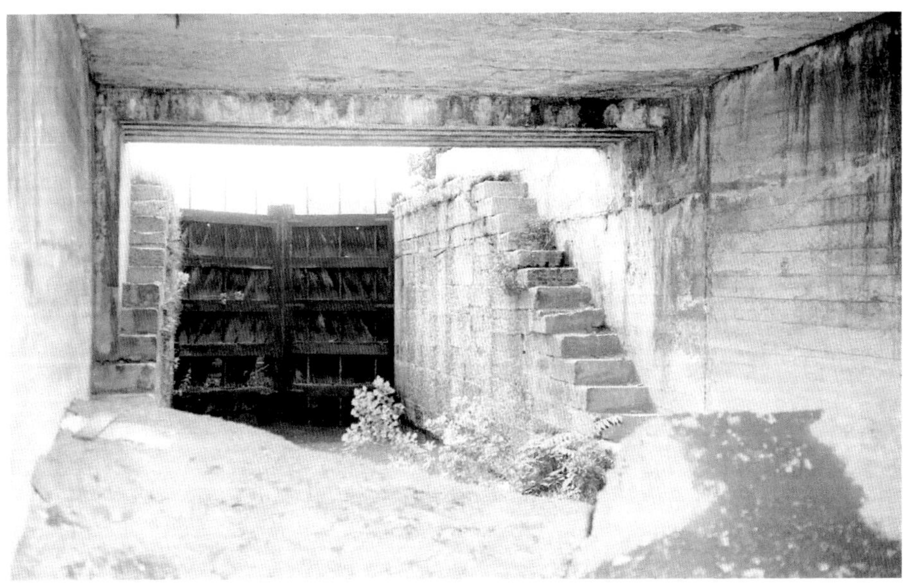

This image is a close-up view under the Western Maryland Railway tracks, which run over the north lock of the C&O Canal. *Corps photograph taken June 19, 1956.*

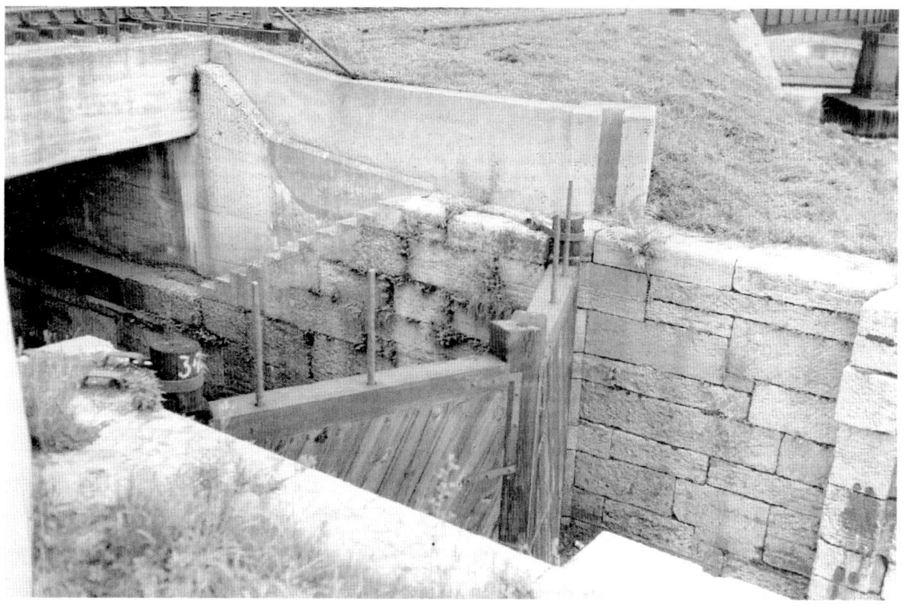

Here we are looking eastward toward the canal steps and canal gates of the south lock under the railroad tracks. *Corps photograph taken June 19, 1956.*

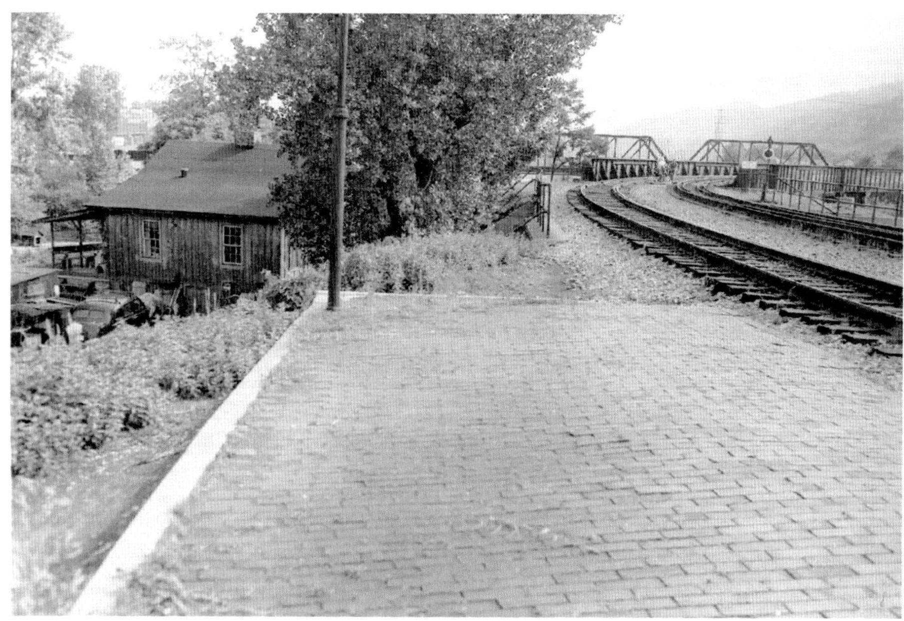

This southward view from the Western Maryland Railway Station platform shows the tracks over the old canal locks and the former one-story frame house between the two canal locks. *Corps photograph taken June 19, 1956.*

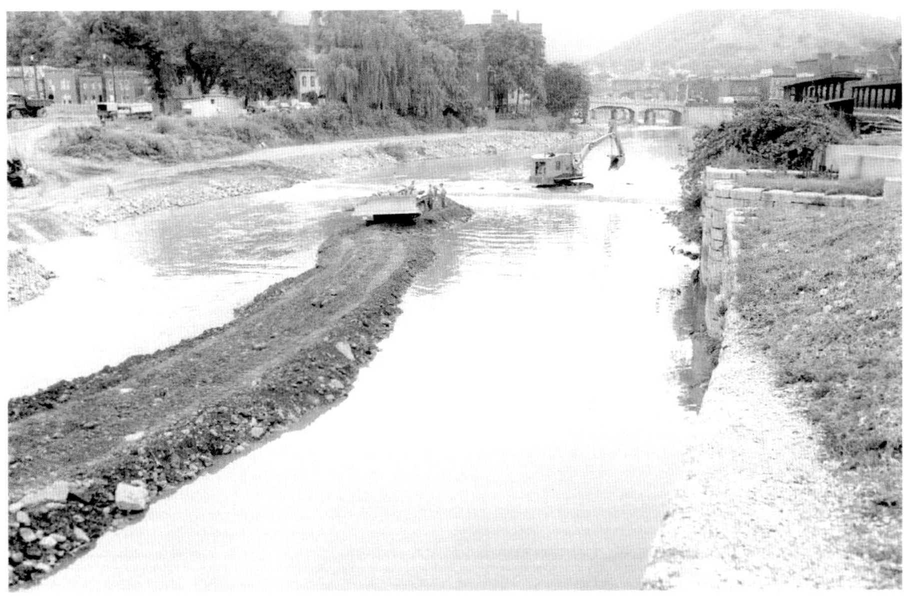

The George F. Hazelwood Company, contractor, is shown here resuming work on the coffer dam. Note Greene Street and Riverside Park on the left, the Chesapeake and Ohio Canal outlet on the right and the old Baltimore Street Bridge in the distance. *Corps photograph taken June 20, 1956.*

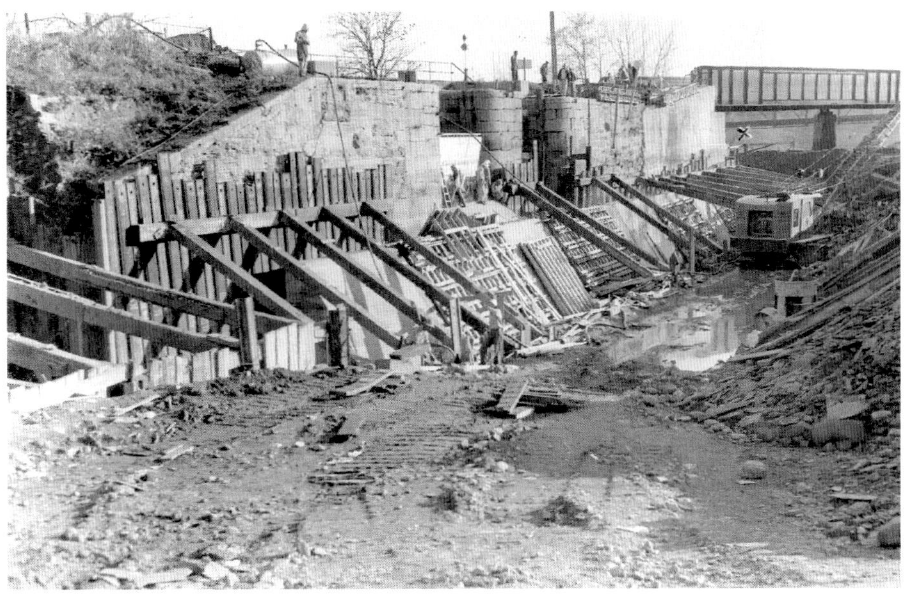

We are looking downstream toward the construction of the tow wall and reinforcement of the old canal locks. *Corps photograph taken November 6, 1956.*

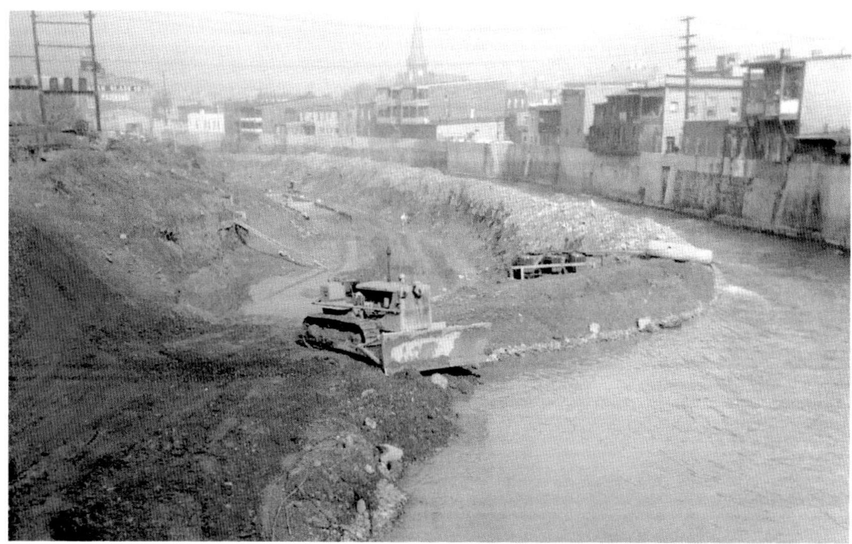

This is looking up Wills Creek from the Western Maryland Railway Bridge at Baltimore Street. The coffer dam is depicted diverting water from the right side of the creek bed with excavations in progress. Note the Sloan Glass Company on the left. Located off Market Street, this glass-cutting and decoration shop operated from about 1935 until 1956. *Corps photograph taken November 7, 1956.*

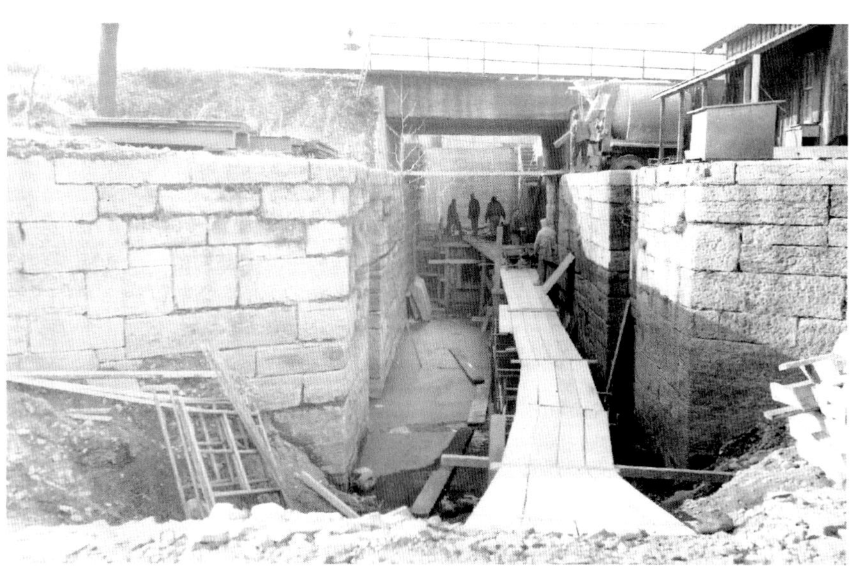

Here is the construction of the four- by four-and-a-half-foot storm siphon through the old C&O Canal Lock. This will carry storm water from west Cumberland to the Mill Race Pumping Station. *Corps photograph taken February 20, 1957.*

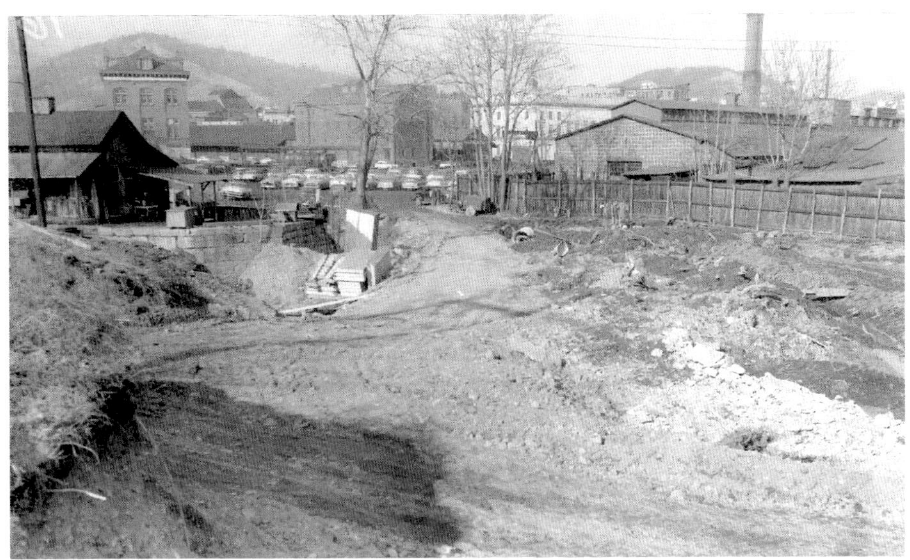

This scene shows the fill in back of the old C&O Canal locks. We are looking north from near the site of the Mill Race Pumping Station. Note the old "inlet guard-keeper's" home on the left. The home was demolished in early 1957, and at the time had been occupied by James "Scat" Eaton, who had driven mules along the C&O Canal towpath during the Chesapeake and Ohio Canal's final years. The Western Maryland Railway Station is in the background on the left. *Corps photograph taken February 20, 1957.*

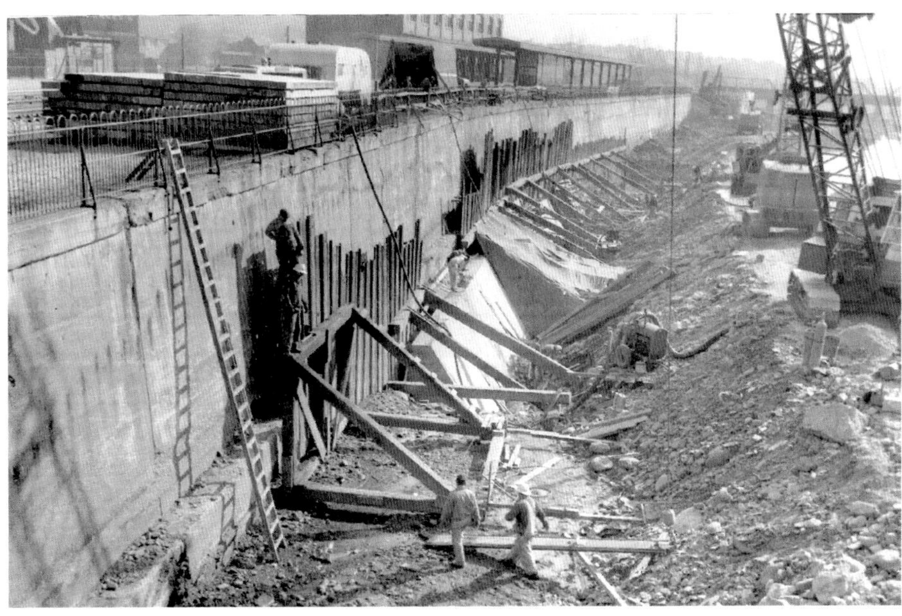

This is a view downstream from the Baltimore Street Bridge along the left bank of Wills Creek. Note the condition of the old wall. *Corps photograph taken February 20, 1957.*

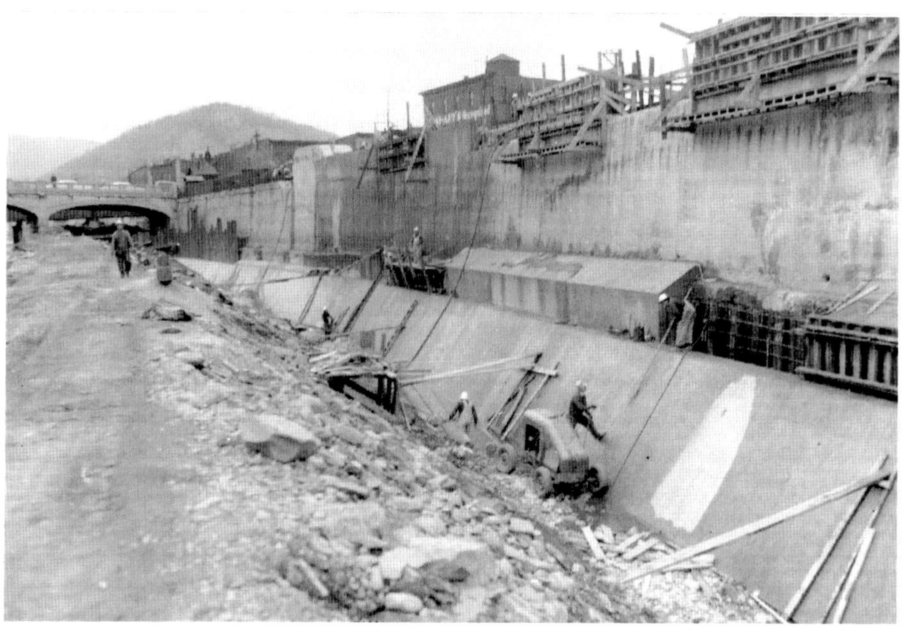

We are looking upstream along Wills Creek from in front of Western Maryland Railway Station to the old Baltimore Street Bridge. *Corps photograph taken April 4, 1957.*

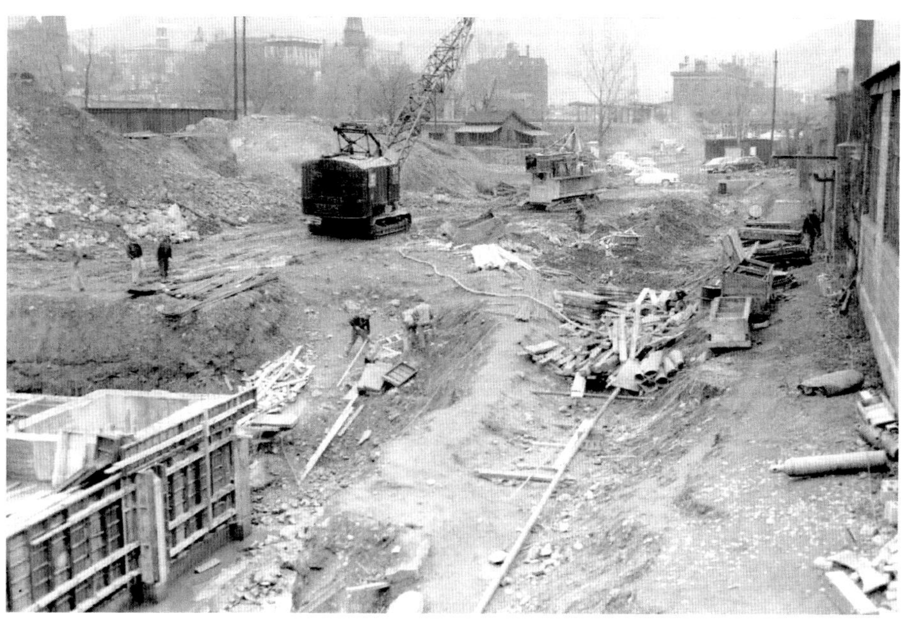

Here is a view looking northerly from the Western Maryland Railway Bypass. *Corps photograph taken April 4, 1957.*

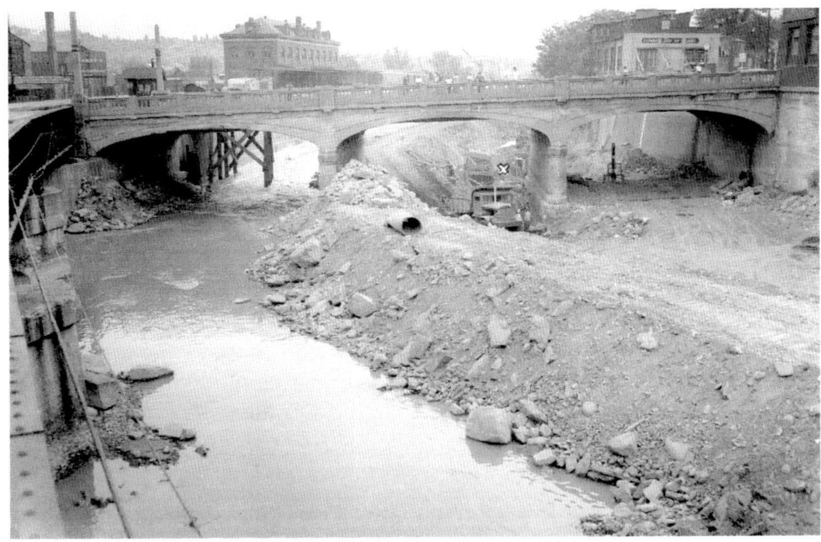

This depiction is from the Western Maryland Railway Bridge, looking toward the old Baltimore Street Bridge. The two primary contractors/construction companies for the project were E.G. Albrecht of Chicago and the George F. Hazelwood Company, Cumberland. *Corps photograph taken May 13, 1957.*

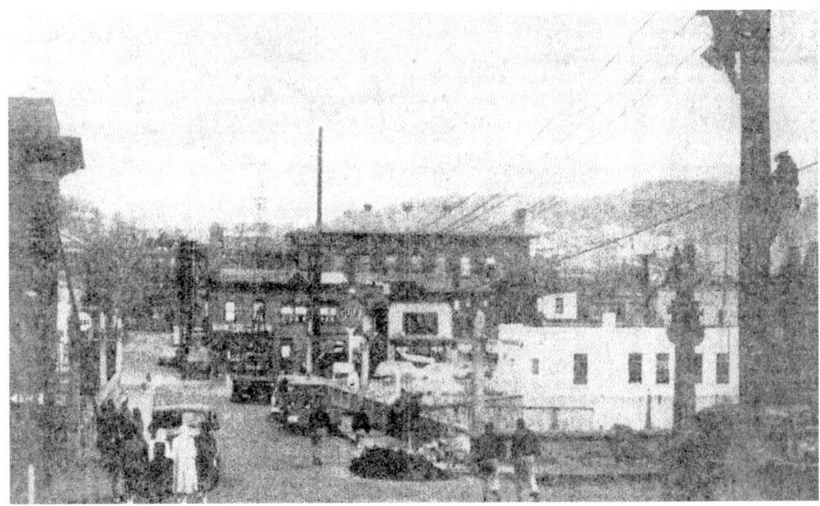

Utility pole removal and other preparations are underway for the rebuilding of a new Market Street Bridge. The large building in the center background is Carroll Hall, which was constructed in 1903. The building originally served as a social hall and sports center and also housed the Carroll Club. It went on to house the all-boys LaSalle Institute that had been established in 1907. Carroll Hall (which became LaSalle High School in 1938) served in this capacity from 1924 until 1966 and the opening of Bishop Walsh. Carroll Hall was razed in 1987. *Courtesy the* Cumberland News, *December 1955.*

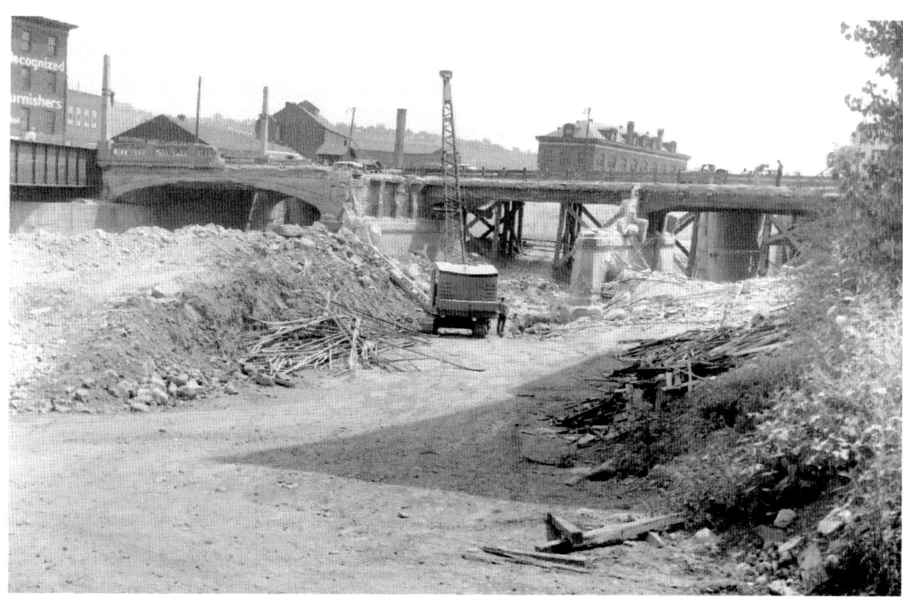

This view is looking downstream along Wills Creek and portrays the demolition of the old Baltimore Street Bridge. *Corps photograph taken August 14, 1957.*

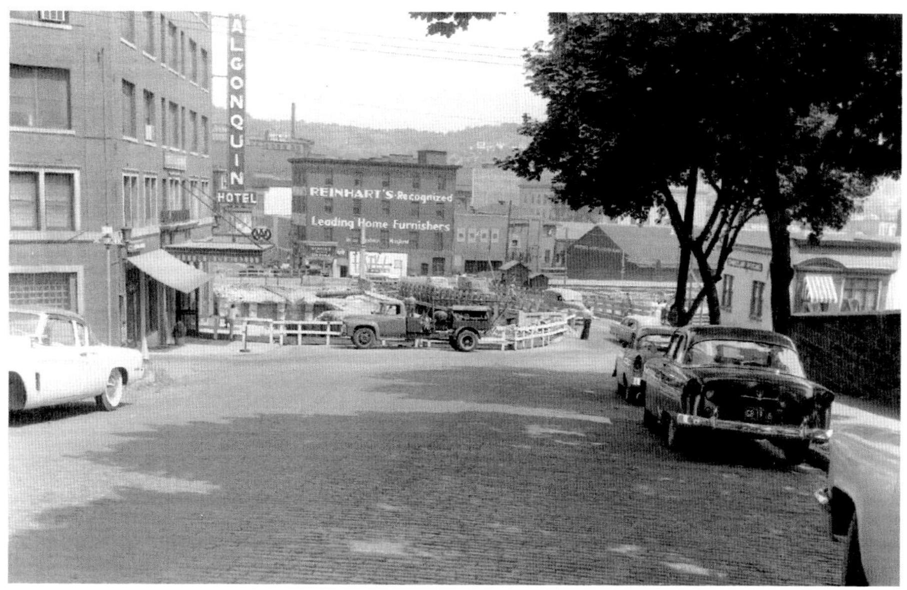

We are at the foot of Washington Street, looking east toward the new Baltimore Street Bridge, which is under construction. Note the temporary wooden bridge to the right. *Corps photograph taken August 14, 1957.*

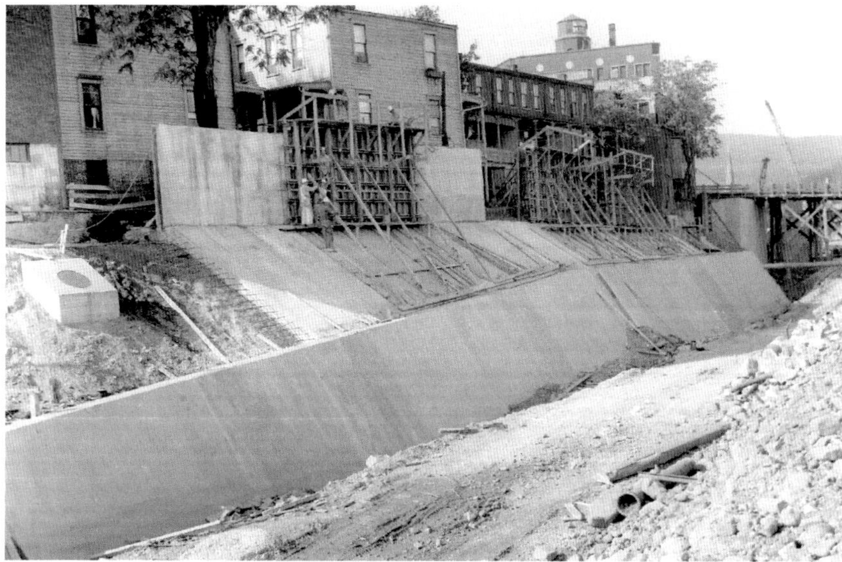

Here is an upstream image along the right bank of Wills Creek from a point opposite the Western Maryland Railway Station. Atop the hill stands the Emmanuel Episcopal Church, which was constructed between the years 1849 and 1851. *Corps photograph taken October 1, 1957.*

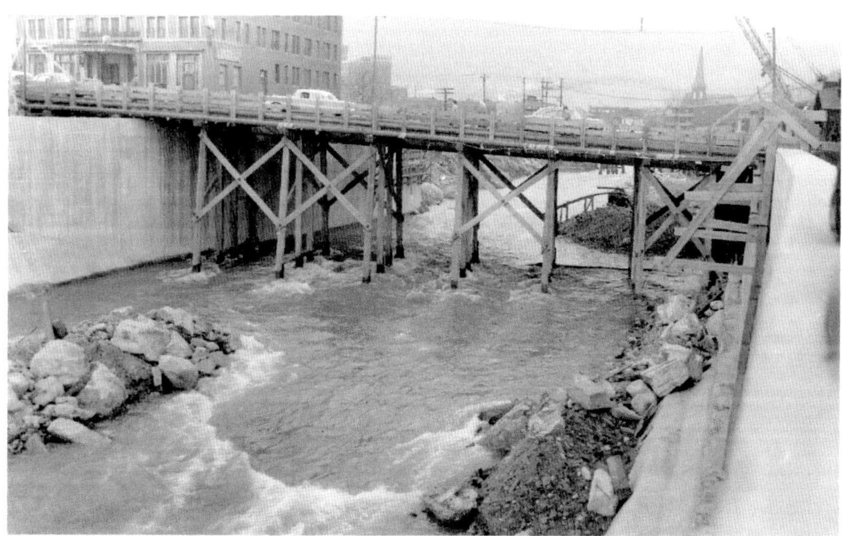

This upstream view along Wills Creek was taken from near the front of the Western Maryland Railway Station and shows the temporary Baltimore Street wooden traffic bridge and water flow. The temporary bridge was opened to traffic on August 5, 1957. It was razed in July 1958 soon after the July 3, 1958 opening of the new concrete and steel Baltimore Street span. *Corps photograph taken March 4, 1958.*

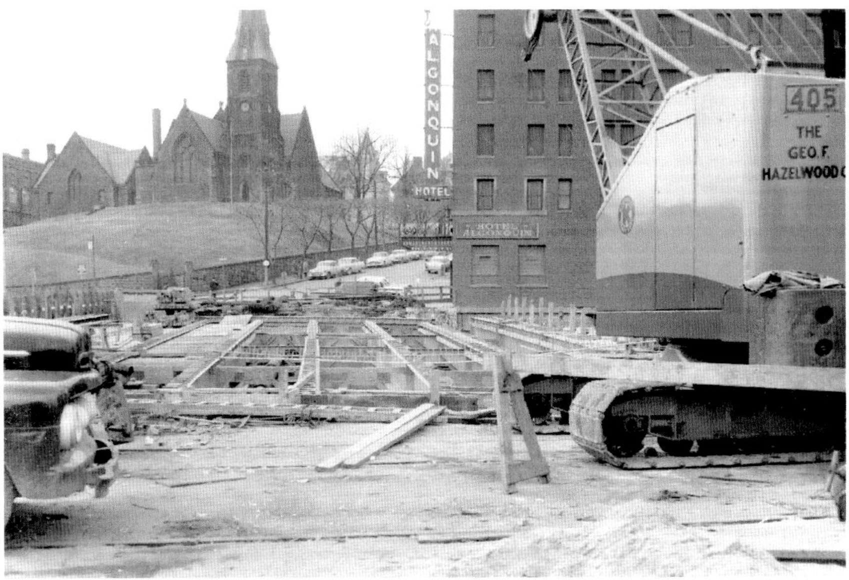

This image of the Baltimore Street Bridge looking west shows the progress being made on deck construction. *Corps photograph taken March 4, 1958.*

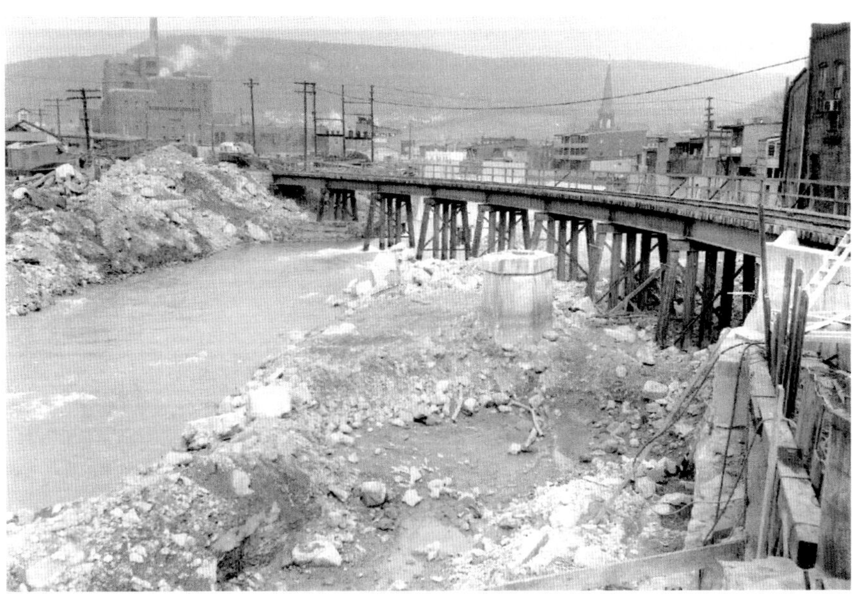

This upstream view shows the temporary railroad trestle crossing Wills Creek at Baltimore Street. At this point, the old railroad bridge has been completely removed. *Corps photograph taken March 4, 1958.*

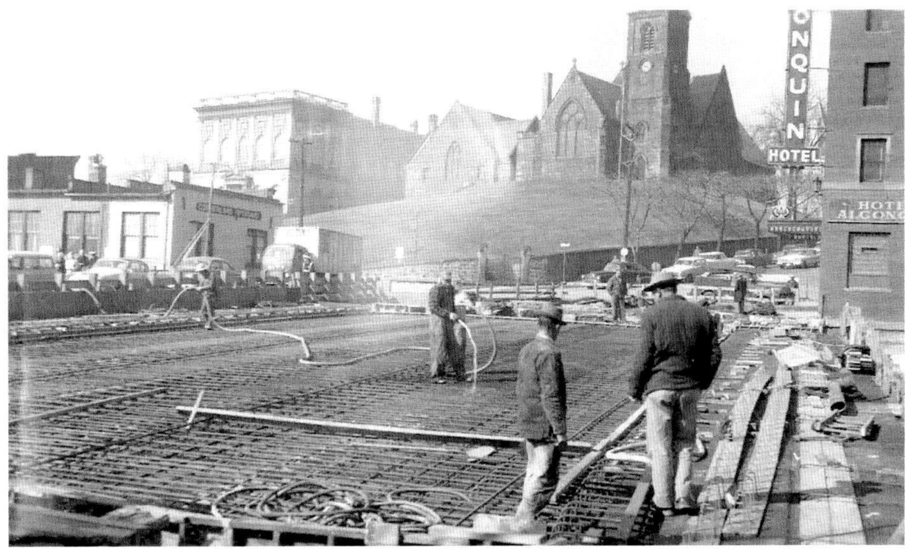

The new Baltimore Street Bridge deck, as seen under construction from the east abutment, is almost ready for concrete placement. *Kington photograph taken March 28, 1958.*

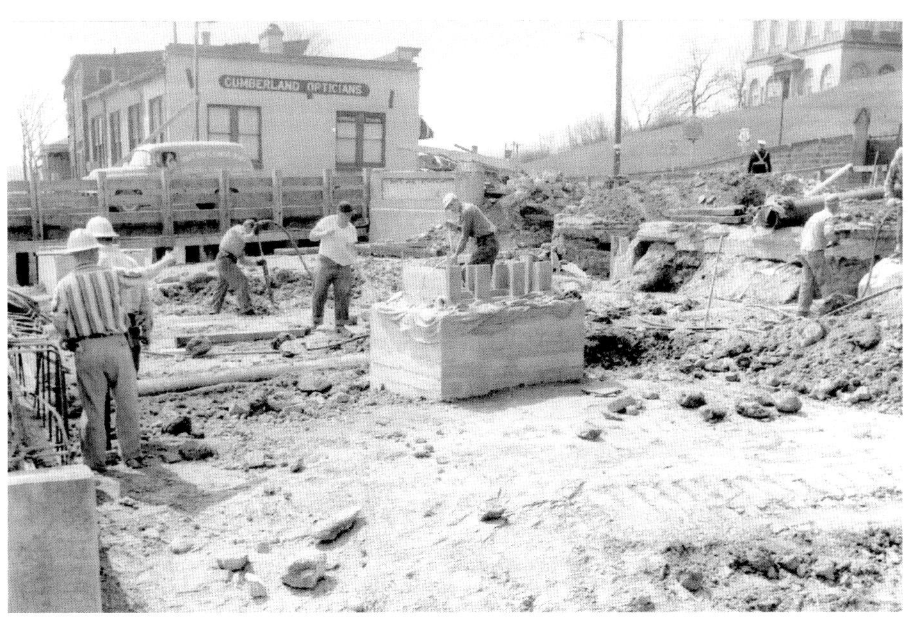

Looking southward, the west approach to the Baltimore Street Bridge is portrayed in this photograph. Cumberland Opticians was at that time located at 8 Greene Street. On the right, atop the hill, is the Masonic Temple, which was built during the years 1911–12. *Corps photograph taken April 14, 1958.*

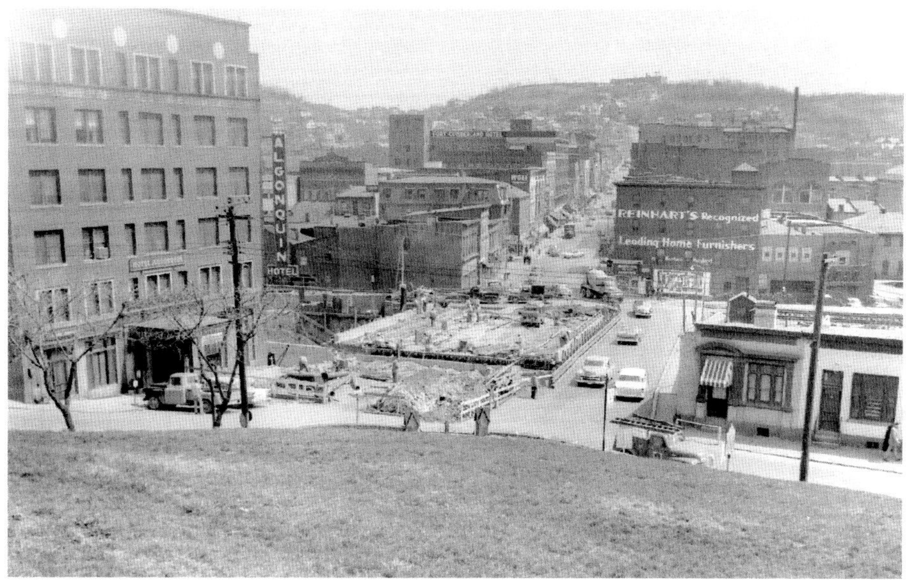

The view in this scene looks down on the new Baltimore Street Bridge, still under construction, from the Emmanuel Episcopal Church grounds. The new Baltimore Street Bridge would be officially dedicated in a ribbon-cutting ceremony held on July 3, 1958. The temporary wooden bridge was razed soon afterward. *Corps photograph taken April 16, 1958.*

BIBLIOGRAPHY

In addition to the following resources, an array of period Cumberland newspapers, city directories, telephone books, maps and other materials from the respective flood eras were utilized.

Allegany High School Social Studies Department. *Reflections of the Silver Screen: A History of Allegany County Movie Theaters*. Cumberland, MD: Allegany High School, 2000.

Feldstein, Albert L. *Feldstein's Fiftieth Anniversary Commemorative Edition of the St. Patrick's Day Flood of Cumberland, Maryland, March 17, 1936.* Cumberland, MD: Commercial Press, 1986.

———. *Feldstein's Gone But Not Forgotten, Volume I (A Graveside Biographical Tribute to Historic Allegany County Figures and Notable Personages from the Past)*. Cumberland, MD: Commercial Press, 1988.

———. *Feldstein's Historic Banner Front Pages of the Cumberland Daily News, The Cumberland News, and Cumberland Evening Times.* Vol. 1, *The Twentieth Century*. Cumberland, MD: Commercial Press, 1986.

———. *Feldstein's Historic Coal Mining and Railroads of Allegany County*. Cumberland, MD: Commercial Press, 1999.

———. *Feldstein's Revised I Remember Downtown Cumberland, 1950–1980.* Cumberland, MD: Commercial Press, 1994.

———. *Feldstein's Top Historic Postcard Views of Allegany County, Maryland.* Cumberland, MD: Commercial Press, 1997.

———. "Task Force Takes on Area's Disastrous Legacy of Floods." *Cumberland Times-News*, March 31, 1998.

Lowdermilk, Will H. *History of Cumberland, Maryland.* Baltimore, MD: Regional Publishing Company, 1976. First published in 1878.

150th Anniversary Committee for the Town of Lonaconing. *Lonaconing: Home in the Hills.* Lonaconing, MD: Town of Lonaconing, 1987.

Rada, James, Jr. *The Rain Man.* Cumberland, MD: Legacy Publishing, 2002.

Renshaw, Richard T. *The Cumberland Shoppers Guide Souvenir History of Cumberland's Flood.* Cumberland, MD: Stanley Fields and William Kaldor Publishers, 1936.

Stegmaier, Harry, Jr., et al. *Allegany County: A History.* Parsons, WV: McClain Printing Company, 1976.

Thomas, Colonel R.S. "Flood Protection for Cumberland, Maryland and Ridgeley, West Virginia." A talk delivered to the citizens of Cumberland, Maryland, on February 13, 1939.

United States Army Corps of Engineers. "North Branch Potomac River Flood Protection Project for Cumberland, Maryland—Appendix, Basis of Design." Washington, D.C.: United States Engineer Office, 1940.

———. A Report on the Construction of the Cumberland, Maryland–Ridgeley, West Virginia Flood Protection Project, 1949–1959. Washington, D.C.: United States Engineer Office, 1959.

ABOUT THE AUTHOR

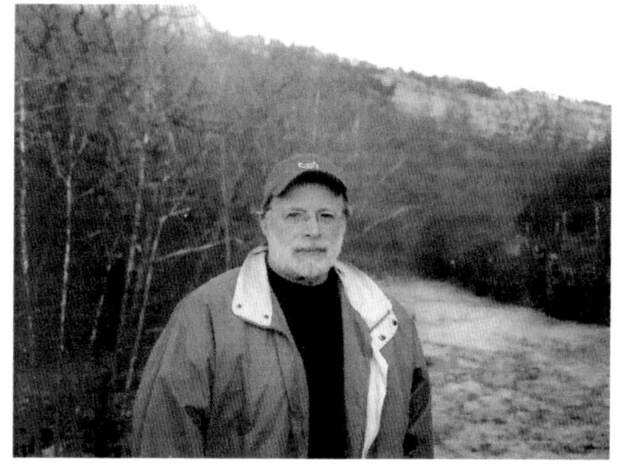

Photograph by Angela Feldstein with Wills Creek and the Narrows in the background.

A multi-award-winning amateur public historian, Albert Louis Feldstein has since 1980 successfully published over thirty books and videotapes depicting the history of all three Western Maryland Counties—Allegany, Garrett and Washington—as well as nearby West Virginia. His works have focused on a wide array of subjects.

A 2003 effort, a political history poster entitled "Buttons of the Cause, 1960–2003," was accepted for exhibit and sale at the Smithsonian's Museum of American History in Washington.

In 2007 and 2008, Feldstein developed three educational websites, all initiated in collaboration with the Western Maryland Regional Library. The first, entitled Historic Women of Allegany, has been linked to several historical and women's history websites. The second, entitled Allegany County African American History, has also been linked to various educational and historical institutions on both the national as well as statewide level. Most recently, Feldstein has developed a website on presidential campaign buttons that has also received national attention.